Computer Analysis and
Qualitative Research

New Technologies for Social Research

New technologies are transforming how social scientists in a wide range of fields do research. The series, New Technologies for Social Research, aims to provide detailed, accessible and up-to-date treatments of such technologies, and to assess in a critical way their methodological implications.

Series Editors:
Nigel G. Fielding, *University of Surrey*
Raymond M. Lee, *Royal Holloway University of London*

Advisory Board:
Randy Banks, *University of Essex*
Grant Blank, *University of Chicago*
Edward Brent, *University of Missouri*
Angela Dale, *University of Manchester*
G. David Garson, *North Carolina State University*
G. Nigel Gilbert, *University of Surrey*
Noel Heather, *Royal Holloway University of London*
Udo Kelle, *University of Vechta*
Edith de Leeuw, *Free University of Amsterdam*
Wim Liebrand, *University of Groningen*
Peter Ohly, *IZ, Bonn*
Bryan Pfaffenberger, *University of Virginia*
Ralph Schroeder, *Chalmers University, Gothenburg*
Eben Weitzman, *University of Massachusetts at Boston*

Computer Analysis and Qualitative Research

Nigel G. Fielding and Raymond M. Lee

SAGE Publications
London • Thousand Oaks • New Delhi

SAGE Publications Ltd
6 Bonhill Street
London EC2A 4PU

SAGE Publications Inc.
2455 Teller Road
Thousand Oaks, California 91320

SAGE Publications India Pvt Ltd
32, M-Block Market
Greater Kailash - I
New Delhi 110 048

British Library Cataloguing in Publication data

A catalogue record for this book is available from the British
Library

ISBN 0 8039 7482 5
ISBN 0 8039 7483 3 (pbk)

Library of Congress catalog card number 97–062539

Typeset by Type Study, Scarborough
Printed in Great Britain by Biddles Ltd, Guildford, Surrey

To our friends in the CAQDAS community

Contents

Acknowledgements

This book is just one outcome of a long-standing collaboration between us. (The order in which our names appear on the title page is alphabetical.) It might, therefore, be appropriate to begin by each of us thanking the other for providing support, ideas, encouragement, and occasional bouts of goal displacement. Among those who have helped us develop ideas and arguments, and who we thank, are Udo Kelle, Wilma Mangabeira and Eben Weitzman. Over the years we have learned much from software developers including: Ian Dey, Sharlene Hesse-Biber, Udo Kuckartz, Thomas Muhr, Lyn and Tom Richards and John Seidel. We have also learned from the evaluative and methodological work of Paul Atkinson and Mike Fisher. It is a considerable pleasure for us to acknowledge the outstanding debt we owe for the support and hard work of Ann Lewins, our project officer on the CAQDAS Networking Project. We thank Maureen Stenning for diligently and accurately transcribing our focus group data. The participants in our interviews and focus groups took time out from their hard-pressed work as social researchers to themselves take on the role of research subjects. We are especially grateful to them and thank them warmly. The University of Edinburgh, the University of Manchester, and Royal Holloway University of London provided fieldwork venues for which we are grateful. Finally, we salute and thank the late Renate Tesch for her pioneering work.

1
Introduction: Computer Analysis and Qualitative Research

Nowadays, it seems, qualitative researchers are as likely to talk about RAM, grep searches and DWIM interfaces as they are to recount their dealings with gatekeepers, informants and the like. This comment is, of course, a playful one, an exaggeration. It points, though, to an observable change. Computers were traditionally used in the social sciences to analyse statistical data. Now researchers increasingly use computer programs to analyse qualitative data, such as transcripts from depth interviews and focus groups, fieldnotes from participant observation studies and so on. CAQDAS (Computer Assisted Qualitative Data Analysis Software) has ceased to be a novelty and has become a palpable presence.[1] Indeed, to exaggerate again, but perhaps only just, we might be seeing the last few generations of qualitative social researchers who still analyse their data mainly 'by hand'.

In part this book emerges out of a conviction that the work of social scientists is being steadily transformed by new technology (Lee, 1995b). Massive increases in computing power at declining cost put onto the desks of social scientists new ways of dealing with problems and topics. Social researchers now deploy a range of emerging technologies to acquire, store and manage data. The rapid development and diffusion of the Internet has revolutionized scholarly communication, and provides ready access to large volumes of widely dispersed information. Of most importance in the present context, the major purpose of the computer is no longer literally to 'compute', that is to do numerical calculations. Instead, computers are increasingly used to manipulate many different forms of information, including text or audio-visual material.

To be convinced about the ubiquity of new developments and to be excited by their potentiality is not, of course, to endorse those developments uncritically. The advent of powerful and easy-to-use statistical packages undoubtedly enhanced levels of *technical* sophistication in quantitative research. Whether *theoretical* sophistication was by the same means enhanced is open to question. Technologies, for example, can interpose themselves in ways which serve to distance the researcher from the data. As Fischer (1994; 199) points out, the computer can also encourage the use of research procedures because they are easy, rather than because they are appropriate, and can isolate researchers from the fundamentals of their methods to the extent that these become poorly understood.

Traditionally, the literature on qualitative research was weighted towards issues of data collection. Miles (1983) reports an analysis of major texts on qualitative methods which were published in the 1970s. While problems of access, field relations, ethical issues and so on were dealt with at length in these books, analytic matters were largely ignored. The volume of material devoted to analysis was typically of the order of 5 to 10 per cent of the total page tally. In recent years the pendulum has swung healthily in the other direction. Analytic issues are increasingly central to discussion and debate (Bryman and Burgess, 1994b; Coffey and Atkinson, 1996). While perhaps not the only factor, we could contend that the advent of software packages for qualitative data analysis has been important in moving analysis issues to the forefront of concern. Paradoxically, new methods have put old procedures under scrutiny. As software for quali-tative analysis has evolved, so has commentary upon computer-based methods. Much of the early literature appeared to be designed to convince readers that computers could indeed be used to analyse qualitative data. Later, discussions about the epistemological implications of computer use, and the possible impact of CAQDAS programs on the craft of qualitative research, began to emerge. There now seems to be a movement away from speculation and towards discussions based on empirical analysis of program use and/or explicit evaluation of software tools (Weaver and Atkinson, 1995b; Mangabeira, 1995). The present book is a contribution to the former; in it we also seek to build on an empirical base a wider commentary on the process, objects and future of qualitative data analy-sis in general.

The Users' Experiences Study

Throughout this book, we draw on a research project into users' experi-ences of qualitative data analysis software.[2] As part of this research we conducted a series of focus groups with CAQDAS users throughout the UK. A little less than half of our focus group participants were contract researchers, a quarter were lecturers and a further quarter postgraduates, the few remaining individuals being employed in computer support or advisory roles. Slightly over three-quarters of those who participated in the focus groups were female.[3] Since no information is available about the overall population of qualitative researchers in the UK, it is difficult to judge how representative our sample might be. We suspect that full-time academic staff are underrepresented. The range of variability is suffici-ently wide, however, to encompass a diverse range of experiences on the part of our respondents.

We chose to use focus group methodology because we have sometimes, although not always, found individual users surprisingly unclear about how precisely they use a program. We reasoned that in a group context the sharing of experiences might promote a more fruitful discussion. A range of topics was covered in the focus groups: how users heard about the program they used, how they used it, the nature of their research and the research environment within which they worked, how they had gone about analysing their data and how far the software they used had aided or hindered the analytic process. Groups lasted between 90 and 150 minutes and were tape-recorded and transcribed verbatim with transcripts fed back to participants on request. In analysing the data we experimented with a number of approaches and with a number of packages. However, the bulk of the data were analysed using Atlas/ti, with additional analysis being carried out in NUD•IST. In addition, for specialized tasks and/or for the purposes of experimentation, concordance packages, text retrieval software, and visualization programs such as Inspiration™ were also used.

Qualitative research is a broad church. It is found in many social science disciplines and is making headway in others, such as human geography and psychology. It is represented by many schools of thought. It embraces many methods. It has many uses, many audiences and many sponsors. The projects on which our respondents used qualitative analysis software were varied. On the evidence of our sample, CAQDAS is used across the range of research from the purely academic to the purely applied. In the main, we conclude that the users in our sample were committed to qualitative methods and tended to employ them as the dominant methods in their projects. Indeed, in several cases researchers with a quantitative background spoke in terms of a 'conversion' to qualitative methods (while others, we should add, questioned the distinction between quantitative and qualitative methods and/or took a pragmatic, tools-for-the-job approach). While interview-based studies predominated (possibly reflecting their place in qualitative research methods generally), the projects reflected overall the rich array of methods available to qualitative researchers. Excluding those largely involved in teaching qualitative software or providing research support, 24 of our focus group participants had used CAQDAS on a purely interview-based project, three on a purely observation-based project, three on a purely document-based project, 19 on a project using multiple qualitative methods, and six on a multi-method project involving both quantitative and qualitative data. Our impression is that these proportions reflect the broad pattern of use of the particular methods generally, rather than an affinity between CAQDAS and any given method.

A non-exhaustive list of the projects undertaken would include a study concerned with children and domestic violence, research on the household economy, studies of the sexual behaviour of young people, the care of the dying, appraisal processes in education, and environmental issues. One informant studied how people talk about dreams. Among the social groups studied by our informants were teachers, nurses involved in providing geriatric care, film makers, and professionals in the construction industry. Of the projects on which we have information, 14 were solo dissertation or thesis projects, 18 were solo projects of other sorts and 16 were team research projects. However, even these distinctions are not rigid. For example, one project we classified as team research was actually described as being 'solo but complicated' (FG3).[4] There were 'four projects in one, each project in a different institution'. Data gathered at each site were passed to researchers at other sites, though researchers in each institution were responsible for their own analysis.

Between them our focus group participants were familiar with a wide range of qualitative analysis software. Programs used included AQUAD, askSam, Atlas/ti, Ethno, ETHNOGRAPH, HyperResearch, HyperSoft, Info Select, Martin, and NUD•IST. Some of our informants had also at various times adapted word-processing or database programs for use in qualitative research. We do not have any precise data on the length of time people had been using particular packages. It is clear, though, that our focus group participants varied a good deal in terms of their experience with qualitative software. Some were novices, but others had followed developments in the field for a number of years and/or had used, and in some cases evaluated, several packages.

Facility with computers in general also varied widely among our focus group participants. On the one hand, some of those we talked to clearly enjoyed working with computers and took a formal approach to analysis because of an affinity with statistical work. Thus, 'I like to have a logic, to look at things and categorize things. I also like computers and I had this sort of pang that because I was going to do qualitative work I wouldn't be able to do SPSS or GLIM and it was some way of compromising my need' (FG2). Another computing enthusiast recorded that learning to use a word processor had helped him to overcome a writing blockage at a difficult point in his career. As he put it, 'word processors suddenly came on the scene [and] I realized I might be an academic, I was going to give it up . . . When you've got those very positive feelings about this piece of technology and what it can do then any other form of software and computer using follows on' (FG1).

Against this there were those who spoke of being nervous about using the computer or of entering a new and unfamiliar world. 'I felt that the computer is actually a language, bit like French, and that the only way to learn it is to immerse yourself in it, and sooner or later you begin to realize what the words mean, so in a way [I] did a course which was . . . learning to speak computer' (FG4). Even those who did 'speak computer' did so sometimes in a less than fluent way which required a jump to be made from a press-the-right-button stage to having the confidence to

experiment. 'I used to do certain things, i.e., CD\WPfile1, you know ...
Even within WordPerfect it was certain functions I did and I did them reli-
giously. Learning [package] was initially a bit of a shock ... It came down
to me learning about how these things work in practice ... It's a simple
thing in retrospect but at the time I didn't really quite understand. "Sub
directory, this should go in sub-directory, what does that mean?!"' (FG5).
In another case, CAQDAS led the respondent to the computer for the first
time. 'I always felt "I don't want to touch, I don't like what that does and
it doesn't do what I say"... It was actually because I wanted to use
[package] that I got the computer ... and it was actually [package] that
liberated me, and I had hated it' (FG1). (Interestingly, exposure to
CAQDAS sometimes also prompted researchers to learn statistical software. As one of our respondents put it, 'All my previous experience is
qualitative but I have actually got into SPSS now because I feel that that
was a missing wing' (FG2).)

Summing up, then, the focus group participants in our study brought
to our discussions with them a range of experience with computers, a
variety of methodological commitments and a diversity of reasons for
using CAQDAS. One important caveat to enter, however, is that the users
we studied were for the most part early adopters of the software.
Programs and users' facility in handling them have developed appreci-
ably in the interim.

Program Types and Capabilities

In what follows we give an overview of different kinds of software
program, and how they can be used to analyse qualitative data. We do not
intend to supplement this sketch by describing in detail the features of
particular programs, or how they work. Nor will we rate programs or
make detailed comparisons between them; readers seeking recommendations to the 'best' program will be disappointed. In this, we agree with
Weitzman and Miles (1995: 9):

> 'What's the best program?' There's no answer in the abstract. Choosing the right
> software for you, depends on your own level of work with computers, on your
> time perspective, on the particular project you have in mind, and on the type of
> analysis you are expecting to do.

Fortunately, information on specific programs and advice on choosing
a package are now quite widely available. For those new to the field,
Weitzman and Miles (1995) provide a particularly useful starting point.
Detailed comparisons of specific packages can also be found in Weaver
and Atkinson (1995b), Stanley and Temple (1995), and Fisher (1997).[5]

As do Weitzman and Miles (1995) and Richards and Richards (1995), we distinguish between generic, usually commercially produced, software which can be adapted for use in the analysis of qualitative data and dedicated qualitative analysis packages.

Generic Software

Under this heading we include programs such as word processors, text retrievers and textbase managers.

Word Processors

Qualitative data analysis does not necessarily require sophisticated software. Much can be done using an ordinary word processor. One method of using a word processor that seems to have been invented independently by many people we refer to as 'embed and retrieve'. It is described, for instance by Bernard (1994), by Fischer (1995) and by Tesch (1990). The procedure is simple. One inserts mnemonic codes directly into the text of fieldnotes or interview transcripts. We might take an example given by Bernard (1994: 199–200). Suppose one had a fieldnote which describes an informant's decision to migrate from her village to the city in order to look for work. If the informant is referred to as MA and the village as XOR, the following codes might be associated with the fieldnote. 412 MA XOR 101290 MIG WOM ECO. The codes MIG, WOM and ECO stand respectively for migration, women and economics since these are topics relevant to the content of the fieldnote. The numerals, 412 and 101290, associated with the codes are tracking devices. The number 412 simply denotes the number of this particular fieldnote in a sequentially numbered sequence; 101290 is the date on which the fieldnote was recorded. Often text segments are also marked by a delimiter, some uncommon symbol, $$$ for instance, which can be retrieved easily. With most modern word processors it is relatively easy to write macros in order automatically to retrieve and write to a separate file requested segments. (For examples of WordPerfect macros, see Ryan, 1993a, 1993b.) In the case of fieldnotes one can usually choose as a matter of personal preference whether to include codes at the head of the note or to format the text in a word processor so that codes appear at the side of the text.

Text Retrievers

As the example above shows, computers are particularly good at simple string searching, so called because the computer is used to find a specific sequence or 'string' of characters. Text retrievers are stand-alone, usually commercial programs that extend in complex ways the ability to find text. Weitzman and Miles (1995) distinguish text retrieval software using an 'internal files' approach from that which uses external files. Software of the latter kind builds an index of all of the files on the users' hard disk. The advantage of this approach is that subsequent searches are performed very quickly indeed. However, the original indexing process can take a long time, the index takes up disk space and one does need to reindex when new material is introduced. Software using the internal files approach searches for text 'on the fly'. It is therefore slower. Increasingly, fairly sophisticated search routines are also being built into dedicated qualitative data analysis packages and it is becoming more common for dedicated qualitative analysis packages to permit what is sometimes called 'autocoding'. Typically, one can request a search pattern and automatically assign a code to the found string(s). In some cases a certain amount of context can also be attached to each hit.

Fisher (1995) suggests that text retrievers are ideally suited for making an 'aerial reconnaissance' of textual data. Using a text retriever one can quickly identify themes, topics and terms within a large body of text, as well as information about their location, clustering, co-occurrence or non-overlap. Such information can be of considerable analytic significance. For example, the low-income women interviewed by George and Jaswal (1993) in Bombay often deployed concepts of 'honour' and 'shame' in talking about their personal, sexual and reproductive histories. Text retrieval showed, however, that the terms virtually never co-occurred, alerting George and Jaswal to an important underlying distinction between personal and collective reputation.

One need not search simply for a particular word. The scope of a search can usually be widened in different ways. One is through the use of so-called 'wild cards'. The term 'wild card', taken from poker, refers to situations where one card, the joker say, can substitute for another. By extension, the term can be used to refer to a symbol which can substitute for sought-for text strings. Thus, if a particular program uses the asterisk as a wild card, it is possible to enter laug* in order to find the terms 'laugh', 'laughs', 'laughter', 'laughing' and so on. *Boolean searches* allow the analyst to find combinations of search terms defined by the Boolean operators AND, OR, NOT. *Proximity searches* find instances where one search term appears within a given distance of another. Distance in these cases is usually being measured in terms of words, lines, sentences and the like. *Pattern searching* involves the matching of a pattern of characters to a search request. For example, one might search for all words beginning with a capital letter followed by a vowel and ending in 'ing'.

Direct retrieval depends, quite obviously, on the sought-for string actually occurring in the text. For example, suppose one was interested in how far users of qualitative data analysis packages felt that the computer-based procedures they now used differed from their previously used manual methods of analysis. One could search across transcripts for the term 'manual'. The problem is that there is no guarantee that informants will make the distinction between manual and computer methods in the way that an analyst might. Phrases that might be relevant such as 'conventional methods', 'the way I was taught to do it' or 'cut-and-paste techniques' would all be missed by a string search. Moreover, searching for 'manual' might also elicit comments about documentation not relevant to the specific purpose of the search, such as 'I like [package] because the manual is very approachable' or 'all it says in the manual is "Look at Chapter 3" '.

As Pfaffenberger (1988) points out, in situations where one can look only for what is in the text, configuring a search request can become a matter of fine judgement. Defining search criteria too broadly means generating a large number of irrelevant hits. Narrowing the criteria too much might simply exclude potentially significant material. A further problem is that text retrieval software, like concordance programs, displays hits within a fixed rather than a user-defined amount of context. The analyst, of course, will – or should – recognize this. However, as Pfaffenberger points out,

> what is suspect here is the *appearance* – a false one I would argue – that the program is retrieving significant units of data; what it retrieves are units of data that are being defined clandestinely by the computer and ripped out of their context. The appearance is powerful enough, perhaps, to hoodwink even an experienced fieldworker into thinking that what appears on the screen is significant data instead of disembodied and artificially biased. (1988: 42; emphasis in original)

Textbase Managers

Text retrieval can be improved through the use of a 'textbase manager' rather than a straightforward text retrieval package. (For more detail on textbase managers, see Rubinstein, 1991; Fischer, 1994; Weitzman and Miles, 1995.) As the name perhaps implies, textbase managers stand some way between dedicated text retrieval packages and database software. Conventional databases are organized into records and fields. For example, in a bibliographic database each record might refer to a book, article or other work. Within each record would be found fields for author, title and so on. In a conventional database there are usually restrictions on the length of records and fields, and the information stored in the database tends to have a relatively structured form. Textbase managers are free of some of these constraints. They typically accept free text of varying length but allow the definition of fields which can be associated with the text. A textbase manager will usually support complex search procedures which will return both structured and unstructured records. Textbase managers are well adapted to the needs of qualitative researchers since they deal readily with the mixture of structured, semi-structured and unstructured data typically generated by field research. They do, though, have some disadvantages (Fischer, 1994). Some programs take up large volumes of disk storage and some at least can be rather slow in searching through large volumes of material.

Some researchers, particularly those who deal with large volumes of textual data or who combine quantitative and qualitative data, find the use of text retrievers advantageous (Wellman, 1990). Typically, these researchers relish the speed and flexibility that text retrieval methods allow. For others, the use of string searching is primarily a filtering and focusing device.

Dedicated Qualitative Analysis Packages

Weitzman and Miles (1995) suggest that software packages that have been explicitly developed for use by qualitative researchers fall into a number of categories. These include: code-and-retrieve programs, code-based theory building programs and 'conceptual network builders'.

Code-and-retrieve Programs

Kelle and Bird (1995) note that the concordance was one of a variety of tools developed in the eighteenth and nineteenth centuries to aid the development of biblical hermeneutics. Biblical scholars also made use of 'synoptic comparison': they took passages from different parts of the Bible, laid them side by side and looked for similarities and differences. As Kelle and Bird go on to point out, the comparison of extracts of text from different sources is a common procedure in the analysis of qualitative data in the social sciences. In this case, however, the text passages come from data such as fieldnotes, memos recording analytic reflections on the material to hand, and interview transcripts.

Before the advent of the computer, social scientists had recourse to a variety of devices for aiding the process of extracting and comparing segments of texts. These included copying relevant passages onto index cards, marking up text with coloured pens or pencils, marking the position of text segments with paper clips or sticky labels, and so on (Knafl and Webster, 1988). With the advent of the photocopier analysts began making multiple copies of field materials. These could then be cut up and pasted onto cards or larger sheets of paper, allowing the extracted material to be evaluated and compared relatively easily. This latter practice seems to have become ubiquitous enough for the phrase 'cutting and pasting' to be used as a metaphor for describing this kind of analytic work.

Code-and-retrieve programs mechanize the procedure just described.

Text to be analysed – fieldnotes, memos, transcripts and so on – is entered into the computer. The data are then inspected and codes assigned to particular segments of text which are of interest to the analyst. The computer can then be asked to recover codes, or combinations of codes, and display them together with the text with which they are associated. Retrievals might involve complex Boolean searches. In other words, the analyst asks the computer to retrieve segments coded X and segments coded Y but not those coded Z. Varying degrees of context can usually be outputted for a particular search, and in many cases information relating, for example, to the demographic characteristics of respondents can be included as search terms. The size of text segments is chosen by the researcher as part of the analytic task, as are the codes attached to the text. Codes might be, in effect, labels which are largely descriptive of themes or topics appearing within the text, or they might have a more analytic cast. In this case, they might reflect more or less elaborated theoretical understandings of the material contained within the data, with particular codes standing in a theoretical relationship to one another and to wider theoretical categories. During the course of analysis, the kind, variety and volume of codes might change as new analytic insights emerge.

Most of the early programs for qualitative data analysis worked in this way. Even though they seem limited today, the advent of qualitative data analysis software was a revolutionary step. As Weitzman and Miles (1995: 18) comment: 'Code-and-retrieve programs – even the weakest of them – are a quantum leap forward from the old scissors-and-paper approach: They're more flexible, and much, much faster.'

Code-based Theory Building Programs

Although some like Lofland (1970) have been unimpressed by the commitment of qualitative researchers to theory development, building theory remains an important (though not exclusive) goal of qualitative research, as instanced by qualitatively based studies which have had a signal influence on theory in fields such as the sociology of deviance or the sociology of health and illness. What Weitzman and Miles (1995) describe as 'code-based theory building programs' extend code-and-retrieve procedures in the direction of theoretical development. Of course, one can build theory with paper and pencil, or while in the bath or walking down the street. What the software does is to facilitate and enhance theoretical development, usually by treating codes applied to text segments as building blocks for the production of a set of interrelated conceptual categories. To put this another way, use of the appropriate software tools allows the analyst to go beyond using codes simply to label or point to relevant themes in the data. Instead, codes become theoretical categories, emerging out of the data, but linked in possibly complex, but theoretically relevant ways.

The routes that programs take to theory building are varied. One route, close to 'traditional' code-and-retrieve methods, provides advanced Boolean retrievals and the availability of 'system closure' (Richards and Richards, 1994). What this means is that the results of searches and retrievals do not simply end up on the researcher's desk, they become available for incorporation into the emerging set of theoretical categories. Other programs take a more formalistic approach. Some draw on artificial intelligence techniques to support a cycle of inductive and deductive reasoning. Using rule-based systems, hypotheses emerging from a set of data cases, and inferences derived from them, can be tested on a case-by-case basis. Yet a different and more explicitly causal approach attempts to associate particular configurations of conditions identified within qualitative data with social outcomes of various kinds. Finally, in some programs theory building is supported by visual representation. The emerging theory is displayed graphically as a network of categories linked by sets of logical relations.

Conceptual Network Builders and Textual Mapping Software

Conceptual network builders appear in two guises: as commercial 'visualization' software and as add-on features to code-based theory building programs. Theory is represented in the form of a 'semantic network' (Jonassen et al., 1993: 11). This is a graph made up of interconnected nodes and lines. The nodes are labelled with the categories that form the conceptual elements of one's theory. These are derived (usually) from higher-level codes that have emerged towards the end of the analysis process. The lines indicate relations between the conceptual categories. Such relations might take the form of 'causes', 'is a', 'is part of', and so on. Textual mapping software is used to elucidate some underlying structure in textual data. The obvious example is where the analysts want to bring to the surface something like the underlying narrative structure in a piece of text. Although they are not widely used, a number of programs exist which allow the user to elicit the structure of interest and to represent the interrelation of its various elements in the form of a flow diagram (see, e.g., Griffin, 1993).

The Development of Computer-based Methods for Qualitative Analysis

It has taken some considerable time for the research community to reach the present (and still somewhat modest) level of software use in qualitative data analysis. Figure 1.1 shows a timeline which displays the development of data analysis software in the social sciences.

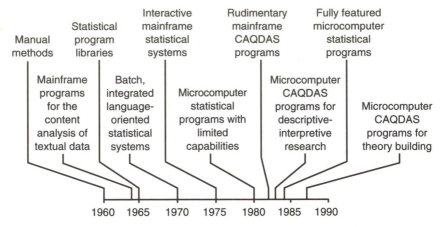

Figure 1.1   *Historical development of data analysis software in the social sciences (Brent and Anderson, 1990; Tesch, 1990)*

The dates given are approximate and the distinctions made between different program types are in places somewhat arbitrary. Nevertheless, some clear patterns emerge. First of all, data analysis software in the social sciences has been oriented towards the needs of quantitative researchers. As Brent and Anderson (1990) show, small-scale, limited programs for performing statistical analyses began to emerge in the middle 1960s. Before long these began to be collected into integrated statistical libraries which could be operated in batch-mode on a mainframe computer using a simplified command language. By the middle 1970s, statistical packages of this kind began to be used interactively on mainframe computers and were soon followed by programs capable of providing at least a limited range of statistical procedures on desktop computers. A decade later, fully featured statistical packages had found their way onto microcomputers.

As the timeline shows, the use of computer software to analyse textual data is not entirely new. Indeed, researchers in the humanities, especially those such as biblical or Shakespearean scholars who must perforce deal with very large volumes of textual material, have long been interested in the use of computers for analysing non-numeric data (Lee and Fielding, 1991). However, in the social sciences, while mainframe-based programs for analysing text appeared relatively early on, they used traditional content analysis methods which looked, for example, at the frequency of word use. Qualitative researchers who needed to analyse fieldnotes or interview transcripts continued to rely on manual methods, perhaps using coloured pens or making multiple copies of relevant segments of field material which were then 'cut and pasted', for example, onto index cards.

From the perspective of qualitative research, the early 1980s appears in retrospect as a period of experimentation. During this time, qualitative researchers explored the use of databases, content analysis programs and word processors. It was at this time too that rudimentary mainframe code-and-retrieve programs, such as the original versions of ETHNOGRAPH, Qualpro and TAP, appeared (Tesch, 1988). Since then growth has been rapid. Dedicated qualitative analysis packages have been developed in a number of countries: the United States, Germany, the United Kingdom, Denmark, Holland and Australia. With some exceptions, development since the mid-1980s has been firmly focused on desktop computers. Programs have mostly been developed for IBM PCs and compatibles although there is also a sprinkling (mostly using the HyperCard author-ing system) for the Macintosh platform. Alongside purely technical developments there has burgeoned an apparatus for the dissemination, support and discussion of the new software tools. An international community emerged of developers, users and others interested in the technical and methodological aspects of CAQDAS. Where information on computers and qualitative research was once hard to come by, there are now regular conferences, user groups, electronic bulletin boards, and a growing literature on the topic.

The software itself has steadily developed. Strikingly, many of the early programs emerged more or less simultaneously from developers unaware that others were doing the same thing. Developers now seem much more aware of each others' work. They seem to have learned from one another, and a case can be made that a degree of relatively friendly competition between developers has raised standards. Some of the early programs have become defunct. Others have gone through a series of revisions, adding new features, often at the instigation of users, and taking advan-tage of developments in operating system design. There has also been a trend towards heterogeneity in program type. Programs explicitly incor-porating facilities for 'theory building' have increasingly joined existing packages based largely on the code-and-retrieve model.

Technical changes apart, software use largely seems to have gained *social* acceptance among qualitative researchers in the social sciences. Tesch (1989) argued that in the early stages of their development com-puter-based methods for qualitative analysis faced resistance based on epistemological suspicion. According to Tesch many qualitative researchers, through misunderstanding and/or ignorance of how computers might fruitfully be used, regarded the computer as an alien device with roots firmly based in the quantitative paradigm. Of course, what might be thought of as suspicion from one point of view might from another be seen as the perfectly appropriate caution of a scientific community faced with a new and untried idea. In the event, Tesch's characterization of the situation seems no longer to be apt. Stephen Cole (1983: 113–14) has distinguished between the core of a discipline, the 'small set of theories and analytic techniques which represent the "given" at any particular point in time', and the research frontier which 'consists of all the work currently being done by all active researchers in a given discipline'. Cole suggests that one can see roughly what comprises the core in a particular discipline by looking at the content of basic graduate education in the field. Judged from this point of view, CAQDAS has moved from the frontier and towards the core in qualitative methodology. Discussions of software packages and their use can now be found in many graduate-level texts and readers (Bogdan and Biklen, 1992; Bryman and Burgess, 1994a; Denzin and Lincoln, 1994; Miles and Huberman, 1994; Emerson et al., 1995; Hammersley and Atkinson, 1995; Lofland and Lofland, 1995; Coffey and Atkinson, 1996). There are also indications that the ability to use a qualitative data analysis package is increasingly seen as a marketable skill in applied research. We have already begun to notice advertisements for jobs or for graduate assistantships that specify a need for the applicant to have or be capable of acquiring expertise in CAQDAS.

CAQDAS in the UK

As we have commented elsewhere (Lee and Fielding, 1991), an extensive international community of CAQDAS enthusiasts developed well before a corresponding *national* community in the UK and – we suspect – other countries. A variety of responses emerged as information about CAQDAS became more widely available in Britain from about the late 1980s onward. A relatively small group enthusiastically embraced computer-based methods and the possibilities they offered. Some people, who had crafted do-it-yourself approaches using word processors or text retrievers, wondered, perhaps with justification, what all the fuss was about. Others adopted a cynical view (which needless to say we do not share), suggesting that those involved in propagating information about CAQDAS were somehow in the pay of software developers, or were trying to build or enhance an academic reputation on the back of the developments. Probably, the most common response was a slightly worried interest. People seemed to want to believe that software could relieve the burdens associated with qualitative data analysis but without losing anything in the process. Many had doubts about their own technical competence or worried that CAQDAS would distance them from their data (Weitzman and Miles, 1995).

Today, we would guess that, roughly speaking, CAQDAS-aware researchers in the UK fall into three broad groups. A fairly small number, perhaps 40–50 people, have a wide knowledge of a number of programs, are aware of current technical developments and are engaged in discussion of methodological and epistemological issues surrounding software use. A large and growing group exists of fairly proficient users of a particular package which they have employed more or less successfully on one or more research projects. The remainder are aware that programs exist, perhaps have attended a course and tried out a package, but are still uncommitted to computer-based methods. Our impression is that the programs which have greatest 'name recognition' in Britain are ETHNOGRAPH, NUD•IST and Atlas/ti. We would judge that for a long time ETHNOGRAPH was the most widely used program. It seems, though, to have lost ground to both NUD•IST and Atlas/ti over the last few years. NUD•IST is now probably the package that most people at least know by name. Other programs, such as HyperRESEARCH, Kwalitan, HyperSoft, TextBase Alpha and so on, appear to have their adherents. It is not uncommon with these packages to find clusters of users in particular locations. What seems often to have happened in such instances is that the program was introduced locally through (sometimes adventitious) contact with a particular developer, and possibly in ignorance of developments elsewhere.

To conclude this chapter, we comment briefly on the place of qualitative research in Britain within one social science discipline, sociology. We will also describe some of the processes surrounding the diffusion of qualitative software in the UK. In this way, we do two things. First of all, we set the scene, particularly for readers from other countries who might be unfamiliar with the context within which our empirical research took place. Second, we signal a theme that will re-emerge later. The diffusion and use of methodological innovations like CAQDAS are shaped by those social and organizational features of the research process that have increasingly informed the means of intellectual production in British social science over the last two decades.

British sociology has been notable both for the vigour of its theoretical debates and for the relative weakness of its quantitative tradition. (Indeed, some would regard quantitative work as the poor relation in British sociology, and the lack of quantitative skills among British sociologists as a clear deficit (Bulmer, 1980).) Bechhofer (1981, 1996) examined the methods of investigation used in articles appearing in the major sociology journals in Britain for the years 1977–9, and for 1992–4. During the earlier period, close to 60 per cent of articles made no reference to empirical data, although by 1992–4 this proportion had fallen to slightly over one-third. For both time periods Bechhofer counted the proportion of articles using quantitative techniques. (The term 'quantitative' is used in a rather broad sense to include any use of numerical procedures going beyond simple counting. Thus, even an article reporting the use of simple descriptive statistics was treated as a quantitative study.) The proportion of quantitative articles increased slightly from the earlier period to the later one. In both periods, however, little use of complex statistical techniques was found, and there was a noticeable tendency for the authors of papers using complex statistics to be based outside the UK. In other words, empirically based research, Bechhofer's work suggests, now forms a substantial element of British sociological endeavour; much of that endeavour is based on qualitative research.

If we look beyond sociology at the total population of those who make their careers in social research, it appears that qualitative research is also well represented in the UK. Some 40 per cent of the organizations listed in a detailed and comprehensive directory of social research organizations in the United Kingdom indicate that they undertake qualitative analysis (Bulmer et al., 1993). One has to caution at once that this might give an over-optimistic picture. There is some tendency for organizations to exaggerate the extent of their expertise in directory entries. Moreover, there is no way of translating the figure for organizations into an estimate for the number of *individuals* involved in qualitative research. Nevertheless, the 1994 membership directory of the Social Research Association, the main voluntary association serving the needs of social researchers in the UK, records that 35 per cent of its members chose qualitative research when asked to pick two out of a list of methodological interests. Let us assume from these figures that about a third of social researchers in the UK do qualitative work. The total number of social researchers in the country has been estimated at somewhere between 10,000 and 20,000 (Social Research Association Working Party, 1993). The range of this estimate is rather wide, and there are reasons to prefer a figure some way above the lower limit (Bulmer et al., 1993). If we assume that in total there are around 15,000 social researchers in the UK, one-third of that total would give an estimate of 5,000 for the number of qualitative researchers in the country. We do not know how many of these are CAQDAS users. Based on assumptions that are far from robust (Lee, 1995a), we think that something like two-fifths of qualitative researchers could be regarded as being 'CAQDAS aware' at the time of writing.

As we have observed in another context (Lee and Fielding, 1995), modest funding investments in events such as training workshops have been quite effective in encouraging the diffusion of new methods and technologies. Discussion of qualitative software has also begun to find its way onto the postgraduate research methods curriculum. The move was hastened by the increasing focus on formal research methods training as an element in postgraduate studies by the principal sponsor of doctoral research in the UK, the Economic and Social Research Council. Doctoral students were expected to devote a portion of their first year to methods training and a number of institutions set up Master's-level methods programmes to cater for this, as well as to address the needs of those wishing to enter the labour market as social researchers trained to Master's level.

The size and mobility of the social research community in the UK, and its growing connectedness through electronic means, has facilitated diffusion of CAQDAS. The compact geography of the country and the relatively small size of the research community mean that a small number of key events such as conferences or workshops can have a relatively large impact. Another factor in spreading knowledge of available software has been the mobility of applied social researchers in the UK. Many work on short-term contracts. In consequence, people move around the system a lot, diffusing new knowledge as they go.

Our focus group material suggests that users rarely use commercial software distributors as a source for packages. It is also noticeable that commentary on CAQDAS has been almost totally missing from software magazines and technical reviews, although for some users these sources did provide information on text retrieval and text management software (e.g. askSam, Sonar). The fairly rapid growth of computer networks in the UK in recent years has also allowed news of innovations to spread quickly and evenly. The ftp and World Wide Web sites at the University of Surrey, and electronic discussion lists, such as qual-software and lists supported by particular developers, have made available a greater volume of information.[6] More recently, Weitzman and Miles (1995) have produced a book in which they compare a variety of commercial and dedicated packages suitable for qualitative data analysis. One possible consequence is that these last developments are beginning to encourage a more 'consumerist' attitude among potential users. This is likely to continue as software becomes more versatile and developers identify new applications for their software.

Informal networks seem to have played an important early role in disseminating knowledge about the software. We documented in our focus group study a number of instances where choice of a package resulted from an enthusiastic referral by an existing user in someone's informal network. There is some suggestion in the focus group data, though, that learning about CAQDAS through informal channels can have its drawbacks. One problem is that, as one of our focus group respondents remarked, informal networks can generate rumour and misinformation. Researchers seeking information often found that people knew of various packages but had rarely used one. In some cases, confident assertions that 'package X is better than package Y' were found to be based on little more than hearsay. An additional difficulty is that because information about a particular development might flow through a variety of channels, people might know that something exists without having relational ties to someone who can give them further information. For example, one of our focus group participants heard about ETHNOGRAPH while standing over the departmental photocopier talking with a colleague about the problems of handling large amounts of qualitative data. As a result of this chance encounter our informant initiated a search for information about the package. This lasted for some months before contact was made with someone who could provide further details. This individual, as it happens, was based at an institution only a few miles away. A second difficulty is that the capacity of informal networks to spread information widely might lead to overload of those capable of giving information. As word spread that they knew something about CAQDAS, early users increasingly found themselves being inundated with requests to give advice, make recommendations about particular packages, or to give talks on their experiences. One user recorded that within days of her obtaining a particular package 'I had already had three people come and ask me and I am completely a baby user' (FG3). Asked if she now felt she was regarded as the local expert on the package, she commented ruefully, 'You turn into the expert.' In other cases, early versions of some packages acquired a reputation for bugs, crashes and quirks. Users then found themselves elevated to the status of expert because 'at least you have got it working' (FG3).

By and large, our impression is that 'involuntary experts' were willing to help because they felt a responsibility to pass on their knowledge to colleagues. Nevertheless, some of those whose interest in the software became widely known clearly felt that the demands placed on them were excessive, and more than one began to be cautious about advertising their expertise too widely because of the volume of enquiries it produced. One applied researcher who had worked on a software evaluation project, but had then moved on to another post, recorded spending 'half my week at the moment trying not to answer the phone, or trying to explain to people that I am no longer employed on this' (FG4). Another similarly placed informant commented: 'I even spent an hour with someone on the phone yesterday trying not to agree to spend five days with her showing how every single package works so she can then make a decision . . . Those of us who have any interest get over-used . . . the vultures begin to descend and you can see them wanting to peck [package A] or peck [package B]' (FG4).

There are also indications in the focus group material that institutions act in 'greedy' ways. In other words, they will often be resistant to innovation unless the costs of gaining information about that innovation are borne by someone else. Some of our informants reported that they were able to acquire software with institutional funding but only on the understanding that they would have to evaluate it and report back what they had found to the organization as a whole. Others found that institutional obstacles previously put in their way disappeared, but only once they had acquired expertise that others could use. One researcher who had faced resistance, both to her use of qualitative methods and to her enthusiasm for qualitative data analysis software, found herself invited back to her former institution (one of the most prestigious in Britain) to inform the generations of students who followed her about developments.

Although the process is not well described in the literature, the kind of 'demand diffusion' we have just described seems to be fairly common. As knowledge of an innovation spreads, 'experts', real and imagined, are deluged by requests for information. (Parenthetically, we suspect diffusion of this kind has increasingly begun to take place via the World Wide Web.) Even if one is prepared to put up with the demands on time and good-will generated by this situation, a dilemma beckons. What does one provide? Simple information or a deeper understanding of what software use might involve? This was an issue that exercised some of our more sophisticated users, especially when it was clear that advice-seekers typically wanted to be *told* what package to buy. One of our focus group participants remarked, 'I start off with what the researcher wants to do in a particular field because I think it is very dangerous to recommend a particular package, and then [I] talk about what particular process of research is put forward by each of the particular packages . . . It very much depends on how much they have thought about the process themselves whether they decide which one to go for in the end' (FG4). According to another participant, a methods specialist, 'With experienced researchers it is possible to go through a half-hour discussion of what kind of data they have and what kind of questions they should ask of their software and to what extent software that they use gives them purchase, but if you invite a less experienced researcher . . . and run [package] up and go through some of their data, I often get drawn into quite fundamental questions about the way they have gathered their data and suppositions they are making about how they should interpret it' (FG5). A further, rather dramatic, illustration of the conflicting expectations that can surround the provision of information is provided by another of our sophisticated users. Together with a colleague who was also familiar with a range of software packages she agreed to run a workshop. Their intention was to emphasize epistemological considerations and the fit of programs to particular analytic purposes. Those who attended the workshop, however, clearly expected training in the narrowest sense. 'We cleared the room by lunchtime of anybody other than those people who were interested in thinking through issues and a lot of people left and two people became quite belligerent when we weren't actually saying "press this button, do that"; they actually became very disappointed' (FG4).

Concluding Remarks

New developments throw up new problems as well as new opportunities. New ways of working force reappraisal of existing methods and approaches and, sometimes, rediscovery of old ones. In the next chapter we go on to examine a variety of approaches to the analysis of qualitative data with a view to indicating the different roles CAQDAS might have. As should be clear, there are distinct 'family resemblances' between a variety of existing approaches to qualitative analysis. In our view, however, there are clear differences in the analytic logic underlying particular strands of qualitative analysis. These differences need to be well understood if one is to assess the role, positive or negative, of computer-based methods in qualitative research.

Notes

1   Having coined the acronym CAQDAS (Lee and Fielding, 1991), we have some mixed feelings about its use. Acronyms are often used, perhaps especially in the field of information technology, to mystify or to lend a spurious importance to some topic. On the other hand, the acronym is usefully compact compared with the original. (We also liked the pun on 'cactus'; the use of computers for qualitative data analysis has sometimes been a 'thorny' issue.)

2   The project was funded by the UK Economic and Social Research Council, Grant No. R000234586.

3   We know of no evidence which suggests differential rates of take-up of computer-based qualitative data analysis by men and women, or that either gender prefers one package over another. Nor are we aware that women use packages differently than men. On the other hand, almost all the developers are male, as are many of those who might be called 'infrastructure developers', people who have established formal means for the dissemination of information and program use. (One shining exception here is, of course, the late Renate Tesch who was indefatigable in her propagation of CAQDAS.) Men are presumably more exposed to opportunities for technical training in fields such as computer programming and may have a more 'technicist' orientation to hardware and software.

4   FG3 designates that this quotation came from our third focus group. We indicate the source of each of the quotations we use as a quality control measure.

5   Some years ago we commented that there was a 'pressing need for research based on field trials where different programs and different applications are compared' (Lee and Fielding, 1991: 13). Although we regard the sources just mentioned as valuable and recommend that those interested in particular programs consult them, we now feel some need for caution. In particular, we would point to three methodological problems in making program comparisons. First of all, evaluations of particular program features are affected by the assumptions evaluators make about the nature of qualitative research. This is not only inevitable, it is probably desirable. Doing so helps often to uncover the tacit assumptions about analysis that the developer built into the program. Nevertheless, we think care needs to be taken to avoid unjust comparisons. To take a slightly overdrawn example, one needs to be careful not to see the problematic aspects of programs associated with favoured approaches as 'rough edges', while those of less favoured approaches are treated as 'fatal flaws'. Second, to the extent that programs are evaluated sequentially the possibility of conditioning effects arises. In other words, positive or negative experiences with one program may carry over into the evaluation of the next. Third, there is also what might be called a 'recency problem'. What we mean by this is that processes of software development often mean that the programs being compared are not at a comparable stage of development. A program that does not fare well in a comparison with other programs may in a matter of months leapfrog them when a new version appears.

6   The CAQDAS Networking Project maintains an ftp site, ftp.soc.surrey.ac.uk, and a website, http://www.soc.surrey.ac/caqdas/ which provide a variety of relevant information. Demonstration copies of a number of well-known packages can be downloaded from both sites. The website contains links to other sites and gives information about the qual-software discussion list. The CAQDAS Networking Project is funded by the Economic and Social Research Council.

2

Approaches to Qualitative Data Analysis

The late Renate Tesch (1990) set out to explore in detail how computer software could be used to assist qualitative researchers. She began by developing a taxonomy of approaches to qualitative research from which she identified the analytic tasks basic to each approach. The analytic needs implied by these tasks she then matched to the capabilities of various types of software.[1] Tesch's thorough and painstaking untangling of the myriad analytic threads that make up the totality of qualitative research stands as a monument to her. We will not attempt anything quite so comprehensive here. Instead, we provide an historical overview of the development of analytic techniques in qualitative research, attempting in the process to draw out the main features of a variety of analytic approaches. This, we hope, will indicate the range of requirements researchers have in respect of software as well as the kinds of criteria they might need to bear in mind in assessing packages.

Analytic Induction

The term 'analytic induction' was coined by Florian Znaniecki. Although not entirely hostile to quantitative research in the social sciences, Znaniecki (1934) was critical of what he called 'enumerative induction'. By this term he meant attempts to generalize by statistical means from a large number of cases across which were aggregated the properties of many individuals. What flows from enumerative induction, in Znaniecki's view, are probabilistic statements often confined to only superficial aspects of a particular phenomenon. Znaniecki contrasts enumerative induction with what he regards as the proper method of sociology, that of the natural sciences. Znaniecki argues that natural scientists in fields such as biology or physics eschew large numbers of cases and probabilistic statements. They work instead with a single case or a small number of cases studied in depth. Such intensive study, typically using experimental techniques, allows for the specification of universals. These are deterministic statements about the properties of phenomena, and the conditions under which they appear. Analytic induction is analogous to this use of the experimental method and aims to produce universal statements about social phenomena. Such statements seek to identify the essential features of a social phenomenon by identifying conditions always associated with that phenomenon. In other words, a universal statement asserts that the phenomenon only occurs in the presence of these conditions. If they are absent, it does not occur.

A good example of a universal statement is seen in the theory of opiate addiction developed by Lindesmith using analytic inductive methods. Briefly, Lindesmith argues that individuals become addicted when the following conditions are present: they (a) use an opiate, (b) experience distress due to withdrawal of the drug, (c) identify or recognize the symptoms of withdrawal distress, (d) recognize that these symptoms will be alleviated if they use the drug, (e) take the drug and experience relief. The important point for the present discussion is that Lindesmith is quite unequivocal about the universality of this theory (1968: 4):

> The theory that is developed is a general one; its applicability is not limited to American addicts, to lower-class users, to twentieth century addiction, to any restricted segment of the problem, to any specific historical period. Consequently, the focus of theoretical attention must be on those aspects of addiction which may reasonably be regarded as basic or essential in the sense that they are invariably manifested by all types of addicts regardless of place, time, method of use, social class, and other similar variable circumstances.

Because explanations produced by analytic induction aim to be complete and universal, negative cases are important (Manning, 1982). Such cases, when they occur, point to the need to modify the existing formulation of a supposedly universal statement. This means that analytic induction is a stepwise procedure. Cressey (1953: 16), who studied instances where those placed in positions of financial trust violated that trust by embezzling funds, describes the steps involved in the method as follows:

STEP 1: Identify the phenomenon you want to explain.
STEP 2: Formulate a rough definition of that phenomenon.
STEP 3: Formulate a working hypothesis to explain the phenomenon.
STEP 4: Study one case.
STEP 5: Ask 'do the facts of this case fit my initial hypothesis?'
STEP 6: If the answer is 'Yes', go on to study the next case. If the answer is 'No', EITHER redefine the phenomenon to exclude the case, OR reformulate your working hypothesis.
STEP 7: Continue Step 6 until you have a 'universal solution', that is until there is 'practical certainty' that the emerging theory has accounted for all of the cases which have been considered. However, the occurrence of any negative case must lead to either redefinition or reformulation.

Robinson (1951) commended analytic induction for formalizing and systematizing the process of generating a causal theory from an initial working hypothesis.[2] He also saw as a strength the insistence implicit in the method that negative evidence should prompt redefinition of the phenomenon. In this way the analyst limits the scope of the theory or the range of situations to which it is applicable. However, in a robust and sustained critique, Robinson points to a logical difficulty with analytic induction. As already indicated, the analyst working by analytic induction looks at instances where the phenomenon of interest is present. The argument, it will be remembered, is that the phenomenon only occurs when particular conditions are present. It does not occur in their absence. Robinson points out, however, that this implies the need to look at cases where the phenomenon is *not* present. In this way, the analyst can be sure that there are no cases where the supposedly universal conditions under which the phenomenon occurs are actually in some cases associated with its absence.

Citing the examples of both Lindesmith and Cressey, Robinson points out that this is precisely what researchers who use analytic induction do *in practice*. Lindesmith systematically studied hospital patients who received drugs over a long period of time but who had not become addicted and compared them with the addicts he had studied. Cressey did not study a sample of non-violators. He did, however, study the personal histories of his informants to see whether the conditions he had identified as producing trust violations had been present earlier in their lives in situations where they had not violated the financial trust placed in them. For Robinson, the difference between analytic induction *as described* and the method as used *in practice* undermined Znaniecki's claims for analytic induction as a method of proof, as a means, that is, for isolating the essential conditions determining a phenomenon. 'The success of analytic induction in producing its complete explanations is due to its procedure, to its systematisation of the method of the working hypothesis, and not to its logical structure' (Robinson, 1951: 816). Indeed, Robinson argues, analytic induction is a special case of enumerative induction.

Despite at least one spirited defence of the method (Manning, 1982), subsequent commentaries on analytic induction, while often sympathetic, have generally acknowledged the force of Robinson's criticisms (Denzin, 1970; Bloor, 1978; Hammersley and Atkinson, 1983; Hammersley, 1989). Compromised by its logical flaws, analytic induction also suffered from a wider shift of orientation in qualitative research, the movement away from procedures based on the analysis of cases and the increasing popularity of analytic approaches involving the coding of textual data derived from interviews or fieldnotes.

The Transition to Code-based Methods

Coding procedures of a kind were not unknown to sociologists in the original Chicago School tradition. Palmer (1928), for example, makes the following rather modern-sounding comment in her early methods text-book, 'Skilled research workers are able to rearrange the data observed in interviews so that remarks concerning one topic can be grouped together without losing the implication contained in the original sequence.' It is also clear, as Platt points out, that in the same period case study researchers in the Chicago tradition used case summary sheets as a data reduction device, and information on such summaries was sometimes further reduced onto file cards (Jennifer Platt, personal communication). Summaries of this kind were attached, however, to the whole case. The practice of attaching 'codes' to segments of data within a body of case material rather than to the case itself seems to have appeared later.

In market research, 'coding' as a term for the classification of responses to open-ended questions on surveys appears to have been in use at least by 1937 (Association of American Marketing, 1937). By the 1940s the term had been extended to the analysis of what now would be called semi-structured interview data. As a product of the New Deal, the US Department of Agriculture set up in the mid-1930s a small-scale unit for interviewing farmers (Converse, 1987). Under the direction of Rensis Likert, perhaps better known today as the begetter of the five-point atti-tude scale that bears his name, this unit operated between 1939 and 1946 as the Division of Program Surveys. One notable feature of the Division – inherited from its very early days – was its commitment to open-ended interviewing. The Division's interviewers were trained in non-directive interviewing techniques, some of which were adapted from the psycho-therapeutic methods of Carl Rogers (Converse, 1987: 196). They also made it a practice to write down verbatim (or as close to verbatim as they could manage) answers to the questions they asked. Material of this kind needed to be coded for analysis. However, Converse comments that the coding procedures used were of a rather simple kind, leading worried staff to feel that some of the richness of their data was not being exploited (1987: 197).

Both the term 'coding' and the procedures associated with it appear to have emerged in a haphazard and unplanned way. Merton developed a fairly elaborate classification system to analyse unstructured interviews from a study of interpersonal influence undertaken in 'Rovere' in 1943. In discussing the classification, which he eventually came to regard as 'logi-cally impeccable, empirically applicable, and virtually sterile' (1968: 445),[3] he does not, however, use the term 'coding'. In the post-war period, depth interview material was gathered, along with a range of standardized and projective methods, for research on the 'authoritarian personality'. In the initial report on this work (Adorno et al., 1950), terms like 'categorization' or 'classification' were used to report results. This usage seems to have given way to the term 'coding' by the middle of the 1950s. For example, in their methodological critique of The Authoritarian Personality, Hyman and Sheatsley – both of whom were survey researchers – continually use the words 'code', 'codes' and 'coding' to refer to the classification process

(1954; see also Guetzkow, 1950). One can also find Riesman and Watson (1964: 290) talking about 'planning a code' for the analysis of pilot interviews for the 'Sociability Project', a study begun in 1955. (In the event the researchers decided to proceed using observational methods rather than interviews so the coding was never done and the interviews remained unanalysed.) The term 'coding' does not seem at this time to have been applied to qualitative data deriving from participant observation.

What is probably the first sustained use of the term 'coding' to refer to the analysis of qualitative data appears in the methodological writing associated with *Boys in White*, a study of the University of Kansas medical school begun in 1956 (Becker and Geer, 1960; Becker et al., 1961). One possible conduit for the use of the term coding could have been David Riesman who, as we have just observed, was familiar with the term and who had some involvement with the *Boys in White* project, during which he reviewed and commented on fieldnotes (Riesman, 1979). This is conjecture, however. Howard Becker does not now recall how or why he and his colleagues used the term 'coding' (personal communication).[4] Becker does indicate, though, that, while the term itself was not in widespread use at the time, procedures for the systematic extraction of material from fieldnotes were hardly novel. One procedure he learned as a graduate student, for example, was to mark up fieldnotes using different coloured pencils to refer to different topics.

Becker observes that *Boys in White* was perceived as a study of higher education, a field dominated at that time by psychologists. To forestall scepticism from this quarter about the evidential basis of their assertions, Becker and Geer needed to make explicit the procedure and logic of what they were doing. According to Becker and Geer (1960), the lack of systematic procedures in qualitative research encourages qualitative researchers to resort to anecdotal data. They suggest as an alternative a systematic sequence of procedures for generating well-substantiated analytic propositions. The basic purpose of this approach is to establish a theoretical model which cannot *plausibly* be assailed on available data. This approach is summarized in Becker and Geer (1960) and in a later paper which, ironically perhaps, assesses the possible impact of computers on qualitative analysis (Becker et al., 1984; see also Geer, 1964 and Becker, 1958). Typically, in the kind of project Becker and Geer describe the bulk of the analysis is carried out after the data have been collected, since it is usually only by then, they suggest, that time is available to deal systematically with the material. However, Becker and Geer assume that analysis begins in the field at least in two respects. First of all, from the beginning of data collection fieldwork becomes a site for the generation of working hypotheses and for identifying major areas of concern (Geer, 1964). Working hypotheses might be very little more than assumptions drawn from theory or from everyday conjecture about what is likely to be important. Primarily, they guide the research in terms of what to look at, who to talk to, and the sort of questions to ask. Other hypotheses – perhaps of a more elaborate sort – emerge in the course of the fieldwork itself. Because they vary in their relevance and complexity, Geer suggests, some kinds of working hypothesis can be tested easily and quickly. Others inform the research over a long period, and are subjected to repeated refinement and testing as the research goes on. Through this elaboration some hypotheses eventually emerge as major themes in the research.

The second way of beginning the analysis while still in the field is for the researcher to maintain a running summary of fieldnote material. These fieldwork summaries are coded using a 'loose inclusive' coding procedure (Becker et al., 1984: 22). Because it has a different purpose, coding of this kind 'systematically violate[s] the principles involved in connection with survey procedures' (1984: 21). In quantitative research the system of codes needs to be exhaustive and made up of mutually exclusive categories and the coding process is governed by strict rules (Lazarsfeld and Barton, 1951). This is because coding is used to transform open-ended material into standardized units. In qualitative research one needs, however, to maximize the inclusion of potentially relevant material. In other words, a code should be assigned whenever there is any reason to suppose that it might bear on the matter in hand. In addition, coding does not initially utilize 'analytic, theoretically defined categories' (1984: 22) in order to avoid premature analytic closure.

Coded materials are used to build analytic propositions about the basic elements of some aspect of social organization, the conditions under which particular phenomena occur or social processes of relevance to theory. The aim is to use a set of systematic procedures to turn up all items of relevance to a particular proposition, especially those which might negate it. This involves the use of quasi-statistics and negative case analysis. Quasi-statistics are in effect simple counting procedures designed to permit judgements about the frequency and range of some phenomenon. For example, in offering support for the proposition that medical students adopt a particular perspective on progress through medical school, Becker and Geer provided evidence on the frequency with which the perspective was invoked, the range of contexts within which it was invoked and the extent to which the perspective could be regarded as being held collectively rather than individually. This last involved the explicit display of the conditions under which the perspective manifested itself. Thus Becker and Geer systematically assessed how far statements or activities indicative of the perspective were volunteered or elicited, and whether they took place only in the presence of the observer, or when others were present. By showing that the perspective was frequent and widespread and that its expression could not be attributed to the prompting of the researchers, they enhanced the plausibility of their analysis.

Negative case analysis involves inspecting all coded fieldnotes which do not support the proposition which has been advanced. As in analytic induction, such instances might be shown to be irrelevant, in which case they could be excluded from consideration. Negative evidence might also, however, force a re-evaluation of the proposition under consideration. The search for negative cases involves analytic work. To identify such cases, the analyst has to seek plausible alternative explanations for the patterns found. If such alternative explanations can be ruled out given the weight of evidence against them, there are grounds, though no proof, for asserting the plausibility of the analysis (Becker, 1958).

Becker and Geer note that the procedures they describe 'bear a family resemblance to the techniques of analytic induction' (1960: 271) in at least two respects. Their method is, first of all, sequential in character, proceeding through the successive refinement of an initial model,[5] and, second, it is partly driven by the search for negative cases. Unlike classical analytic induction, however, the aim is not to produce statements of universal applicability. Instead, recognizing the logical weaknesses of analytic induction, Becker and Geer propose as the analytic end of qualitative research the establishment of a model based on strongly plausible inference; one in which the means by which the conclusions are reached are visible and difficult to assail on purely evidentiary grounds. Although they recognize parallels between their attempt at systematization and the attempt by Lazarsfeld and Barton (1951) to codify qualitative procedures (Becker and Geer, 1960: 272), the coding procedures Becker and Geer used were clearly different from those employed in survey research. The latter aimed to allocate information to exhaustive and mutually exclusive categories. Becker and Geer's strategy was to code in a way that allowed all relevant material on a particular topic to be retrieved for inspection and further possible differentiation; a procedure of the kind still used by qualitative researchers (Becker et al., 1984).

It is probably no accident that the transition from case-based to code-based analysis occurred at a time when researchers were moving increasingly to 'real-time data capture' methods. The tradition of participant observation which grew up in sociology after the Second World War was quite clearly influenced by developments in anthropological research. Malinowski had reoriented fieldwork practice away from a 'verandah model' (Wax and Cassell, 1979) which utilized professional informants towards what Sanjek (1990b) calls 'situated listening', the detailed contemporaneous recording of everyday life. In the methodological appendix to *Street Corner Society* Whyte comments that as he began to develop his own research methods 'the social anthropological literature beginning with Malinowski . . . seemed closer to what I wanted to do' (1955: 286) than the existing community studies tradition in sociology. In particular, Whyte cites the influence of Conrad Arensberg who had just returned from anthropological fieldwork in a rural Irish community. It was Arensberg, Whyte records, who 'worked with me on field research methods, emphasizing the importance of observing people in action and getting down a detailed report of actual behavior completely divorced from moral judge-ments' (1955: 287; emphasis added).[6]

Related to this change was a move towards recording interview responses verbatim. In her early methods textbook Vivian Palmer (1928) indicates that Chicago School sociologists typically jotted down notes during an interview which were written up afterwards in more detail. Although she mentions recording devices, it is only to indicate that, 'So far no extensive use has been made of these mechanical devices, and their use should, of course be confined to the study of the interview and to exceptional research studies.' In other words, she seems only to have regarded phonographic recording as a potentially useful tool for methodo-logical research, or in unusual circumstances, rather than as a routine aid to substantive research. However, Bulmer (1984) records that Clifford Shaw made use of a stenographer for recording interviews, and by the war years Kluckhohn (1945) was enjoining researchers to develop skills in shorthand or speed-writing techniques in order to record interviews. There is an indication that at least some of the interviews carried out by the Division of Program Surveys were phonographically recorded (Skott, 1943). Tape recording of interviews only apparently became common, however, by the end of the 1940s and beginning of the 1950s (Bucher et al., 1956), once commercial production of tape recorders resumed after the war (Rowe, 1953). By this time, Chapoulie (1987: 270) comments:

> Instead of briefly summarizing fieldnotes and remarks gathered by interview-ing, or even simply referring to these data, many . . . accounts cited them word for word, which forced researchers to construct finer categories of analysis and to explain their interpretations of remarks and behavior in more detail.

This offers early evidence of the interplay between technical develop-ments and analytic refinement.

Grounded Theory

If Becker and Geer introduced the term 'coding' into qualitative practice, its subsequent popularity is probably due to Glaser and Strauss (1967), who use it repeatedly and without comment, as do both Strauss and Glaser in later works (Glaser, 1978; Strauss, 1987; Strauss and Corbin, 1990). According to Strauss and Corbin (1994: 275) Glaser and Strauss's book *The Discovery of Grounded Theory* had three main aims. The first was to provide a rationale for theory that was empirically derived (i.e. 'grounded'). Largely this aim emerged out of the frustration Glaser and Strauss felt at the turn taken by American sociology in the 1950s and early 1960s. Reflecting both the expansion of the discipline and its insecurity, that period fell prey to what C. Wright Mills (1959) derided as 'grand theory' and 'abstracted empiricism'. This was the tendency to produce, on the one hand, intricate macroscopic theoretical schemes, largely devoid of empirical content, and , on the other, attempts to verify in a usually quantitative manner relatively modest deductively derived hypotheses. Related to this rejection of existing trends was a desire on Glaser and Strauss's part 'to legitimate careful qualitative research' (Strauss and Corbin, 1994: 275). This emerged from an awareness that, by then, the qualitative tradition, judged incapable of verification, had an increasingly low status within the discipline. A third aim of *The Discovery of Grounded Theory* was to suggest a 'logic for and specifics of grounded theories'. In other words, Glaser and Strauss wanted to provide researchers with a guide to the methods and procedures by which a theoretically grounded analysis could be produced. (These are variously detailed in Glaser and Strauss, 1967; Glaser, 1978; Strauss, 1987; Strauss and Corbin, 1990.)[7]

Although the basic outlines remain clear, it has become progressively more difficult to give a succinct and adequate account of grounded theory. As time has gone on, shifts in emphasis appear and new terminology emerges. Latterly, too, Glaser has seemingly entertained serious reservations about how Strauss had developed the grounded theory approach. In essence, Glaser seems to feel that Strauss has abandoned the constant comparative method at the heart of grounded theory in favour of a system of analyst-generated, rather than data-generated, conceptual development. In what follows an account will be given of the method as it was originally articulated in *The Discovery of Grounded Theory*. This is followed by a description of 'open coding' based on a detailed example of the procedure given by Strauss. The basic features of Strauss and Corbin's development of the method are then outlined. Finally, attention is directed to Glaser's critique of Strauss and Corbin.

At the heart of grounded theory is the 'constant comparative method'. This is set out in detail in Chapter V of Glaser and Strauss's (1967) book, which reproduces an article originally published by Glaser (1965) in *Social Problems*. One begins constant comparison by examining 'incidents' recorded in one's data. In the account of the constant comparative method given in *The Discovery of Grounded Theory*, the term 'incidents' is not defined. Glaser's *Social Problems* article, however, contains a reference back to Becker and Geer's (1960: 281) work, where incidents are defined as 'complete verbal expressions of an attitude or complete acts by an individual or group'. Each incident in the data is coded into as many theoretical categories as possible. Categories are of two kinds: 'sociological constructs' and '*in vivo* codes', as Glaser (1978) describes them. The former derive from the language of social research. On the other hand, *in vivo* codes are based on the language of research participants. For example, Glaser and Strauss note that nurses often talked of maintaining their 'composure' when discussing how they dealt with the death of a patient. 'Composure', therefore became in their analysis an *in vivo* code. In contrast to the procedure adopted by Becker and Geer, which involved the running allocation to new incidents of codes developed early on in the research process, coding in constant comparison is governed by a basic rule: 'while coding an incident for a category, compare it with the previous incident in the same and different groups coded in the same category'. That is, before you do further coding you should recall or go back and look at all incidents previously coded using the same category.

Codes at this stage are conceptual labels, usually written in the margins of fieldnotes or interview transcripts (though other forms of recording might also be used). As one proceeds from incident to incident, looking back at previously coded incidents in the process, one inevitably explores the theoretical properties of a particular category. In other words, the analyst embarked on the constant comparative method will soon begin to think of different types of category, and to explore categories in terms of their conditions and consequences, as well as their relation to other categories and their properties. This is essentially a process of conceptual clarification, through which the nature of a particular category and its properties are delineated. Precisely because the delineation of categories and their properties is a process which reflects emerging conceptual awareness, Glaser and Strauss set out a second rule of constant comparison. Coding should periodically be interrupted in order to record a memo on the present state of theoretical understanding associated with a category.

Glaser and Strauss argue that, from the beginning of the research, the processes of collecting, coding and analysing data should go on at the same time. Data collection in this situation is guided by 'theoretical sampling'. The point of theoretical sampling is to select sources of new data in ways that permit the further development of theory. The procedure is quite unlike statistical sampling where one must define a population, and a procedure for ensuring random selection. Instead, in theoretical sampling successive reformulations of theory inform and are informed by the 'ongoing inclusion' (Glaser and Strauss, 1967: 50) of groups, settings or situations thought to have comparative relevance for the generation and clarification of conceptual categories.

The second stage of constant comparison Glaser and Strauss refer to as 'integrating categories and their properties'. Having generated a set of categories from the initial comparison of incidents, the analyst now compares further incidents against those categories. Glaser and Strauss argue that this process leads to developing theory. Categories are further clarified, their properties are further specified and the interrelation between categories and their respective properties becomes progressively clearer. Again, to follow Glaser and Strauss's example, coding of incidents relating to how nurses dealt with dying patients generated a category of 'social loss' related to how the nurse perceived the social value of the patient. Also generated was a category of 'composure' related to nurses' strategies for coping with the emotional impact of a patient's death. Comparisons of incidents to categories led to an emerging theory which linked a property of the first category, 'high social loss', to how nurses maintained their professional composure under trying circumstances.

As coding proceeds, theory emerges, but in the next phase of constant comparison the nature of that theory changes as it becomes 'delimited'. In the first place, the theory itself 'solidifies'. Major modifications become fewer in number. Rather, changes made to the theory involve clarification, simplification and reduction. Reduction is an important step on the way to grounded theory. 'By reduction we mean that the analyst may discover underlying uniformities in the original set of categories or their properties, and can then formulate the theory with a smaller set of higher level concepts' (Glaser and Strauss, 1967: 110). Reduction allows categories to be expressed at a greater level of abstraction, and therefore, generality. Indeed, one can see here the possibility of moving from substantive theory to formal theory. In other words, a theory of how nurses maintain their composure faced with the death of patients having varying degrees of social value might be stated more generally, and formally, as a theory about how professionals allocate their services in relation to the implicit social worth of their clients. In making such a move, Glaser and Strauss add, one achieves two important goals of theorizing. On the one hand, the theory produced is parsimonious, attaining maximum explanatory power based on a relatively small number of variables. On the other, it has wide scope by virtue of being applicable across a range of situations. In addition, the theory is well grounded. There is a close relationship between theory and data.

All of this has implications for further data collection and the time needed for analysis. Because one has reduced the range of categories relevant to the range of emerging theory, it is now possible specifically to focus one's attention on those categories in analysing further incidents. Furthermore, categories become *theoretically saturated*. One can quickly see whether a subsequent incident is likely to force a modification of an existing concept. If it is, then the concept is coded and compared to existing categories. If not, it can be passed over without coding, because to do otherwise 'only adds bulk to the coded data and nothing to the theory' (Glaser and Strauss, 1967: 111). This kind of logic can also be extended to situations where a new category emerges some way into the coding of data or where information from other sources appears to be relevant to the emerging analysis. If new material rapidly leads to theoretical saturation, the need to go back and recode existing coded materials is obviated. A lack of theoretical saturation, on the other hand, might require a reworking of existing categories.

Memos are a crucial tool in the production of grounded theory. Strauss and Corbin summarize the role of memos like this: 'Memos contain the products of actual coding, plus theoretical sensitizing and summarizing notes, and give direction for sampling' (1990: 223). The aim of memoing is to provide a loosely structured forum within which to develop theoretical ideas. Memos exhaust 'momentary ideation', as Glaser (1978: 84) puts it. They are a vehicle by which the process of raising descriptive material to theoretical significance can be begun and pursued. Memos, in other words, are the site for categorizing, dimensionalizing, hypothesizing and integrating theoretical ideas. Thus, a rule in grounded theory work is that the analyst should always break off from the coding process to record a memo. Memos provide a 'free' context for theory emergence. That is, considerations of style, voice, elegance and analytic closure are subordinated to the production of the memo. In Glaser's words, 'The idea is the thing.' Inscribing ideas about one's material as and when they occur avoids the loss of ideas through forgetting and provides a set of new materials which can be refined, elaborated, rewritten and commented upon; processes, of course, which can be continued through further coding.

What emerges from the immediate and recurrent recording of ideas in memo form is a 'sortible [sic] memo fund' (Glaser, 1978: 86–7). The sorting of memos provides a spur to theoretical thinking and might spark further ideas through the juxtaposition of previously separated material. The need to sort memos has consequences for data management. Memos need to have a physical form that makes sorting easy and which permits categorization and cross-referencing. This also implies having procedures for making categories clearly visible, for example through highlighting or underlining. An important rule is that memos and data should be held separately though nearby. Attaching memos directly to data, through writing memos directly on transcripts, say, risks confusion about the analytic level of marginal annotations.

Open Coding

In the writings which appeared after *The Discovery of Grounded Theory*, the initial process of coding the data became known as 'open coding'. The term 'open coding' has a rather benign ring to it. Notice, however, that rather violent language is often used to describe the process. Strauss (1987: 29), for example explains that, 'Open coding quickly forces the analyst to fracture, break the data apart analytically . . .'. In other words, the purpose is to force open the research by encouraging the analyst to get into the data, to make some initial, if only tentative, interpretations and to gain a sense of where to go and what to do next. Another way of putting all of this is to say that open coding involves a dialogue with a generative purpose. This dialogue is often an internal one as the analyst confronts and records reactions to the data, but it can also be a dialogue with colleagues.

Glaser (1978) and Strauss (1987) present a series of guidelines for open coding. First of all, one should constantly question the data. What, for example, do the data say about the emerging topic focus of the study? What theoretical categories can be generated from the data? How do those studied deal with the problems that confront them? A second guideline is that the data selected for open coding must be treated microscopically, coded line by line, sentence by sentence, even word by word, if need be. A third guideline follows on from the role of open coding in generating theoretical ideas. Coding should be interrupted immediately to record memos detailing the theoretical implications of what is being coded. Finally, the analytic importance of any category should always be demonstrated rather than assumed (Strauss, 1987: 32). This means, for example, that, 'The analyst should not assume the analytic relevance of any "face sheet" or traditional variable such as age, sex, social class, race, until it emerges as relevant. Those, too, must earn their way into the grounded theory.'

Strauss (1987: 59–64) gives an example of open coding based on an observation he carried out in a cardiac recovery unit. Specifically, the observation refers to a nurse working with a barely conscious patient who has just returned from surgery. Strauss takes the first four sentences he recorded in his fieldnotes during the observation and shows how they would be dealt with through open coding. The analysis consists of a detailed rumination on the data, captured in an almost stream-of-consciousness style. Here we consider only the first sentence Strauss deals with: 'She changed the blood transfusion bag', in which he focuses on how the nurse works with the blood transfusion equipment attached to the patient. The sentence analysed contains only six words. It yields 73 lines of explication, generating in the process a variety of potential analytic categories, speculations and hypotheses.

Strauss immediately identifies three analytic categories associated with the changing of the bag. 'She *changed* the blood transfusion bag' suggests a *task*. This category, Strauss suggests, is drawn from common experience. '*She* changed the blood transfusion bag' suggests *division of labour* as a category, this time drawn from the technical literature. Finally, 'She changed *the blood transfusion bag*' suggests *supplies* as a category. Having generated these categories, Strauss sets the last two aside in order to focus on the task of changing the bag. In considering the changing of the blood transfusion bag, Strauss first asks himself what properties the task has. It is visible to others, is simple, quick, does not require much skill or present much of a challenge. Each of these aspects of the task is a dimension along which any task might be characterized. A question about the frequency of the task leads on to a further chain of speculation: 'What would happen if they temporarily ran out of the bags of blood?' Strauss notes the relevance of this question to the safety of the patient, and hypothesizes that, were a safety issue to be present, organizational procedures would be present to ensure blood bags were always available.

At this point Strauss sets the issues of task and the related issue of supply to one side. He proceeds instead to an analysis of the division of labour involved in changing the bag. This immediately sets up a series of comparisons. It is a non-working relationship. Since the patient involved is barely conscious he cannot help the nurse. Neither, however, can he hinder her. This sets up a further more explicit comparison with situations where patients, when conscious, might be anxious about the possibility of receiving contaminated blood. In this case, anxiety is identified as a condition of potential non-cooperation on safety grounds which Strauss regards as a consequence of being conscious when blood transfusion work is being done. This relates too to the integrity of supplies.

Strauss then moves to an explicit consideration of the supplies issue, again asking a series of questions and making implicit comparisons. Unlike supplies for the maintenance of equipment, blood is a natural product which has to be taken to the patient and must be stored safely. It must also find its way into the patient, something that implies a body–equipment connection and a process of body invasion. Again, for each of these categories, a range of dimensions needs to be considered: how is the connection made?, what effect does it have on the patient?, how far does it need to be monitored? and so on. This issue of monitoring raises in its turn issues about safety: how far might infection result from the body–equipment connection?, who monitors that risk?, and what might happen if monitoring fails? The question of safety also brings the question of supplies into focus again, and reminds Strauss of the need to look at a later date at issues to do with the sources and storage of blood. Only then does Strauss move on to the next sentence in his fieldnotes.

A number of comments about this exercise are in order. First, the analysis produced by open coding is not fixed or immutable. There is not one, single privileged reading of the data. Indeed, it might be a useful exercise for the reader to consult the original example and to attempt to extract from it elements Strauss did not consider. Second, it might be that much of what arises from this sort of close questioning of the data is banal, dross even, having little long-term relevance. The point, however, is to extract what is of potential theoretical value, to use open coding as a 'springboard' (Strauss, 1987: 63) to think more broadly about the implications of the material both for developing theory and for collecting relevant data in the future. Note, too, how material is 'banked' for future use. (For a different use of banking strategies – in the writing process – see Becker, 1986: 142.) As Strauss emphasizes, part of the point of open coding is its provisional character. The intention is to generate *initial* formulations since they can always be modified as the research progresses. As Strauss puts it (1987: 45):

> So at every step you're asking about opposites, variations and continua. Sometimes in actual research you don't follow all of these leads – sometimes it is just

too exhausting and sometimes a phenomenon just forces itself on you from the nature of what you are seeing or hearing, day in and day out. Or you see something on one day and on another something fits with it. But at every step this is what you are doing. That is why you don't want to rush out and get a lot of data, because you would get submerged. You get a little data, then you stop and think! At every point in your initial fieldnotes or interviews, you must do this kind of thing.

'Straussian' Grounded Theory

Apparently driven in part by the difficulties students have with open coding, Strauss and Corbin (1990) present a range of heuristic strategies for open coding. As might already have been guessed from the example of open coding given earlier, one set of techniques for breaking open data revolves around the asking of simple questions. These include the litany of factual questions taught to every budding journalist: who? what? why? where? when? how much? The example Strauss and Corbin give has to do with the relief of arthritic pain. One might ask, for example, who provides pain relief to people with arthritis? What gives them relief? How is pain experienced and handled? How much relief is needed? When does pain occur and when is relief sought? Why is pain relief important? Besides such questions a range of temporal (and implicitly quantitative) questions might also be asked concerning the frequency, duration, rate and timing of the pain. A second technique involves an extensive interrogation of a particular word or phrase. An example of this has already been seen, but there are other possibilities. All the possible meanings associated with a specific word might be listed in order to sensitize the analyst to the various ways in which a particular utterance might be relevant.

Strauss and Corbin suggest a variety of techniques for open coding based on comparisons. One is the engagingly named 'flip-flop' technique. Think about 'creeping featurism' in the computer industry. Commercial software companies keep on adding more and more features to a particular program to keep it ahead of the competition. Now do the flip-flop and think about software development in a non-competitive market. The development of CAQDAS programs is a good example. Does the absence of competition mean that creeping featurism is absent? The answer is no. Programs keep on adding new features (although development cycles are longer in non-competitive software markets than in competitive markets). In the case of CAQDAS programs, creeping featurism is driven by the interpersonal relationships which come into being between developers and users. The flip-flop technique has enabled us to tease out something analytically relevant from our knowledge of the data.

Two further kinds of comparison are possible according to Strauss and

Corbin: systematic comparison and far-out comparison. An example of systematic comparison comes from a study one of us did of Catholic–Protestant intermarriage in Northern Ireland (Lee, 1994). In developing a scheme for coding interview data from this study, systematic comparisons were made between relationships where the male partner was a Roman Catholic as opposed to the female partner, situations where parents were hostile to the marriage compared with those where they were not, situations where couples had formed a relationship very quickly versus those where it had developed over a long period of time, and so on. Using far-out comparisons has something in common with the flip-flop technique. As the name implies the analyst looks, not for the obvious comparisons, but for those which are unusual in some way. Exploring how body-builders use equipment, Strauss and Corbin make a comparison between violinists and body-builders. The comparison draws attention in Strauss and Corbin's analysis to the portability of equipment, its supply and ownership, and how people are taught to utilize their equipment.

A final technique Strauss and Corbin recommend is referred to as 'waving the red flag'. What they mean by this is that analysts should treat with caution statements of absolute certainty made about the social world. To put this another way, statements such as 'Everyone knows that . . .' or 'It's always the case that . . .' are in fact invitations to consider the conditions under which the alleged uniformities actually occur. Everyone knows, for example, that parents in Northern Ireland oppose the marriage of their son or daughter to someone of the 'opposite' religion. Yet instances can be found where parents accept the possibility of out-marriage with equanimity (Lee, 1994). Very hostile parental reaction does occur, but is often associated with particular circumstances to do with the social environment within which parents are located.

Growing out of and feeding back into open coding is the process of 'axial coding' (Strauss, 1987; Strauss and Corbin, 1990). In axial coding one takes a category produced by open coding. Through rather intensive coding one attempts to build around it a texture of conceptual relationships. (The category is therefore treated as an 'axis', thus the term 'axial coding'.) Strauss and Corbin give a very detailed account of axial coding. Briefly, the properties of a phenomenon to which a category applies are dimensionalized. These properties and dimensions are progressively linked to each other through the operation of the 'coding paradigm' (Strauss, 1987; Strauss and Corbin, 1990). In other words, it is assumed that one can relate together categories, properties and dimensions by specifying the *conditions* which generate a phenomenon, the *context* and *intervening conditions* bearing on it, the interactional *strategies* and *tactics* of those involved, and the *consequences* that result from all of the above. 'The analyst hypothesises about and increasingly can specify varieties of conditions and consequences, interactions, strategies and consequences (the coding paradigm) that are associated with the appearance of the phenomenon referenced by the category' (Strauss, 1987: 64).

All of this is carried out through a complex web of questioning, comparing, dimensionalizing and hypothesizing *involving a constant interplay of inductive and deductive thinking.* The status of categories, properties, dimensions and relationships is a provisional one. Through a continual process of open and axial coding, those relationships which are not supported by the data are progressively discarded. As Strauss and Corbin (1990: 112) put it, 'Your final theory is limited to those categories, their properties and dimensions, and statements of relationships that exist in the actual data collected – not what you think might be out there but haven't come across.'

Selective coding is the process by which a fully grounded theory emerges. According to Strauss and Corbin, the procedures involved are rather like those used in axial coding. The difference is that they take place at a higher level of abstraction. Selective coding begins with the attempt to establish a 'story line'. This is a brief descriptive account which encapsulates the essence of what the research is about. Strauss and Corbin give an example from a study by Corbin which looked at the management of pregnancy by women suffering from chronic illness. The basic story line which emerged out of the open and axial coding of interviews with a sample of women in this situation was as follows: women with chronic illness play an active role in managing the risks associated with pregnancy out of an overwhelming desire to have a healthy baby. The production of a grounded theory depends on the transformation of this descriptive account into an analytical story (Strauss and Corbin, 1990: 142). The process of telling an analytical story depends on establishing a central or *core* category around which other categories are integrated. Just as in axial coding, categories are then related to the core category by reference to the coding paradigm. Corbin used the core category of 'protective governing' to refer to the way in which women with chronic illness actively managed the risk to the health of their unborn child. From this a theory was developed in terms of whether the pregnancy trajectory was on-course or off-course and whether the conditions producing risk were high or low, critical or non-critical (Strauss and Corbin, 1990: 131).

We have already mentioned the importance of memos in grounded theory. According to Strauss and Corbin, memos are of three kinds: code notes, theoretical notes and operational notes. Code notes contain information relating to categories, properties and dimensions. Theoretical notes serve to alert the researcher to emerging conceptualizations. Researchers write operational notes as reminders of what to do next, who to see, what to ask and so on. At the stage of open coding, code notes record the initial dialogue with the data. Identified in a memo of this type are categories, dimensions, initial speculations and hypotheses. Code notes written off axial coding might have a similar character, although the concern here is much more with relating categories, properties and dimensions with one another. The purpose of theoretical notes is to sensitize the analyst to emerging aspects of the theory in order to guide theoretical sampling. Again the difference between theoretical notes associated with open coding and those related to axial coding probably has more to do with their level of abstraction than their actual content. At the stage of selective coding, code notes are likely to be relatively sparse while operational notes will be quite directive. Instead of an exploratory character, they direct the analyst towards situations and contexts which aid the verification of emerging aspects of the theory. Theoretical notes at the stage of selective coding are likely to focus on the emerging descriptive and analytic story line.

The status of Strauss and Corbin's book poses a difficulty for any assessment of grounded theory. From one perspective the book can be seen as an accessible introduction to the method, and a much-needed manual detailing the procedures involved in grounded theorizing. Glaser (1992), however, has subjected Strauss and Corbin's work to a sustained and robust critique. Glaser excoriates Strauss and Corbin for deviating from the received principles of grounded theory. Specifically, Glaser charges, Strauss and Corbin substitute a series of procedures for forcing meaning from data in place of authentic grounded theory procedures which, Glaser argues, ensure theory emergence. For Glaser, the procedures advocated by Strauss and Corbin produce 'full conceptual description' rather than grounded theory. Instead of letting theory emerge from the data, Glaser argues, Strauss and Corbin constrain the data into a variety of predetermined templates. Glaser's rebuttal of Strauss and Corbin's methods is too exhaustive to be detailed here. What follows is a brief indication of why Glaser objects to the procedures set forth by Strauss and Corbin.

Glaser (1992: 50) acknowledges that the various techniques Strauss and Corbin advocate for breaking open data provide some degree of theoretical sensitivity. He goes on to argue, however, that outcomes produced by such procedures will emerge out of constant comparison anyway. Moreover, in doing so they will have been driven by the data and their relevance to emerging theory will be assured. Deploying Strauss and Corbin's procedures before one has demonstrated the relevance of the answers they produce merely forces the data, Glaser claims, into a preconceived package.

Glaser argues that the paradigm model in which the analyst looks for causes, consequences, interactional strategies, intervening conditions and so on is another example of forcing the data into a prepackaged pattern. He does not deny that such aspects are relevant but, again, he insists that their relevance should emerge out of the data by means of constant comparison. Glaser contends that what Strauss later came to call the 'coding paradigm' is one of a large number of 'code families' detailed in his (Glaser's) book *Theoretical Sensitivity* (1978). Glaser's account of code families is not altogether clear. Code families, it seems, are made up of sets of related theoretical codes. 'Theoretical codes conceptualize how the substantive codes may relate to each other as hypotheses to be integrated into the theory' (Glaser, 1978: 55). The list of coding families represents a thesaurus, as it were, of conceptual connections between different categories and between categories and their properties. Code families include not only causes, contexts, contingencies, consequences, covariances and conditions familiar from the coding paradigm. Glaser also identifies, among many others, a process family and a degree family. The former, for example, is concerned with stages, progressions, transitions, trajectories, etc. In the latter, properties are identified in terms of limits, range, intensity and so on.

A further point of contention between Glaser and Strauss and Corbin refers to the notion of the core category. The generation of a core category is a goal of theory generation (Glaser, 1992: 75). According to Glaser, Strauss and Corbin see the core category as referring to a central phenomenon around which narrative and conceptual description are woven. In Glaser's eyes, the core category is a central and recurrent conceptual entity, substantially and richly connected to other categories, and with considerable analytic power. As such it accounts for most of the variation in a pattern of behaviour 'which is relevant and problematic for those involved' in the situation being studied (Glaser, 1978: 93). Since the core category reflects what is of major concern to research participants, it is actually difficult, according to Glaser, not to uncover it. The core category will emerge eventually out of the coding and sorting of data and memos. Again, for Glaser the procedures of axial and selective coding advocated by Strauss and Corbin actually hinder, rather than ensure, identification of the core category.

While these are significant controversies they represent dispute about particular emphases and components of what is now a highly developed approach to qualitative data analysis. Although, as we claim in Chapter 7, the use of grounded theory might not be as ubiquitous as sometimes thought, the approach clearly has a dominant position in the analysis of non-numeric data at the present time.

Miles and Huberman

Matthew Miles and Michael Huberman have extended in a very considerable way the range of procedures available to qualitative researchers. Their approach, which they continued to refine up to the point of Miles's untimely death, is described in Miles and Huberman (1984, 1994), and is summarized in Huberman and Miles (1994). According to Miles and Huberman, qualitative analysis has a number of characteristics. First of all, qualitative research designs cannot be taken 'off the shelf'. They need to be developed in relation to the problem at hand and are subject to modification and customization as the research proceeds. Miles and Huberman, both drawing on extensive experience as evaluation researchers, do not take this to mean that qualitative studies must inevitably proceed in a loose, inductive way. They also envisage situations where relatively 'tight' deductively driven designs might be appropriate, for example where the research site is a familiar one and a range of well-defined concepts is available to the researcher. In either event, Miles and Huberman see the analytic choices the researcher makes in selecting particular settings, problems or a conceptual framework as a form of 'anticipatory data reduction' (Huberman and Miles, 1994: 430), giving direction and focus to the research, and out of which emerge the later explanatory stages of the analysis.

A second feature of qualitative analysis according to Miles and Huberman is that it has an 'interim' quality. Qualitative studies have 'a peculiar life cycle' as they put it (Huberman and Miles, 1994: 431). The relative weight put on data collection and on data analysis shifts as the research proceeds, and different phases of the research call forth different analytic strategies. The advantage of this is that understandings emerging from the analysis feed into and modify further data collection so that, 'Unlike experimental studies, changes in observational protocols or interview schedules in a field study usually reflect a better understanding of the setting, thereby heightening the internal validity of the study' (Huberman and Miles, 1994: 431). Alongside this, however, is a disadvantage. The more one learns about a situation, potentially the more one realizes how much one has yet to know. Analysis, in other words, has an inflationary character. As the analysis proceeds, more and more material might need to be taken into consideration. It is this, in part, which makes qualitative data an 'attractive nuisance', as Miles (1983) calls it. The richness, detail and depth that inhere in qualitative materials are offset by the difficult, time-consuming and potentially *ad hoc* character of qualitative data analysis.

The third characteristic of qualitative research Miles and Huberman highlight is its iterative character. Qualitative analysis is inherently cyclical. Patterns, hypotheses and themes are discovered inductively. Possible verification of the emerging patterns is then sought using deductive strategies. This in turn potentially yields further inductive insight. Miles and Huberman suggest that a wide variety of tactics is appropriate to this iterative process. Such strategies range from noting emerging themes in the data, through the making of contrasts and comparisons between analytic elements, to the construction of an extensive and coherent conceptual and analytic schema.

Miles and Huberman see analysis as involving three linked processes which reflect the anticipatory, interim and iterative character of qualitative research. These are: data reduction, data display and what they describe as 'conclusion drawing/verification' (Huberman and Miles, 1994). By data reduction they mean an initial process by which material is selected and condensed on the basis of an emerging conceptual framework. Data display is the 'organized, compressed assembly of information' (1994: 429). That is, data, already reduced, are arranged in ways which make it easier for the analyst to identify, focus on, and select potential interpretations of the data. In their various writings, Miles and Huberman have strongly emphasized the utility of devices such as structured case summaries and synopses, the use of vignettes, network diagrams and matrix displays. The term 'conclusion drawing and verification' describes what Miles and Huberman see as the process of drawing broad, but substantiated, interpretations from displayed data.

Miles and Huberman describe three broad strategies for data reduction: the use of summaries of various kinds, coding and memoing, and review procedures. Summaries are used to render into a compact and easily retrievable form fieldnotes associated with particular contacts, informants, interviewees and the like, and for the information contained in documents about the field site that might come into the possession of the researcher. The aim is to produce such summaries soon after the contact is made or the document received. Usually a single side of paper is used so that the main features of the summary can be immediately apprehended. Summaries guide the planning of future activities and, where there is more than one fieldworker, aid project co-ordination. Inspected at a later date, summaries help to refresh the fieldworker's memory of a particular contact or document. They can be coded and analysed like other data, used either to develop preliminary codes or as the basis for revising existing codes.

Coding is a fundamental part of data reduction. Codes are 'astringent' (Miles and Huberman, 1994: 58). They pull together material and signal potential themes in the data. Miles and Huberman distinguish between first-level and second-level coding. The aim of first-level coding is to produce a working set of codes. At this level codes might be merely descriptive. As such they 'entail little interpretation'. The analyst is simply 'attributing a class of phenomena to a segment of text' (1994: 57). Miles and Huberman differentiate descriptive codes of this type from those having a more interpretive character. Although their discussion is not entirely clear, interpretive codes reflect a greater familiarity with the field setting; such codes also relate, not just to the data, but to other codes. The example Miles and Huberman give refers to the motivations school principals have for adopting an educational innovation. Accounts of their motivation, say from interview transcripts, might be coded in an abbreviated form as 'MOT' for 'motivation'. As data collection and analysis proceed, accounts of motivation might be seen interpretively as involving elements of public relations as opposed to individual commitment. The initial descriptive coding might then be elaborated in an interpretive manner by distinguishing between public motivation, 'PUB-MOT', and private motivation, 'PRIV-MOT'.

First-level coding involves a process of naming and classifying what is in the data. Second-level coding marks regularities in the data. Such regu-larities are captured in 'pattern codes'. Pattern codes 'are a sort of meta-code' (Miles and Huberman, 1994: 69). They have an explanatory status, serving to identify themes emerging from the data, configurations of events, persons or processes, or explanation. As the term 'pattern codes' might imply, the researcher begins second-level coding by looking for threads, leads, commonalities or recurrences that suggest some under-lying pattern. According to Miles and Huberman, pattern codes 'usually turn around four often interrelated, summarizers: themes, causes/expla-nations, relationships among people and more theoretical constructs' (1994: 70). Thus one might classify instances of informal rule-following as a theme, the reasons given for some particular activity as an explanation, the existence of a social network as a relationship, and a tentative analytic idea as an emerging construct. Pattern codes can be used in a variety of ways. Their robustness can be checked out by seeing whether or not they fit readily with new data. They might be written up in memo form as a basis for further conceptual development, or laid out graphically as a way of seeing the potential relationships between the various patterns identi-fied. Finally, pattern codes might be used in an inferential way as the basis for working hypotheses capable of being checked out in a further wave of data collection.

Miles and Huberman (1994) give a set of guidelines for coding. The analyst writes code words in one margin of transcribed fieldnotes or inter-view using the other margin if necessary for comments, reflections or expansions. Reflective comments can also be embedded within written-up field materials. Miles and Huberman suggest creating a start-list of codes prior to fieldwork. They note that such a procedure would not find favour with all qualitative researchers. Those committed to grounded theory, for instance, favour approaching a research problem without a predetermined structure to their thinking. Codes here emerge after data collection has begun. By contrast, Miles and Huberman argue that a start-list helps to orient the researcher to the conceptual purposes of the study. As Miles (1983: 119) put it in earlier writing, 'The risk is not that of "imposing" a self-blinding framework, but that an incoherent, bulky, irrelevant, mean-ingless set of observations might be produced, which no one can (or even wants to) make sense of.' The start-list is a provisional list; it is open to change and modification as the study proceeds.

Miles and Huberman make the important point that a code list is a conceptual structure. 'Codes should relate to each other in coherent study-important ways' (1994: 62). It is important in consequence to steer a course between developing, on the one hand, a code structure which is logically neat but ultimately ossified (what in another context John Seidel has described as 'finding the codes and losing the data') and, on the other, simply agglomerating a tangled and disorganized collection of disparate codes. One's code list should have a structure but be capable of being revised. It is therefore also important to have neither too many codes nor too few. Too few codes produce a lack of analytic richness; too many are difficult for the analyst to remember. As a practical matter Miles and Huberman suggest that a list of codes should fit as far as possible on one sheet of paper. Codes need to be defined in a way that makes them clearly understood and provides a basis which allows them recognizably to be attached to segments of text. Coding should be combined with other more reflective comments.

Echoing Glaser and Strauss (1967), Miles and Huberman suggest that memos are a fundamental tool for data reduction in qualitative analysis. Memos are a conceptual device for making sense of data. They serve as a repository for ideas, and for commentary upon them. In the kind of multi-site, multiple investigatory study of the kind favoured by Miles and Huberman, they also have an important communicative role, being useful for conveying information and analytic ideas to other team members. Memos have many uses. They can be used as a vehicle for working out concepts, as 'placeholders' for storing ideas for later elaboration, and to integrate data and emerging concepts in a fruitful way. Again, following Glaser and Strauss and congruent with their own ideas on data management, Miles and Huberman recommend that memos should always be dated, that they should be labelled with relevant concepts, and linked to data, previous discussions or case summaries.

As the outlines of an analysis emerge, a variety of review strategies can be used. Typically, what one is doing here is rendering into a condensed form provisional understandings of existing data so that they can be accessed in a systematic way. The focus of reviews is on (a) what has emerged so far in analytic terms, (b) the quality of the data already collected, and (c) possible next steps. The various review strategies Miles and Huberman propose will be described here very briefly. They might include any or all of the following. One strategy is simply to meet with team members, or in the case of the lone researcher, with sympathetic colleagues to discuss a statement of progress. Miles and Huberman also recommend the writing of 'interim case summaries'. An interim case summary is a provisional statement, perhaps 10 to 25 pages long which synthesizes what the researcher knows at a given time about the study in question. Other strategies include, alone or in combination, developing a propositional inventory, a data accounting scheme, or the production of vignettes. The first of these involves the compilation of lists of statements generated out of the research process. Items on the list are then clustered and displayed in ways which make them capable of systematic evaluation in the light of available evidence. A data accounting scheme describes what data have already been collected from what sources, and what still needs to be obtained. Miles and Huberman describe a vignette as a 'focussed description of a series of events taken to be representative, typical or emblematic' of some case (1994: 81).

Qualitative research depends on careful description; 'What is going on here?' is a fundamental question. However, in itself description does not, in their view, provide explanation, particularly where a researcher wants to make strong explanatory or causally based claims. As indicated earlier, Miles and Huberman have extensive experience as educational evaluators. Much of their work focuses on the consequences of educational innovation. Perhaps not surprisingly therefore, Miles and Huberman assert that qualitative researchers should be interested in exploring causal relationships, a demanding objective that remains uncommon in contemporary qualitative research. Indeed, they argue that qualitative research is uniquely suited to exploring the dense and multiple chains of 'local' causation to be found in changing organizational settings. To do this the analyst needs to see the full range of data systematically arranged in a form which allows for a detailed interrogation of the material. It is for this reason that Miles and Huberman stress the importance of data display. Displaying data, for example in a matrix or network form, adds iterative momentum to the analytic process. Inspection of the display tends to suggest patterns, and this leads to analytic reflection and writing. Such writing in turn suggests further ways of displaying the data.

The iterative interplay of display and analysis advocated by Miles and Huberman is designed to fulfil a number of objectives. It makes a potentially difficult and cumbersome process easier to manage. The payoff here is not simply in terms of productivity or the comfort of the researcher (though these factors should not be discounted lightly). The process ensures that the emerging analysis is firmly based on the data, and that all relevant material is examined and given due weight. In this way, material irrelevant to the matter in hand is excluded, while the impact of the merely dramatic, unusual or exotic is reduced. Finally, the processes Miles and Huberman advocate are intended to be self-documenting, ensuring that analytic judgements and decisions are made visible and explicit.

If Miles and Huberman have a motto, it is surely 'Think display' (1994: 240). They present a compendium of methods for data display, some of their own devising, others adapted from existing methods, and give detailed suggestions about different display types, their construction and their use (Miles and Huberman, 1984, 1994). Detailed description of the various display types proposed by Miles and Huberman is far beyond the scope of this chapter. In outline, Miles and Huberman distinguish two major formats for data display: matrix display and network display. In the former, data are arrayed in rows and columns. The aim here is to partition data in a way which facilitates the recognition of patterns, configurations and associations. Networks are graphical representations. They are made up of nodes and links (at their simplest, points connected by lines), and are particularly useful for showing flows and structures. What is entered into a display is not restricted, as it would be in quantitative research to numbers. Instead, whatever is relevant to the purpose in hand might be utilized: quotations, references to source data, comments, abbreviations, ratings and so on. Neither are displays produced mechanically. The basic rule is that 'form follows function'. In accordance with a basic principle enunciated by Miles and Huberman, displays are iterative productions. A data display is meant to be evolved in the direction of greater clarity. Sometimes, for the purpose at hand, more complexity might be needed; at other times less. Finally displays are frequently ordered in some way, for example by time, by case or through the application of a conceptual framework.

Miles and Huberman note that qualitative researchers have commonly embraced the one-shot case study as a mode of research. They also note, however, the growing importance of studies based on multiple sites. In identifying strategies for qualitative analysis, they explore issues which arise both for within-case analysis and for analysis between cases. Studying across cases enhances external validity. One can identify, for example, configurations of elements which occur in some cases but not others. Each case, moreover, provides a potential site for the replication of emerging findings. There is a danger in multi-site work. One might lose the particularity of particular cases, ending perhaps 'with a smoothed set of generalizations that may not apply to any single case' (Huberman and Miles, 1994: 435). Miles and Huberman argue that data displays, especially of a matrix form, are important tools for cross-case analysis. Again, the strategy here is an interactive one as data are sifted, sorted and displayed in the search for cross-case configurations.

Verification for Miles and Huberman consists of checking for biases which commonly affect qualitative studies. Such biases might include paying too much attention to dramatic incidents or mistaking co-occurrences for causal relationships. Miles and Huberman advocate using a variety of tactics for dealing with potential bias. These include checking data for representativeness and the extent to which material collected might have been affected by reactivity. As analysis proceeds, one can actively seek out in the data potentially relevant contrasts, comparisons, outliers and extreme cases. More elaborately, the researcher can try to replicate key findings, look for negative evidence and assess rival explanations. In part, these strategies are also designed to make qualitative research more 'transparent'. According to Miles and Huberman, the clear and explicit reporting both of one's data and of the procedures used in analysis allow the reader of a research report to have greater confidence in the findings of the study. Transparency also makes possible further uses of the data; secondary analysis and auditing procedures both become possible.

Discursive Approaches

A number of qualitative researchers have sought alternatives to what they see as the 'scientistic' conception of research embedded in traditional methods of qualitative data analysis. Encompassed within this alternative strand is a wide range of different approaches: conversation analysis, deconstructionism, discourse analysis, dramaturgical analysis, ethnomethodology, narrative analysis, phenomenology, semiotics, structuralism and poststructuralism. As Atkinson observes (1992: 38), these approaches have 'roots in diverse philosophical, theoretical and methodological inspirations'. What they share is a commitment to the interpretive or hermeneutic understanding of social life. From this standpoint language does not describe an external reality. Rather, social worlds are socially constructed in and through language. Analysis involves the interpretation of cultural representations treated as texts. Placed in the foreground, therefore, is 'the relationship between the "text" as a social construction and its form or its imputed audience-derived meanings' (Manning and Cullum-Swan, 1994: 464).

Alasuutari (1995) has suggested that many of these approaches can be collected together under the rubric of 'cultural studies'. Given the substantive rather than methodological tenor of the term it is unclear whether this is a useful label or not. Certainly, to date, there has been relatively little codification of analytic procedures. There are signs, though, that some researchers have begun to see interpretive approaches as providing an analytic repertoire for qualitative analysis (Manning and Cullum-Swan, 1994; Alasuutari, 1995; Feldman, 1995). Here different approaches, such as narrative analysis or semiotics, are deployed, either separately or in combination, to illuminate facets of some research situation.

Narratives are a ubiquitous form occurring, for example, in literature, folklore, the mass media and in people's accounts of their own lives. In disciplines like sociology and anthropology it is this last, 'elicited personal narratives' (Mishler, 1986: 77) that has been of most interest. There is, however, no commonly agreed definition of narrative (Riessman, 1993: 17). Discussion of the concepts tends, however, to cohere around a number of assumptions. Narratives, which often take the form of stories – but need not – tend to have a beginning, a middle, and an end. As such, they usually form a distinct unit capable of being analytically detached from surrounding discourse. Narratives are frequently organized in a sequential manner. Riessman notes, however, that this is not inevitable. Stories might have an episodic rather than a chronological character, organized by theme rather than sequence. Nevertheless, as Hydén (1995) remarks, 'Common to most of [these] definitions is an emphasis on the temporal ordering of events that are associated with change of some kind.'

There are no standard procedures for carrying out narrative analysis. Narratives can be studied in functional terms. Hydén (1995) has suggested, for example, that chronically ill individuals can use illness narratives in various ways, to construct or reconstruct their own biography, assert or project a certain identity, to understand the illness, or to transform it from something affecting the individual into a collective phenomenon. More broadly, analytic approaches vary in the extent to which 'the internal coherence of the text is defined in advance with reference to codes, syntax, grammar, or forms' (Manning and Cullum-Swan, 1994: 464). In many cases, analysis has a rather loose and intuitive character. Riessman enunciates the important principle that the process of analysis cannot be detached either from the transcription of recorded speech, or from its elicitation. To analyse a narrative, it has to be 'reduced' to a summary form (Riessman, 1993: 60). What can be reduced, and how, depends on how the elicited speech was transcribed. What is available for transcription and what is left out reflect the researcher's analytic assumptions. These might vary in the extent to which, for example, the vocality of the elicited speech is retained in the transcript. Researchers vary, too, in the extent to which they have what is essentially a political commitment to the co-production, or otherwise, of the narrative.

A summary might reflect the 'plot' of a given narrative, the sequence of events as they are rehearsed by the informant, the twists, turns and transitions from one part of the story to another. Considered across narratives, deriving, say, from interviews with people in the same situation, transitions might reveal contingencies, cultural expectations and background conditions which shape people's lives (Riessman, 1993). As an alternative to this kind of approach, Riessman describes her own attempts to analyse narrative accounts of the process of going through a divorce, using an approach derived from poetics. Using as an example part of an interview transcript which describes the troubles besetting a respondent, Riessman shows how the material can be set out in a stanza form. The rule for identifying a stanza is that it should deal with a single topic, and that the recorded speech relating to that topic should be delivered at much the same rate and with little hesitation. Riessman pays careful attention to the structure of stanzas and their relationship to one another. By doing so, she is able to develop a structural analysis which ties together the essential, externally produced, tensions in the respondent's life and links these to their experiential meaning for the respondent. Analytic strategies of this kind are obviously facilitated by writing tools which permit the easy reordering, condensation or annotation of text.

Other forms of narrative reduction might involve coding-type procedures rather more like those used in conventional qualitative analysis. In narrative analysis, though, the intention of coding is to delimit the narrative and its constituent parts, and to retain its sequential character. This is an important difference between narrative analysis and conventional coding. The latter, in effect, fragments the text, seeking segments of transcribed speech that can be lifted out of their original context to be compared with other segments similarly obtained. A second difference is that what are attached as codes in narrative analysis are indications of narrative functions. One influential strand in narrative analysis starts from the assumption that narratives have formal properties. A narrative, in other words, can be thought of as being made up of a set of pre-specified elements, theoretically or empirically derived. These elements occur, often in standard sequences, with each element having a function in relation to the narrative as a whole. The codes attached to a narrative typically, therefore, mark off these functional elements. An approach of this kind is seen in 'eidochronic analysis' (Colby et al., 1991) which seeks to find the basic 'eidons' or plot constituents and the rules governing their sequence within particular cultural genres, the folktales of a particular group, for example. For a given genre, eidon types are coded onto the text. Further analysis seeks to establish how eidonic structures are stable across a particular genre. The ultimate aim of this work is to identify a cultural grammar for the group under consideration, that is 'the cultural logic that people use to interpret events and behaviors in their world' (Colby et al., 1991: 383).

Event structure analysis, developed by the sociologist David Heise, seeks to develop a model for the relationships between events in a sequence, such as that recounted in a narrative (Heise, 1991). These relationships are assumed to be subject to logical constraints: for example where an event is the product of certain preconditions, it cannot recur unless those preconditions are once more present. Computer software can be used both to elicit a user-generated model and to test that model for the completeness and implicative correctness of its logical structure. Heise notes that his approach has affinities with Abell's theory of comparative narratives (Abell, 1988). Abell's work is partly concerned with the relationship between individual and collective action. A narrative or story in this context refers to a patterned sequence of connective actions and 'forebearances'. Sequences of this kind, according to Abell, can be depicted as a weakly connected acyclical digraph. Adopting this representational form allows one to compare narratives since it becomes possible to generate (though not necessarily easily) 'homomorphic translation rules' for graphs being compared. Such rules 'permit us to say of two or more structures that they are sufficiently similar to be regarded as embodying a generalization' (Abell, 1988: 187).

For writers of an interpretive cast of mind whether a narrative is 'true' or not is beside the point. Narratives are inevitably partial, shaped by dramatic convention, and by the identity and audience of the teller. Thus the criteria for judging narratives might more properly be informed by literary or artistic judgements than by social science concerns about validation (Riessman, 1993: 64). Riessman suggests that, if one reconceptualizes validation in terms of the trustworthiness of narratives rather than their veracity, a number of not entirely unproblematic criteria suggest themselves as being of use to the social scientist. The first is persuasiveness. Riessman argues that interpretations of narrative are persuasive to the extent that they are plausible. Of course, the plausibility of an account might owe much to the rhetorical skill of the person presenting it, and rhetorical factors are never absent from interpretations. Nevertheless, the plausibility of an interpretation is enhanced where it is seen to be consistent with informants' accounts and where alternative interpretations have been considered and rejected. A second criterion for judging the adequacy of narrative interpretation, Riessman refers to as 'correspondence'. Work can be taken back to those from whom the material was originally collected. Member check procedures not only provide this opportunity, but are also a reciprocation honouring the original involvement of the research participants. Member check validation can, however, be problematic. The stories people tell about their lives and the understandings that underpin those interpretations might change. Furthermore, how and in what way individuals might judge interpretations based on narratives collected across informants is not clear. What Riessman terms 'coherence' refers to the extent to which the content of what is narrated, the way it is narrated and the reasons for the narration hang together. Riessman suggests, for example, that the divorce narratives she studied were coherent because certain thematic elements were juxtaposed as a justification for the decision to seek a divorce. A final way of enhancing the trustworthiness of narrative analysis is to provide information to others about how an interpretation was produced. This is a strategy which is 'future oriented, collective, and assumes the socially constructed nature of science' (Riessman, 1993: 68). Narratologists should describe how they produced their interpretations, specify how narratives were transcribed and reduced, and make available primary data to other researchers.

Conversation analysis shares with narrative analysis an interest in the sequential organization of transcribed speech. Unlike narrative analysis, it is often (though not exclusively) concerned with short spans of talk centred on routine and mundane, naturally occurring activities. It is also governed by a rigorous methodology committed to producing reproducible results (Psathas, 1995). Indeed, Psathas goes on to suggest that the term 'conversation analysis' is a misnomer. 'It is not conversation but talk-in-interaction that is the broader and more inclusive characterization of the phenomenon of study' (1995: 2). With its roots in phenomenology and ethnomethodology, conversation analysis is concerned with discovering, describing and analysing in a formal way the procedures and practices by which the meaningfulness of social action is produced and displayed.

A particular focus of conversation analysis has been on small-scale, everyday interactions. These have included the exchange of greetings, or compliments, or the giving of directions. Work can also be found on more extended sequences of interaction, doctor–patient encounters, for example, or the interactions between controllers and assistants managing the day-to-day running of the London underground (Heath and Luff, 1993). Analysis is based on recordings of naturally occurring interactional phenomena. Psathas points out that conversation analysts exclude from analytic consideration 'ethnographic particulars of persons, places and settings' (1995: 45). Nor do they consider the motivations, ideas or emotions of those studied unless these matters are explicitly attended to by the participants in the course of the interaction. Conversation analysts consider there are no empirical means by which to gain access to such mental states. Interactions are audio- or video-recorded and transcribed, typically according to a set of transcription conventions. These conventions are designed to help make visible the organizational features of talk by providing representational devices for designating, for example, the sequencing of talk, intervals between and within utterances, intakes and exhalations of breath, and so on.

Recordings are used in conjunction with transcriptions to allow for repeated listening or viewing, a process which allows what might be subtle and unnoticed aspects of the interaction to come into view. According to Psathas (1995: 48),

> Analysts are oriented to the discovery, identification, description and analysis of such matters as the audio-spatial temporal course of interactional phenomena; their constituent elements; their patterns, synchrony, and co-ordination; their sequential properties; and the betweenness of their production, that is, the ways in which other parties are interrelated in the ongoing course of interaction.

The sequences of interaction studied by conversation analysts are not regarded as samples. To do this would require the analyst to pre-specify what is unavailable, the relevant population which has yet to be discovered. A single instance might be sufficient to draw attention to a feature of analytic interest. That instance is to be studied in its specificity and in relation to the formal properties of the situation which produce the interactional feature instanced. Further instances might then be sought from already available or freshly gathered sources, again not with the aim of producing empirical generalization. Rather, the intention is to reveal complexities, variations, or instances of phenomena different from those previously analysed.

A further discursive approach, semiotic analysis, takes language, regarded as a system of signs, as a model for analysing other sign-systems. A sign is made up of a signifier, or expression, and what is signified, the content, that is, what is conveyed. Semiotics, the science of signs, seeks 'to explain how the meaning of objects, behaviors, or talk is produced, transformed and reproduced' (Manning, 1988: 82). The relationship between expression and content for a given sign is understood in terms of the rules or principles that govern how the connection between the two is made. Metaphor, metonymy and opposition are commonly identified ways through which the connection between sign and signifier produces meaning (Feldman, 1995). Eco (1976: 280) describes metaphor as involving 'substitution by similarity', thus, to take Eco's example, as a dog is faithful to its master, mendicant friars in the twelfth century could convey their fidelity to the Church through the appellation 'dogs of God'.

Metonymy, on the other hand, involves what Eco calls 'substitution by contiguity'; the drawing of a mortar-board on a road sign to indicate the turning for a university would be an example. A sign in some instances takes its meaning from its contrast with or opposition to another sign. Think, for example, of the distinctive uniform worn by referees or umpires in many sports. Such uniforms mark them out as having a different (and more formal role) than players.

According to Manning (1987: 35), semiotics provides 'a conceptual apparatus for the analysis of culture'. The meaning of a sign can only arise from its relationship to other signs. The ordering of signs within a given cultural domain into an integrated system can be thought of as a code. Such codes can be identified, formalized, and analysed in a systematic way. The analyst begins by identifying a particular cognitive domain. Manning, for example, studied safety as a domain within the UK Nuclear Installations Inspectorate. Derived from open-ended interviewing, 'safety' in this context is a 'head term', a thematic label to which are attached a variety of denotative meanings; the meanings, in other words, associated with its routine understanding and use (Feldman, 1995: 23). Attached to the denotative meanings associated with a particular term are further connotative meanings. These might be based on metonymy, metaphor or opposition. In analysing the meanings attached to a student residence complex she studied, Feldman notes that connotative meanings were sometimes metaphoric. On occasion, person-like qualities such as reputation, need or uniqueness were attributed to the buildings. Connotative meanings such as 'home' and 'neighbourhood' are based on metonymy when applied to a residence, but also contain an implicit opposition between 'home' and 'institutional' life. Both Feldman and Manning point out that connotative meaning can be further related to wider organizational or institutional concerns. In this sense, semiotic analysis involves a sequential process of deconstructing the original set of denotative meanings and their reconstruction in a way which aids an understanding of the interrelationships between social organization and socially constructed meanings.

Feldman (1995) identifies three different display strategies which might help researchers to perform a semiotic analysis. Semiotic clustering, the technique used by Manning to analyse 'safety', involves listing in column format the various denotative meanings associated with a particular head term, their corresponding connotative meanings, and the wider organizational or institutional concerns to which they are putatively related. Semiotic chains are used to lay out the implicative relations between denotative and connotative meanings within a domain. To do this, denotations and connotations are arranged alongside their opposites and nested within a hierarchy of relevant wider domains. Semiotic squares are used to explore the rules governing the relations between signs. Such relations are assumed to involve prescription and proscription as well as the absence of each. These relations are vertically and horizontally juxtaposed such that each rule is located at the corner of a square. Horizontal and vertical comparisons are then made to see what kind of relationships are implied by the pattern mapped onto the square.

Manning (1987: 35) argues that semiotic analysis is 'consistent with the avowed intentions of the family of sociologies, such as symbolic interactionism, phenomenological-existentialism, and ethnomethodology... to explicate social meanings'. In this regard, it is especially appropriate to the analysis of 'loose belief systems'. Within such systems, beliefs, meanings and the contexts within which they are invoked are only loosely coupled, and need to be identified ethnographically. Manning suggests that traditional approaches to fieldwork have many weaknesses. They are often descriptively focused, for example, on a single case or small segment of a wider social system. However, detailed fieldwork provides a 'rich ethnographic texture' indispensable to semiotic analysis (Manning and Cullum-Swan, 1994: 470). Traditional structuralist approaches in anthropology to the formal analysis of myths, for example, or within ethnoscience approaches to lexical domains, display a tendency towards empty formalism and the analysis of arbitrarily selected cultural codes. Without the deeper cultural understanding elicited by fieldwork techniques such as depth interviewing and participant observation, semiotics has a 'limited capacity to explain change, the interaction of self and group, the history of an individual or group experience with a symbol system, or changes in sign systems themselves' (Manning and Cullum-Swan, 1994: 469). Like other components of the wider practice of qualitative data analysis, semiotic analysis might be regarded as a practice in its own right or as an element in an elaborated division of analytic labour. It must be said, though, that few practitioners entertain the notion of a generic theory of qualitative data analysis in which a range of techniques, interpretive practices and analytic approaches are harnessed together.

Content Analysis

Content analysis techniques are widely used in the humanities, for example in studies of authorship attribution, and in disciplines like political science and media studies. Content analysis is essentially an enumerative strategy based on listing, counting and categorizing the individual words within a text. Analysis of the content of a text often begins with a count of the number of times each word appears within it. Frequency counts of this kind reflect an assumption that how often words appear reflects their salience. Of course, one needs immediately to qualify this statement to take into account the fact that the words most frequent in a text, like 'a' and 'the', are usually of little interest to social scientists (though they might hold considerable significance for language scholars).

To give an example, one transcript we analysed contained 10,728 words in total. The number of unique words was 1,536. Of the unique words, 30 per cent appeared 100 times or more, while slightly over 7 per cent of the words appeared only once. The most common word, 'the', appeared 431 times, making up 4 per cent of the transcript. Content analysis packages usually contain a facility for omitting words on the basis of their frequency. Typically, social scientists treat very frequent words as 'noise' to be excluded, and focus instead on the rank ordering of words defined as 'significant' for analytic purposes.

Lists are a second basic tool of content analysis. One familiar kind of word list, the index, shows not only which words appear in a text but also the *position* of each. A concordance lists the words in a text, showing for each the immediate *context* within which it appears. Concordances are often generated in key-words-in-context (KWIC) format. This shows each word, usually centred on a page, surrounded by the words which appear immediately before and after it in the text. The analysis of collocates (i.e. co-located words) looks at how words in a text are associated with one another. In specific terms the analyst looks at the range of words which appear within some specified distance of the words of interest. An example can be found in Hansen's (1995) account of how British newspapers covered BSE (bovine spongiform encephalopathy or 'mad cow disease'). Hansen found that words such as 'scientist' or 'expert' were typically accompanied by terms like 'top', 'senior' and 'leading'; words used by the newspapers, in his view, to buttress the authority and legitimacy of one set of commentators on the disease.

Content analysts mostly work with 'found' texts such as newspaper articles or political speeches. (Indeed, as Hansen (1995) points out, the increasing availability of such sources in electronic form is set to transform areas such as the study of newspaper content.) In fact, one rarely finds content analytic techniques being used to analyse data from, say, interview transcripts. This is because counting and listing techniques have some serious drawbacks as far as qualitative researchers are concerned. Weber (1985: 53) notes that word frequencies can be misleading if context is ignored. Because words have different meanings or vary in their meaning across context a simple count can overestimate the salience of a particular word. Conversely, if one pays no attention to synonyms or words such as pronouns which can be substituted for other words, word frequencies can underestimate salience. Weber also points out that, since a concordance is usually many times longer than the text which produced it, content analysis involves 'data expanding rather than data reducing techniques' (1985: 48). It might be necessary to go through a number of iterations in order to focus in on relevant data. From the point of view of qualitative research, a further serious problem with content analysis is that, although concordances display words in context, usually that context is fixed, a certain number of words, a certain number of lines or whatever. Although this poses few problems in linguistically oriented studies, a qualitative researcher would rarely want to be constrained in this way. The context for an utterance in an interview, say, might well be a word, a few lines or several paragraphs. Qualitative researchers, in other words, often want to work with user-defined 'chunks' of text.

Against this, as Werner points out, content analysis can be heuristically useful in situations where material is piling up and analysis time is short (1992: 6):

> interviews and lengthy journal entries tend to follow each other in short succession. We are lucky if we manage to keep up with transcription. But even then, given the fast accumulation of pages and pages of text, we have only our imperfect memories to remind us what was actually recorded. Faced with this dilemma, it is useful to have a method to show us the contents of our texts. I have found that a word frequency count can be very helpful.

Interestingly in this regard, Werner suggests inspecting, not only words that appear recurrently, but those that occur only once. Rare but seemingly salient words might reflect areas not covered in sufficient detail in the interview and which might need to be probed in subsequent fieldwork. (Hansen (1995) makes a similar point in respect of newspaper stories. Looking at infrequent words can on occasion provide leads to new twists in the story or journalists' emerging understandings of the issues involved.) For someone like Werner, who is a cultural anthropologist, and thus concerned with indigenous terms and their relation to wider cultural domains, word counts and the like are particularly useful. Other researchers might find them less helpful. Nevertheless, given a transcript, word counts and a concordance allow one to focus very quickly on a number of key terms and the contexts in which they appear. This might be sufficient at least to show how adequately particular interview topics are being covered, and might be enough to alert or remind the researcher about possible future fruitful lines of enquiry.

Computer-based content analysis is a rapidly developing area. In particular, the increasing use of expert systems (Heather and Lee, 1995) and 'clause-based content analysis' (Roberts and Popping, 1993), based on the linguistic parsing of text, promises to make such methods much more useful to qualitative research.

Conclusion

This chapter has sought to demonstrate the heterogeneity of existing approaches to qualitative analysis by tracing their historical development. Failing to recognize that heterogeneity discourages careful analysis of what qualitative researchers actually do when they analyse their data, whether they use computers or not. Jennifer Platt (1996) has argued that the history of qualitative research has been mythologized. Although we cannot do full justice to her argument here, the message we take from Platt's careful debunking of qualitative methodology's 'creation myth' is that we should be careful not to accept a mythologized version of history and to insert computerization into it. If researchers are to use new technologies effectively it is important that they understand clearly the analytic bases of the procedures they use. We are now in a position to better understand how CAQDAS has been received by the research community.

Notes

1   Despite our admiration for her work, we have reservations about the classification system Tesch developed. One problem relates to the categorization of particular research traditions. Tesch, for instance, regards symbolic interactionism as an analytic tradition concerned with the cultural understanding of language use, a characterization some of its proponents might find too narrow. A further difficulty is that certain kinds of qualitative research are not necessarily distinguished by their *analytic* posture at all. For example, some researchers prefer qualitative methods because they have ethical or political commitments to a particular kind of relationship between researcher and researched – the obvious example is feminist research. Yet, it is difficult to fit such a stance into Tesch's classificatory system.

2   We might note here that the development of causal theory is a relatively uncommon aim of contemporary qualitative research studies. With the demise of analytic induction causal analysis came to be associated with quantitative research, where statistical methods can be seen as providing an approximation to experimental controls. Some have noted, however, that causal assertions are more common in qualitative research than might appear at first sight (Kidder, 1981).

3   We discuss later the possible dangers of over-elaborate coding arising from computer-based methods (see also Seidel, 1991). Clearly, though, this example suggests that one does not need a computer to generate analytic sterility.

4   Neither could the late Anselm Strauss, who was also involved in the research.

5   Indeed Becker and Geer explicitly refer to the method as 'sequential analysis'. That term has been avoided here because it seems too general to capture the range of procedures used.

6   This is not to say, of course, that the influences ran entirely in one direction from anthropology to sociology. See Platt (1983: 393).

7   Interestingly, although Strauss and Corbin remark on the similarities between grounded theory and other qualitative approaches, they do not mention that Glaser and Strauss also criticized in their book existing qualitative approaches such as analytic induction.

3
Why Use Computers in Qualitative Research?

Justifications for using the computer as an analytic tool in qualitative research are inextricably tied to the character of qualitative data. Qualitative research often produces an 'assemblage' of data (Lee, 1993). Typically, this assemblage is multi-stranded, derives from multiple sources, and frequently has multiple forms: transcripts, fieldnotes, documents and so on. Researchers might often also work with a range of data types: jotted notes of various kinds, fieldnotes organized according to topic, diaries, chronologies, card indexes, questionnaires, maps and diagrams, not to mention photographs, video or audio recordings and even artefacts (Ellen, 1984; Levine, 1985; Fischer, 1994). The emergent character of qualitative research also tends to encourage 'data promiscuity'. Because one cannot specify in advance what might eventually be significant, data of different kinds are collected 'just in case'. As a result of all this, qualitative researchers tend to accumulate large volumes of data. It might be helpful to visualize. Suppose a researcher carried out a fairly small-scale qualitative study consisting of 20 depth interviews each lasting about an hour. Assume each interview produces 25 pages of transcript. Data from the interviews will amount to 500 pages or a stack of paper 10 centimetres (4 inches) thick; approximately two volumes of the current London telephone directory. (Of course the density of data in the transcripts is much less than in the directory. On the other hand, the complexity of the data in the transcripts is much greater.)

One consequence of volume is that there is a good deal of redundancy in the data. Alongside material relevant to the task in hand, there is usually much non-relevant material that has to be sorted through and set to one side. Probably every qualitative researcher has had the experience of knowing that there is a vital piece of information buried somewhere in a great mass of material, without it being immediately apparent where it is to be found. The sheer volume of material produced by qualitative research also makes data vulnerable to disruption. An obvious solution to having lots of material is to spread it out on the floor. Doing so, however, renders it vulnerable to draughts, children, pets and over-zealous cleaners.

As well as being voluminous, qualitative data are also typically unstructured, context-specific and recalcitrant. In survey research, responses to questions are pre-structured by the response categories the researcher builds into the questions. This is not the case with qualitative research. Indeed one of the justifications for using qualitative data is precisely that one is *not* imposing an *a priori* analytic structure on the data. This is not to say, of course that qualitative data are devoid of structure. Rather that structure is usually implicit. The researcher attempts to discern or elucidate a structure that is regarded as emerging out of the data as the analytic task proceeds. This 'post-structuration' of the data is much more difficult than the pre-structuring of responses that takes place in a survey. Meaning in qualitative data is contextually dependent. In other words, how one interprets a particular utterance in an interview, say, depends on the context within which that utterance is made. An implication of this is that it is important to be able to retain the original context in the analytic process and to be able to switch back and forth between one's analytic material and the original data. Finally, qualitative data are 'recalcitrant' in the sense that they do not yield up their meaning easily. One constantly needs to refer back to the data. Moreover, the process of returning to the data time and time again in itself transforms the analysis. This is so, because, as one's familiarity with the data increases, one's analytic understanding of it is transformed. It becomes important therefore to be able to impose and discard successive analytic schemata on the same basic data.

Not surprisingly in the light of this, one justification for computer use in qualitative data analysis is that the machine can facilitate the task of *data management*. Tesch (1990), an early CAQDAS enthusiast, argued that the mechanical difficulties inherent in working with qualitative data inhibited the analytic process. Mechanizing manual procedures in qualitative research, she argued, potentially offered considerable benefits in terms of time, efficiency and more thorough analysis. Computers are fast and flexible. One only has to think, for example, about how easy it is using a word processor to reorganize a piece of written text or to find a word or phrase in a lengthy document. The computer, Tesch argued, could bring some of this capability to the analysis of field materials. Tesch also pointed out that storing data on a computer means having less paper to shuffle around. This in turn makes it easier to keep track of material and to find specific items when they are needed. Decreasing the amount of time devoted to managing data makes the analysis process less tiresome. The analyst becomes less fatigued and in consequence can devote more time and mental energy to the analysis itself. A related and important aspect of this, according to Tesch, is that using a computer for qualitative analysis allows one to 'play' with the data. It becomes possible to look at data in different ways, and to try out new analytic approaches even though there is no guarantee that they will work. This kind of activity is important because it potentially increases creativity in dealing with one's data. It can be difficult to do with manual methods.

A second justification for harnessing the computer to the needs of qualitative researchers is that in so doing one is potentially extending the *capabilities* of qualitative research. The computer in other words provides analytic possibilities difficult to accomplish by 'traditional' methods. For example, replication becomes a possibility (Conrad and Reinharz, 1984). Qualitative analysis can seem a mysterious and non-reproducible process. There is sometimes a suspicion that the analyst has done little more than string together a series of 'juicy' quotes extracted from transcripts. By contrast, the computer encourages users to be clear about what they are doing. It can also be used to keep a log or trail of analytic procedures. Both these features make it easier for a second person to replicate an existing analysis. Computer assistance might also conceivably make team research more feasible in qualitative research (Conrad and Reinharz, 1984). Lone-hand research is common among qualitative researchers. Indeed, it is the norm for graduate-level research. But restricting research to settings which can be handled by only one researcher produces a bias in the total universe of studies towards small-scale social entities; the factory rather than the business, the school rather than the education system. The bias in survey research is in the opposite direction, towards large-scale social aggregates. It might be – and this is just speculation – that social science leaves out of the picture those intermediate structures of social life which arguably form a crucial link between the micro and macro levels of social organization (Fielding, 1988). If there is such a bias, team-based studies might help to overcome it. In a similar vein, Ragin and Becker (1989) argue that the advent of desktop rather than mainframe computing might help to bridge the traditional gulf between 'variable-oriented' (quantitative) and 'case-oriented' (qualitative) researchers. For both groups the microcomputer encourages closeness to data and an intensive, interactive analytic style. This in turn might encourage a certain degree of methodological convergence as quantitative researchers find the detailed analysis of subpopulations easier and qualitative researchers are able to examine comparative contrasts within their case materials more fully.

A third justification for software use is that it can enhance the *acceptability and credibility* of qualitative research. Some of the early enthusiasm for CAQDAS in the United States seems to have been driven by a concern to make qualitative research appear more 'scientific', and in this way to destigmatize it within a not entirely sympathetic academic environment. While we would judge this to be less true of the UK, qualitative research is not always well regarded by policy makers. Social researchers of all kinds in the UK have for some years faced sustained pressure to deliver research findings in a comprehensive and timely manner. For example, the principal funding body for graduate study in the United Kingdom, the Economic and Social Research Council, has consistently pressed the academic social science community to secure better completion rates for doctoral studies, where 'better' is construed primarily as adhering to a three- or, at most, four-year timetable. One justification for software use is that, by offering efficiencies and the possibility of more sophisticated analysis, it gives the qualitative researcher some leverage in dealing with such pressures.

Evaluating the Advantages of CAQDAS

Claims that CAQDAS can bring about an advantageous transformation of analytic method in qualitative research have of course generated counter-claims which stress the possible disadvantages of software use. Some of these counter-claims will be discussed in detail later on. The general point we would make at this juncture is that the claims advanced for and against CAQDAS use need to be evaluated in a processual manner. Different advantages and disadvantages are manifest at different stages of the researcher's exposure to CAQDAS. Nor is it simply a question of there being clear and unambiguous advantages or disadvantages; different benefits and disbenefits might be experienced, and these might register differently with different users. It is also sensible to differentiate what we might call 'anticipated' and 'experientially validated' advantages and disadvantages. As we will see and as we have implied above, it is not simply a question of the perceptions users have of what the software does or does not do for them; the perceptions of others are also important. A processual perspective accommodates the dynamic character of the research environment and of the negotiation of the place of CAQDAS within it. This is particularly important when we examine criticisms arising from early experience. In a number of cases technical solutions to problems experienced by the users who participated in our focus groups have emerged which were not available at the time of our fieldwork. Users themselves also become more sophisticated.

Analytic Uses of CAQDAS

Taking a processual view, we begin by considering what factors persuaded users to take up CAQDAS in the first place. Often it was the prospect of working with a lot of qualitative data: 'I started working with [package] to help sort out that amount of data' (FG2). Variety of data sources is an associated consideration. 'I had transcripts, law reports, courtroom scripts, solicitors' case files, fieldnotes, and to use such a diverse body of data . . . I felt putting it on computer would be much easier' (FG2). Experienced researchers drew on their knowledge of the time-consuming aspects of qualitative analysis. 'It was expediency really, I knew that I would have about 50 interviews, some going on to two hours perhaps, and I knew that I had a very limited amount of time. Having done a previous project very similar [where] I ended up with 100 interviews to sort and sift and it was cut-and-paste and photocopy . . . I just knew how much space you need for a start. Piles of files and papers everywhere, and marking different categories in different coloured pens, just seemed to me that this would be a mechanical way of doing all that, to give me more time to look at the actual interview data' (FG2). Another respondent remarked that she had often done cut-and-paste during her long daily commute but had lost data as she sifted and sorted it on the train. Another user felt she could not 'keep it all in my head, so I wanted something that was a filing system. I'd been to a seminar in France suggesting ways of doing content analysis by hand and I wasn't at all convinced, just seemed a complete mess and I just couldn't imagine ever being able to do it myself with that amount of data' (FG5). A pragmatic view that CAQDAS would make cut-and-paste easier was also expressed. 'I saw people doing cut-and-paste, and chucking out bits and piles of comments there, and I thought there must be an easier way of doing this' (FG1).

In such cases, the prospective user approaches CAQDAS less as a means of conducting a formal, systematic analysis than as a means of organizing voluminous data. Initial expectations might presage patterns of use, in particular a failure to fully exploit the conceptualizing features of the package. In other cases, systematic analysis was the goal: 'I thought it would help me to be more organized about how I went about my analysis' (FG2). Also oriented to a particular feature was this account: 'I knew looking at my data and the ideas I had before that I did have hierarchical codes, but that I might not be quite sure what they were going to be at the initial stages and I might want that flexibility of being able to move things around' (FG5). An applied researcher had 'worked on fairly small-scale projects and my data sets were quite small so I had always used a cut-and-paste method', but then 'there was a project to look after a national-scale data set and that leapt from fifteen to hundreds' (FG3). This researcher made heavy use of display matrices (Miles and Huberman, 1994) in her doctoral research, 'and as a result of my PhD I had been thinking of what ways I could use to analyse this data' (FG3), so that CAQDAS offered a new means to make analysis systematic.

While convenient, the distinction between 'clerical' data management and analysis is somewhat artificial. After all, the task of 'organizing' involves looking ahead to the likely contours of the analysis. Also oriented to analytic considerations are users who have from the first been dissatisfied with the established approach to qualitative data analysis. 'I started off when I was an undergraduate being not very satisfied with the teaching I got on how to analyse the qualitative material. We were given lectures on how to do interviews and how to think about what codes might be, but it never got further than that. I was getting very interested at that time in how to do statistics and SPSS, and just playing around on the computer, I thought there must be a better way' (FG6). Another user initially obtained CAQDAS for teaching purposes 'because I wanted to show students there was a systematic way of analysing qualitative data'. He felt that students did not respect qualitative analysis relative to statistical analysis because it seemed *ad hoc*: 'the qualitative teaching was unconvincing. The analysis side was underdeveloped, you had an interview and trying to transcribe it all, but then what do you do with it?' (FG6). In another case a sophisticated user's enthusiasm rubbed off: 'not many people in the university were using [package] but this person had been working with it for two years and was impressed' (FG2). These routes to CAQDAS involve an unfavourable comparison between the systematic procedures of statistically based analysis and the less clearly articulated, intuitive and less-reviewable character of qualitative methods.

Users typically anticipate both practical and analytic benefits. The idea that CAQDAS might help make analysis more systematic was frequently expressed. None of the users were dissuaded of this likely advantage as a result of experience with CAQDAS, yet the time-saving expectation was one that few were able to confirm. For people with a keen interest in qualitative analysis it can, as users often said, be a boost to creative work to have features available that prompt new approaches to the data. 'One of the things that fascinates me is the different ways in which it is possible to analyse text, and . . . text of all sorts, and fine grains of analysis, exciting looking at other ways of analysis' (FG1). To another it was a question of discouraging 'this view that qualitative analysis is something magical . . . By having to think about the categories, codes . . . it forces you to think about the systematic process' (FG3). However, it was a question of CAQDAS being an aid or encouragement rather than the *sine qua non* of good practice. Manual qualitative analysis could be rigorous too, it was simply that mechanical cumbersomeness might interfere. One respondent made the point that 'You have to think very clearly about what you are doing', going on to comment: 'You should have been doing that anyway' (FG3). Another remarked that using a computer was no guarantee of rigour: 'if you are unsystematic without computers I am sure you can be unsystematic with them' (FG3). This was one reason that respondents involved in methods teaching were committed to the idea that qualitative analysis principles should be grasped before introducing the software. It was also the case that, without exception, they now included the software in their qualitative methods teaching. Some felt that it helped to convey the principles of qualitative analysis, dividing the analytic process into a series of stages, each of which was accessible for discussion.[1] 'The initial getting-hold of [package] was for teaching purposes, because I wanted to show students that there was a systematic way of analysing qualitative data' (FG6). Another element of the encouragement to be systematic was the idea that qualitative analysis was iterative and therefore subject to much reformulation, requiring reconfiguration of the data, elaboration of category systems and so on. CAQDAS could not only track the development of one's thinking but provide facilities to automate recoding and repeat patterned retrievals as new data became available. 'I knew we would want to go back into it over and over again because there would be different things that we would want to do with it' (FG6).

These advantages were not immediately apparent, however. It was often a case of anticipating help with managing and organizing data and then coming to appreciate the facilities for various retrieval strategies and working with the category system. 'I assumed people must be using computers to take a lot of the physical grind out of the analyses. I was amazed when I found out that some of them not exactly put together theories for you but connected things up in search ways that you could thread' (FG4). One user offered an apt process description of how the speed of the computer aided code development. 'In the process of coding a transcript for an interview and then being able to very quickly locate that code at each point through the transcript, [it] enhances my abilities to really think through the material, because there . . . almost isn't a time gap between locating one thing and the next. And therefore you are on that roll mentally and then you see the next chunk of text that's about that area and you are still with it . . . It's in those very practical ways that it's an enhancer' (FG4). Similarly, 'it allows you to be flexible and try things out and scrap them or move them around or change them without committing yourself' (FG5). Another boon was that it allowed careful checks of the proportion of a sample expressing a given view, which tightened practice and controlled glib summaries from the data. 'It's made us more thorough. When you are interviewing you say "everybody I've interviewed seems to say this, this is what is happening" and [when] you actually go through much more thoroughly in checking [you find] "actually that was only two very articulate people who said that, all the other people [are] saying X", it's made us do that' (FG4). A doctoral student felt that 'it has made me much better organized than I was when I started. It is very easy to shut the door on pieces of paper and scissors and go away, whereas when you produce tons of files with all the different extension names and millions of printouts, you have to have some sort of organization scheme just to know which the latest one is and how you've revised it' (FG4). While non-users sometimes express the reservation that CAQDAS takes researchers away from the data, users often referred to an enhanced grasp of the data as they repeated searches and so on. It made it harder to 'gloss' the data with abstractions. Looking back on projects whose analysis was done 'manually', a qualitative computing advisor remarked that she was now 'rather unsatisfied both with the depth and quality of handling of the unstructured elements of people's data sets and the tendency to produce abstraction in order to legitimate what you are doing' (FG5). Thus do data management issues shade into new, more demanding criteria for data analysis.

Transparency

An effective data management system potentially encourages researchers to produce analysis which is explicit, systematic and documented. Doing so enhances the transparency of the research process. In other words, the researcher and/or others can trace the paths by which a particular analysis emerged. Transparency affects both the process and the product of the research. Some indication has already been given of how transparency makes the analysis process more fruitful by avoiding underinterpretation. If data are manageable, the potential for confusion and muddle is reduced. So too is the temptation to over-rely on the exotic, the near at hand or the voluble. However, the explicit, systematic and documented management of data also helps to avoid overinterpretation. It becomes easier to detect instances where the data have been forced or subjected to premature analytic closure. Transparency also aids analysis by indicating when and how further iteration through the data might be appropriate, and might promote creativity by making anomalous findings more visible. (Miles and Huberman, 1994, detail a variety of innovative strategies for making analytic procedures in qualitative research explicit, systematic and fully documented.)

A variety of audiences have an interest in the published products of research: other researchers, research participants, funders, stakeholders and the public at large (Miles and Huberman, 1994: 280). For each of these audiences, concerns might arise about how conclusions have been reached. Some concerns revolve around the veracity of the research. In other words, the question asked is 'Have research data been misrepresented?' Concerns of this kind are most likely to arise where research participants feel they have been subjected to false, malicious or unflattering portrayals of their lives, or where stakeholders encounter unwelcome findings from evaluation studies. Veracity might also be an issue where scientific fraud is suspected although, as Miles and Huberman (1994: 287) comment, 'we rarely consider this eventuality in qualitative studies'.

A second set of concerns about the transparency of data arises from attempts at secondary use. It is typically easier to reuse date which are well managed than those which are not. One indication of this is given by Lutkehaus (1990). Before embarking on her ethnographic study in Manam, an island close to Papua New Guinea, Lutkehaus read the fieldnotes Camilla Wedgewood had made in the same location 50 years earlier. Lutkehaus observes that Wedgewood carefully recorded, annotated and indexed her fieldnotes. In this, Wedgewood was partly following the promptings of her mentor, Malinowski. Lutkehaus also notes, however, that Wedgewood might have been influenced in her practice by the difficulties she had encountered using the fieldnotes of a deceased anthropologist, Bernard Deacon, who had left behind a set of field materials that were incomplete, unindexed and fragmentary.

Although secondary analysis is often couched in terms of sharing data (Sieber, 1991), 'sharing is useful if the user is provided with meaningful information rather than data' (White, 1991). To put this another way, data sets which are well documented facilitate secondary analysis better than those which are not. Miles and Huberman (1994: 281) point out that qualitative researchers 'don't report clearly on their methodology because there are no shared conventions for doing so'.[2] Miles and Huberman's assessment is an understatement when it comes to fieldnotes. As Atkinson maintains, 'their construction and interpretation has been part of the tacit craft knowledge that is handed on from generation to generation as part of the oral culture of various disciplines' (1992: 19). The privacy of fieldnotes is a recurrent theme in major anthropological treatments of fieldnotes (Sanjek, 1990b). Indeed, some anthropologists seem to treat fieldnotes as 'sacred texts' with powerful and dangerous properties.

A third set of concerns relate to the analytic (re)assessment of the research. Here are issues to do with audit, meta-evaluation (the evaluation of evaluation studies) and replication. Schwandt and Halpern (1988) have advocated the use of audits to determine how far the findings produced by a qualitative study are dependable, confirmable and credible. The analogy here is with financial auditing where a third party attests to the financial health or otherwise of a company by examining its records and procedures. Auditing depends on the existence of an audit trail; a well-organized system of record keeping through which is documented the planning and progress of the research together with a contemporaneous running record of the investigator's actions, thoughts and feelings. Miles and Huberman note that auditing of the kind Schwandt and Halpern endorse is rare. They go on to observe that the audit metaphor with its connotations of 'an external, stern, obsessive expert' (1994: 282) is a forbidding one. However, they concur with Schwandt and Halpern in asserting the benefits which flow from audit-like procedures. From this point of view, operating as if research procedures are open to independent, external scrutiny improves quality by encouraging systematization, openness and reflection. Because establishing an audit trail depends so heavily on systematic and highly structured record keeping, it is costly in terms of time and effort. (Indeed, audits of this kind, if they are to be undertaken, probably need to be incorporated into the research process from its inception.) Computer-based methods in themselves encourage systematization and, to a degree, are self-documenting. They might, therefore, alleviate to some degree the burden involved in maintaining an audit trail. Moreover, qualitative analysis packages increasingly incorporate facilities for producing analytic memos and for allowing codebooks to be maintained. So far, however, the utility of computer-based methods to the auditing process has been asserted rather than demonstrated.

Computer-based Methods and the Credibility of Qualitative Research

To some of those we interviewed considerations of *demonstrable* rigour were clearly important. 'In certain places it [package use] is much more systematic [than manual methods], and you can actually say "here is something rational", you have done this' (FG1). This theme has several aspects. One is that computer use involves an element of laying bare the analytic process to critical inspection. It also, however, bears the implication that procedures similar to those always available are now seen in a new, more flattering light precisely because a computer is being used. Perceptions of this kind are important in fields or disciplines where qualitative research is looked on with relative disfavour. The credibility of what is seen as a 'soft' methodology producing interesting anecdotes but unable to establish their generalizability is boosted by association with that 'hard' research tool, the computer. Two researchers, one a psychologist, the other a geographer, independently noted that qualitative methods were increasingly visible in their respective disciplines. Each made the additional point, however, that such methods faced criticism for their supposed lack of rigour. As one of these respondents put it in terms that were closely echoed by the other, 'People are desperate to find more rigorous ways of dealing with data, they are fed up with being accused of being soft and woolly. They are looking for ways to demonstrate to their colleagues that they have gone through a rational process and with [CAQDAS] they can hold it up and say "this can be done on the machine" ' (FG1). In some disciplines, and in some countries, this view is established in academic as well as applied research. Moreover, there is a perception that using a package gives one not only respectability but also leverage. Thus a respondent from Latin America studying in the UK said of her country, 'there is a strong tradition in quantitative research because that gives more power to negotiate, to say you are doing hard research, and we can get more funding' (FG2). An educational researcher who worked in a department that was 'very statistically based, [with] obviously a lot of software around' found that using software made a difference in securing resources. 'My department was very willing to stand $100 so we bought three copies [of package], one for each of us. They were quite sympathetic' (FG1). Of course, there are 'credibility' issues within disciplines, too. Even though many researchers might be uncomfortable with the quantitative/qualitative distinction, it remains an abiding division. As one user suggested, 'people . . . using qualitative data analysis packages said that they have always thought it gives them more ammunition to quantitative people' (FG3).

But disciplinary change and an interest in pushing forward the tenets of particular methodologies are not the only foci of the credibility issue. We encountered a number of cases where supervisors, despite their own lack of knowledge or expertise, had suggested to graduate students that they might look into using computer software to analyse qualitative data. Other supervisors, though, could be hard to convince of the merits of software use. An element here seemed to be what one respondent described as the ' "we've done it our way, what's wrong with you doing it our way?" argument' (FG6). Supervisors sometimes also harboured the kind of suspicions that people less comfortable with computers often bring to information technology, especially when confronted by a younger and more knowledgeable enthusiast. For example, the respondent just quoted encountered problems getting through her upgrade review because 'they wouldn't believe that qualitative methodology could be combined with quantitative methodology and both could use computing. So "you can't be using [quantitative package] *and* [qualitative package]!" ' (FG6). In the event, this student got through the review, even if she felt that she had not entirely convinced her committee. In this, in fact, the computer aided her. In her qualitative work she had used the computer to document how her analytic thinking had evolved. 'I felt threatened that someone was going to take my thesis away from me [if] I didn't do it in the same way I did my quantitative stuff as well, tracking how I created variables' (FG6). In a similar vein, a different respondent commented, 'That's what convinced my supervisor. Once I came out with a list of code words, "this is what I had a week ago and this is what I've got now" and "look, this is how it works" . . . He said, "Gosh! Quite neat, isn't it" ' (FG6).

Some research sponsors encourage use for quite other reasons. 'The first piece of [CAQDAS] software I heard about . . . was quite a few years ago, when I was working in a research unit at [university] and my contact . . . wasn't from a research point of view but from an administrative and cost point of view' (FG3). The research sponsor commended the package as saving analysis time. In a similar case, the department held a licence for a given package and standardly did all its applied research using it, so the researcher was 'stuck with it to some extent because the department has a case for using [package] . . . and there was a resource element to it as well' (FG3). In other cases it is not a question of a sponsor imposing a requirement but of researchers feeling they are more likely to be seen as credible by sponsors if they use CAQDAS. 'One of the other attractions was the rigour that it imposed, not necessarily imposed because . . . we were used to doing quite rigorous analysis with pencil and paper, but it was convincing outside people, government departments that we were doing research for. They're difficult to convince that qualitative research has anything to offer policy-relevant research for government. Because civil servants have a great turnover you are continually having to educate them. Someone else comes up who has never heard of qualitative methodology and you have to go through the whole process again, so we found it quite attractive that we could say "look, we use this but we are doing it this way" and that impressed them in their naive, ignorant way, which is useful for us. Wasn't all bluff from us, but it was a way, not of imposing rigour but emphasizing the rigour of it' (FG6).

While CAQDAS had been useful in justifying the credibility of qualitative research, it was suggested that at later stages the 'concreteness' of qualitatively based reports led to few queries from applied sponsors about what lay behind the analysis. 'No one has ever challenged us much about the analysis of qualitative data, from government departments . . . It seems paradoxical because they seem to be unwilling to accept it and we have to educate them to see it as a valid method but then when we come to present results it is, you are using quotations or whatever, concrete, they can understand it. And they go "oh yes", big pennies dropping all over the place but when you are presenting statistical [data] to them, my God, they'll go through it with a fine tooth comb! . . . We have never had to defend qualitative output in the sort of depth we have to on numbers . . . It's much easier to present qualitative data because it's grounded in everyday language and if you write about it clearly it's very accessible' (FG6). Respondents were clear that the business of CAQDAS lending credibility was a phenomenon associated with non-academic sponsors. With applied research sponsors there seemed to be greater anxiety about legitimacy in general. 'It's respectability they are looking for, they ask "can I put your name on [the report]" or "can I say that you will do some consultancy on this" and "can you write which guides you have written about this and give a more scientific look to the whole thing" so I am finding increasingly my time is being taken up with making projects look more respectable so if you use a computer it must be better than if you don't' (FG4).

However, some respondents felt that there might in future be similar pressures on graduate students. 'It is also going to be a pressure for students because, as part of research training maybe, [it] makes it look more respectable if it's on a computer' (FG4). Against this was the peer review mechanism, which acted as a brake on innovation. 'I have put up three projects to [funding body] where I have had bum reader's comments based around the software, based on their absolute total and profound ignorance' (FG4). It is also worth recalling the apocryphal tale about the package that was allegedly banned in its country of origin because it made gaining a PhD too easy. The alternative version was that 'people were warned about saying "I will do qualitative analysis and I will use [package]." [It] would not earn many marks in their application for research grants. It was not considered a particular advantage any more because everyone was doing it' (FG5). Thus, CAQDAS might lend credibility at an early stage for reasons of innovation, but once the innovation is established the issue is one of how well the research is being done.

Boosting credibility is perhaps a narrow way of looking at the matter. Anything that heightens the sponsor's interest in the workings of the research and the basis of the analysis is to the good. Two users offered examples of CAQDAS having such an effect. 'I work with [police force] at the moment. They are actually coming in to query the database themselves and I am finding that works very well, I am not driving the analysis in any way. They are getting what they want out of it. It's been quite easy to show them how to use the package. I was somewhat concerned that their interest in the research project, which after all they are funding, might have got completed. By the person driving the computer, by making it easy for them to come in and either follow what I'm doing or actually do it themselves has had a great payoff in the satisfaction they are getting out of the research' (FG4). Since the police were also the subject of the study it is not just a heightened involvement of sponsors but of subjects which was facilitated. In like vein, 'when I have got people I am working with to the point where they can articulate what they want then I can hand it over to them, but it is just the simple process which every researcher knows, you do need to be in almost continuous contact with them' (FG4). Thus, there is more to the matter than a 'philistine' applied scene and a 'pure' academic one. CAQDAS users appear every bit as concerned about preserving the canons of qualitative enquiry as are non-users. Here is a comment from a user in an academic setting: 'once there is a link to real, theoretically informed research that is going on it doesn't really matter what program. It stops being an issue of advocating [package], it's about enhancing methodology, enhancing analysis, allowing a researcher to maximize their time' (FG5).

As we indicated, several respondents felt that CAQDAS stimulated thinking about criteria of proof, adequacy and so on. 'It actually inspires and motivates debate, it makes you revisit issues around qualitative and quantitative philosophy, and puts these issues back on the table. And thinking about technology in the social sciences' (FG4). The phrase 'puts these issues back on the table' suggests that CAQDAS puts familiar epistemological debates in a new light. We must be careful to use verbs like 'encourage', 'stimulate' and 'prompt' when we are considering the impact of software on qualitative analysis. Agency remains with the user, not the package. There is testimony from our respondents to the practical and analytic advantages of use. There is further a recognition that good practice principles are achievable manually. These principles were laid down before computers. But there is also a recognition that there is more to be gained from CAQDAS than the practical benefits of data management. It is perhaps like the introduction of any significant innovation: it helps us question and explore our assumptions anew. We have also seen that, here again, the research environment mediates the benefits. It will be a similar story as we turn to disadvantages.

Disadvantages

We have made the point elsewhere (Lee and Fielding, 1991) that, by and large, proponents of CAQDAS have been relatively modest and non-utopian in their claims, at least when compared to 'computerization movement' enthusiasts in other fields (Kling and Iacono, 1988). Never-theless a variety of cautions, objections and criticisms have been advanced against the use of computers in qualitative research. We examine here some suggested disadvantages of computer-based methods in qualitative research. These are (a) that problems exist in relation to the accessibility and availability of CAQDAS programs, (b) that the practical benefits of computer-based methods have been exaggerated, (c) that computer use distances qualitative researchers from their data, and (d) that the intro-duction of computer-based analytic methods in qualitative research might encourage users to emulate some of the more problematic aspects of survey research.

Accessibility and Availability

Russell and Gregory (1993) have drawn attention to factors that in their view restrict the accessibility and availability of CAQDAS packages. They point out, for example, that the move to computer methods has financial implications. While costly of time, manual methods of qualitative data analysis impose little monetary burden. As Russell and Gregory indicate, the hardware requirements – and therefore the cost – of machines capable of running CAQDAS programs are not always trivial. Especially where the software used is complex, the user will typically need a machine that has a hard disk, a fast processor and a substantial amount of RAM. More-over, there seems to be a trend for requirements of this kind to creep upwards over time. This is not necessarily undesirable since increasing hardware needs often reflect the growing sophistication of the software. Nevertheless, developers and software companies are frequently over-optimistic about hardware requirements. The question is not how much RAM is needed simply to run the program, but how much does the program need to be used productively? Among our focus group partici-pants, graduate students especially had suffered the frustrations of using relatively powerful programs on low-end machines. In the end, they became adept at finding other things to do while waiting for the computer to finish some lengthy process. One respondent, for example, reserved the early morning for certain procedures. After setting the computer to work, she had breakfast, leaving it to grind away at its allotted task. Eventually moving to a more powerful machine, this informant reported that she could now do comparable analyses in minutes.

On the other hand, although software costs are hardly negligible, Russell and Gregory's (1993: 1810) suggestion that the 'cost of . . . quali-tative analysis programs is often prohibitive' seems wide of the mark. Weitzman and Miles (1995) provide information on 23 packages poten-tially of use to qualitative researchers. Taking into account educational discounts, the average cost of a package described in their book is

US$238.25. (The cheapest package, priced at $25 and of a somewhat specialist character, was excluded from the calculation to avoid artificially depressing the mean.) On average, text retrievers, almost all of which are commercial packages, are somewhat more expensive than dedicated qualitative analysis packages produced by academic developers. Perusal of advertisements in computer magazines suggests that high-end word processors had a 'street price' of around US$290 around the time Weitzman and Miles were writing. Given the relatively small size of the overall market for qualitative analysis software, one judgement might be that their pricing is in fact quite competitive.

Another way to look at this question is to explore the issue of software piracy. We found little evidence that CAQDAS software is widely pirated in Britain (Lee and Fielding, 1995). Obviously in our focus group research we dealt with people who were non-pirates by definition; they had registered their software. We enquired, however, if they knew of pirated copies of software and asked them about their own reasons for not pirating software. There seemed to be general agreement on three points. First, the generally low cost of CAQDAS programs – at least relative to commercial business-oriented packages – discourages piracy. To put the matter bluntly, at current pricing levels users do not feel ripped-off. Second, in the British context at least, recent legislative changes seem to have shifted the culture in universities towards one that is anti-piracy. Departments, it seems, are increasingly concerned about illegal copies of software and are policing their use. Having said that, the temptation to pirate software seems in part to be related to the availability of the software. Several focus group participants noted that packages had taken a long time to arrive from abroad and one researcher had resorted to using a pirated copy of unknown provenance while waiting for a legal copy to be delivered.

Russell and Gregory observe that there are difficulties associated with the portability of specific packages and the transferability of data. Researchers reliant on mainframe packages for qualitative analysis may have difficulties, for instance, if they move to a site which does not support the package. Russell and Gregory (1993: 1811) also suggest that 'manual data management systems are often more flexible with regard to data sharing' than are computer-based systems. Qualitative analysis software came of age as, or even after, the desktop revolution in computing occurred. Since mainframe packages are presumably now used only by a small minority of users, portability would not seem to be a problem of major dimensions. Certainly, it was not an issue that had affected any of our focus group participants. Given the physical awkwardness of paper-based data, we would question Russell and Gregory's contention that manual systems allow data to be shared more easily than computer-based systems. Having said that, as some of those in our focus groups reported, problems in transferring data occur in mixed hardware and software environments. The co-ordinator of the project mentioned elsewhere in which four different researchers collected data for each other recorded, for instance, that 'researchers in other institutions are supposed to send me disks with the file in Word which I can read . . . In fact they don't use [an interchange format], they send it in other things, which then have to be re-done' (FG3). Others reported difficulties where some team members used Macintoshes and others used PCs, while for one research team program use was impeded because they had to share a single PC between three researchers.

The Possible Exaggeration of Practical Benefits

How far the potential benefits of CAQDAS have been realized in practice can be questioned. Implicit in claims that computer use in qualitative research fosters paper reduction, the speedy finding of material, and flexibility in the coding process is an assertion that using a computer increases access to one's material. As Weitzman and Miles (1995: 335) point out, however, in practice things were somewhat different. Some programs have awkward interfaces. Others have features like facilities for quasi-statistical output or for hypothesis testing which leave many researchers feeling uncomfortable. In some cases, too, developers fitted 'governors' to their programs. These were ways of working, such as the need to code data off-screen before input to the program, which were built into the software. Almost always the intention was to make matters slightly more difficult for the researcher so as to inhibit facile analysis. Very often, however, as our focus group data clearly show, these were simply perceived by users as a hindrance.

There are no clear estimates of how long it will take a researcher to obtain a good working knowledge of a particular package. The experiences of our focus group participants suggest, however, that at their present stage of development CAQDAS programs offer troublesome, though by no means insurmountable, barriers to self-teaching. One user testified to being 'stuck at the first hurdle, had many phone calls to [developer] before I sorted it out, had to write myself an idiot's guide, which was stained with blood, sweat and tears . . . not knowing whether things were going wrong through my own stupidity or mistakes I was making' (FG3). Another user described encountering bugs in the program she used, which even the developer proved unable to resolve. Told of a fault, his disarming response was simply to express surprise – 'he wasn't even aware that it wasn't doing it, which was even worse!' (FG3). In some instances, users found themselves being thrown back onto local support services. In many cases this proved to be unsatisfactory. Although we are aware of sterling exceptions to the general rule, computer support staff are often not entirely helpful. CAQDAS programs are not well known outside the qualitative analysis community. Moreover, many computer support staff have backgrounds in the natural sciences or in statistics and some-times have difficulty in relating to qualitative analysis.

Since later versions of programs are generally easier to use than the earlier ones, it might be that some of our users paid a penalty for being relatively early adopters. Weitzman and Miles (1995) rated each of the 23 packages they reviewed on a three-point scale: strongly user-friendly, OK, and weak. Inevitably, of course, judgements of this kind are subjective. What is to an expert a minor inconvenience capable of a 'workaround' can seem a terrifying and insuperable problem to a novice. Nevertheless, Weitzman and Miles rated 14 out of the 23 programs as 'strongly user-friendly'. In only four cases did they rate the user-friendliness of a package as 'weak'. The proportion of strongly user-friendly programs falls some-what if one counts DOS versions of programs rather than their Windows counterparts. This in itself points to a trend which has become increasingly apparent in recent years. As is true more generally in the computing world, the developers of qualitative analysis software are moving in the direction of interfaces which are easier to use and which conform to indus-try 'look and feel' standards. These developments make considerably easier transfer of learning from one package to another. (Of course, developments of this kind might have to be bought at the cost of more substantial hardware requirements.)

The computer's ease of use can have possible paradoxical conse-quences. Russell and Gregory (1993) contend, for example, that because the computer is easy to use 'researchers may perform meaningless queries instead of focusing time and energy on productive directions'. None of our respondents reported this as having been a problem for them. Some clearly recognized, though, a downside to the creative play aspect of using a computer: 'I can spend an afternoon just playing with it, put together codes . . . and see what I get' (FG3). (It might be possible to argue that the unproductiveness of a particular line of enquiry is likely to become more evident earlier when the computer is used than in a manual analysis.) To take another example, claims that computer analysis takes less time than manual analysis might not be entirely justified. Because coding data is easy in a computer-based system, the time saved during analysis can be lost again if users do more extensive or more sophisticated coding than they would have done manually. (One of our respondents reported that coding in full an admittedly lengthy transcript – over 100 pages – took seven hours.)

Subject to time pressure, use might be suspended (Lee and Fielding, 1995). But users were loath to say they were abandoning CAQDAS. While there was a degree of disillusionment on the part of some respondents, most said they would continue use. One user remarked, 'I always intend that I am going back and use this thing and interrogate it more. I am sure I will' (FG4). Another who had been very frustrated with her experience of CAQDAS commented, '[Y]ou were asking whether [package] has actually affected the project . . . [I]t has affected us detrimentally, and I think it is partly because of our inexperience, but the psychological block that we have developed as a team . . . killed a lot of the enthusiasm and interest . . . The whole thing became coloured by our hatred and resentment [of] the bloody program' (FG1). (We consider this case in detail in Chapter 5.) Despite these remarks, however, the respondent was still strongly committed to CAQDAS and saw her problems as arising as much from the team research environment as from the software: 'I can still see it has got value and I still am irritated by this thing and I don't like being beaten by it.' She had 'always had a love/hate relationship with computers' and planned to use the package again on her next project, but allowing more time for data entry and coding. Others, who had struggled with large data sets, were less likely to consider using the computer again for small-scale projects, because the set-up time is considerable with CAQDAS and manual methods can cope with limited data sets without being swamped. However, even here there were exceptions. 'Now I think with small data sets I wouldn't [work manually], because I would think that's easy on the machine' (FG1).

For some applied users, the advanced analytic features available in some packages were 'overkill, [package] was too good, it was often too much for the sorts of work you were doing' (FG6). Others worried, however, that they were failing to realize the full potential of the software. Some referred to using the package in 'quite a manual way' (FG3). Thus, 'I have been totally unadventurous with it, all I have been asking it to do is to give me a print-out of all the answers to question one together, all the answers to question two, and there I stop. Last year I tried to categorize it and it took such a long time to sort out I wouldn't dare do it again' (FG3). Some of our focus group participants felt that program documentation often did not give enough emphasis to more sophisticated features. Many of the process descriptions offered were of a straightforward retrieval strategy, recovering the data coded with a given category. There appeared to be a gap between this approach, which is the basic use to which a code-and-retrieve package can be put, and work on category development. 'I find I use the very basic sort [procedure] . . . Partly coward's way out but also some of the things are fairly subtle and complicated and it would take so long to organize the material' (FG3).

Closeness to Data

A worry for many qualitative researchers is that computer methods discourage involvement in and engagement with data, inviting the analyst instead to skim the surface of even the richest material. Agar, for example, encapsulates this anxiety by recounting a metaphoric nightmare. Two studies take place side by side, 'a lousy computer analysis and a beautiful analysis done by hand'. In the nightmare, however, the 'community of scholars would immediately gather round the printout and celebrate its form rather than its content' (1991: 185). This is not an idiosyncratic concern. Fears that using a computer distances analysts from their data are recurrently expressed on electronic bulletin boards relating to computers and qualitative research. As Weitzman and Miles (1995: 335) comment, 'Judging from the electronic mail we've seen, many users place high value on "staying close to my data".' In assessing these concerns, we concur with another observation by Weitzman and Miles; what we are dealing with here 'is a complicated issue'. Raising the issue of closeness to the data in relation to computer use implies that not using a computer will ensure that the analyst stays close to the data. Yet dissatisfaction with manual methods and associated worries about being overwhelmed by the data suggest that manual analysis does not of itself guarantee a rich and fruitful closeness to the data. A further complication is that the phrase 'being close to the data' has a wide range of possible meanings most of which are rarely explicated.

Staying close to the data can mean being able to recover the sights, sounds and experiences of being in the field. Data, in other words, have an evocative character for some researchers. This is nicely, indeed evocatively, captured in the comment made by one of the anthropologists Jackson interviewed: 'For example, you write about a sacrifice, how it's done. When reading my notes I remember how it smelled . . . everyone's really pleased when it comes time to eat it' (1990: 13). For others, 'closeness to data' seems to be related, not necessarily in a very explicit way, to ideas about retaining the holistic character of data. At least for some of our focus group participants there remained an ineffable quality to data which software could not capture and that they experienced as a loss. 'There is something missing from data perceived in one way which was present in data perceived in another way, and software can't manage that' (FG3). For others, computerized code-and-retrieve based procedures fragmented the data in ways that made it difficult to see the wider picture. One said: 'because it was much easier to churn it out in little segments, that took away your interest with the whole transcript' (FG2). As Dey (1995) points out, the problem here is that in code-and-retrieve procedures text segments coded in the same way bear an apparent conceptual relationship to one another. Once retrieved, however, each segment appears divorced from the context in which it originally appeared. Focus group participants clearly felt that seeing results in context remained an important part of the craft of qualitative research. One user who declared 'I don't trust computers. I still do manual calculations' felt that the same held true for CAQDAS: 'if you just go into it and get the results you can't understand them unless you can contextualize the information you get' (FG3).

Having said that, to our mind some of the concerns about data fragmentation expressed in the literature might be overdrawn. The notion of 'context' implies boundedness. If it did not, the only context we could have for a segment of text from an interview transcript, say, would be the entire transcript. Presumably, in fact, most analysts work with an implicit idea of local context, and it is this which determines where the boundaries of a given segment are located. Thus in classical grounded theory open coding is based on an indicator-concept model (Glaser, 1978). Presumably, the boundaries of coded segments are determined in this case by how far the degree of fit between concept and indicator is compromised by extending the segment. Alternatively, in the kind of 'loose, inclusive coding' advocated by Becker and Geer (1960), segment boundaries are left deliberately wide, but subject to revision – presumably based on an understanding of context – as an analytic model is pieced together. What we would concede is that the concerns about fragmentation are clearly relevant whenever sequence is a consideration in data analysis. When something of interest is embedded within a narrative, refers back to something said or observed at an earlier juncture, or where one is interested in transitions from one topic to another, fragmentation *is* a problem. One solution might be to develop more complex coding approaches (Riessman, 1993). On the technical side, developers have experimented both with proximity searching (Drass, 1989) which allows the recovery of sequences of coded text, and the use of hyperlinking techniques (Dey, 1995), the non-linear and associative character of which readily permits the recovery of context.

Sometimes, when researchers refer to being close to their data what they have in mind are the tactile and perceptual aspects associated with data handling. Jackson (1990: 13) notes that 'quite a number' of the anthropologists she interviewed reported that they derived pleasure from handling their fieldnotes. In a similar vein, Seidel records that a researcher who had begun to use ETHNOGRAPH 'called me up and said he missed having his piles of xeroxed copies and note cards lying around' (1991: 114). Staying close to data in this sense implies that material gathered in the field retains a tangible character capable of being experienced in a tactile way. Receiving positive tactile feedback from a task presumably makes that task more pleasurable. This in turn sustains interest, aids motivation and increases one's sense of accomplishment. Interestingly in this regard, Converse (1987: 383) indicates that when in survey research computers replaced counter sorters as an analytic tool, researchers felt that some of the craft was lost. Presumably part of the source of these feelings was that analysts could no longer handle their punch cards or literally see distributions emerge as the machine differentially sorted cards into receiving bins.

The depth of the perceptual field an analyst is able to bring to data is affected by the form within which those data are encapsulated. A computer screen contains only something like 24 lines of text. It becomes almost literally a window, framing data in possibly useful, but always constraining, ways. It is less easy to see, for example, the structure of a text on a screen than on a set of printed pages which can easily be flipped back and forth (Pfaffenberger, 1988: 19). In an article provocatively entitled 'The right brain strikes back', Michael Agar describes how in the early stage of a fieldwork project he eschewed computer use in favour of finding an empty university classroom with a number of blackboards in it. He would write and erase ideas on the boards, turning from one to another to scan the current state of his thinking on the assumption that 'simultaneous visual access to material is what makes ideas happen' (1991: 193). C. Wright Mills advocated periodically spilling file folders out onto the floor and re-sorting them as a method for stimulating creative reflection on one's data. Such a procedure allows for 'perspective by incongruity' (Mills, 1959; Burke, 1969), the possibility that by juxtaposing seemingly dissimilar objects one will discern a non-obvious relationship between them. It is hard to think of a computer analogue of this procedure. Many common types of computer program contain a sort facility. Rarely, however, do they allow one to sort in a random order.

Quite a number of our focus group participants were clearly anxious about the impact computer use might have on their tactile and perceptual relationship with data. Speaking of an early concern, a user reported worrying 'that I might end up looking at the screen more than I was looking at my transcripts, the hard copy was the thing that I clung to, I was very concerned that I would be diverted to getting lots of neat piles of categories with this, that and the other, and forget about that first inter-view' (FG2). Or: 'unless I can hold this in my hand it's not real. I find it very difficult to read things for meaning on the screen' (FG6). The solution was to balance on-screen work with work using hard copy. Several users suggested that this issue could be resolved if one had done the transcription oneself. If so, there was sufficient familiarity to work largely on-screen. 'If you have done the transcription you can code it straight into the screen much easier but if you haven't then you need to go through the process of coding it all off-screen to get in touch with it' (FG1). In any case, as a number of users indicated, 'manual' elements were far from absent when they used the computer to analyse their data. 'I spend a lot of time reading the transcripts and getting them into shape [so] they are ready for [package], and I still do a lot of memoing and scribbled-down notes' (FG3). Others said: 'I don't think it is possible to rely on it [package] entirely' (FG3) and 'does anybody actually advocate doing everything on the screen? Never picking up your pen, that would be impossible' (FG3). Interestingly in this context one focus group participant who had a computer support role made a contrast with SPSS. In her view, SPSS was a good instance of software that required a high degree of abstraction. CAQDAS, on the other hand, was helpful because it supported either formal abstraction or close-to-the-data approaches. In general, 'one has got to evaluate the context of any given project, how far one wants to take

the application of a rigorous structure. There must be room for accommo-
dation of research styles' (FG5).

Some of the distancing effects which inhere in current packages might
be ameliorated by developments in operating system capability and inter-
face design (Weitzman and Miles, 1995). Such developments would
include the simultaneous display on screen of codes and data and what
Weitzman and Miles call 'pencil-level richness', the ability to mark and
annotate screen displays in flexible ways. We would also add to this what
we suspect will be an important development in promoting a rich and
close involvement with data: the substitution of digital video for analogue
audiotape as a data-logging medium in qualitative research. Beyond this,
as Bryan Pfaffenberger (1988) has astutely observed, the only protection
against the power of the computer to shape work in hidden ways is critical awareness. This requires reflection on the analytic process itself, independent of the computer, as well as awareness of what it is about the
technology that operates in undesirable ways.

One final comment about the issue of closeness to data is that, whether
or not the computer does distance researchers from their data, it challenges researchers to be clear about their assumptions. In earlier writing,
we used the metaphor of Frankenstein's monster to refer to the fear some
researchers felt about the impact of computer methods on the craft of
qualitative research (Lee and Fielding, 1991: 8). When we used this
metaphor we had in mind the standard cinematic representation of a mute
and horrible creature visiting mayhem and destruction on those who had
created him. As many commentators have pointed out, this is far from
Mary Shelley's original conception. That story can be read as counterpos-
ing an enlightenment view of science, reason and progress typical of the
eighteenth century with 'early nineteenth century Romantic perspectives
that probed beneath the tranquil face of Nature and man to confront the
dark and passionate powers therein' (Smith, 1994: 58–9).The desire not to
be distanced from one's data in part reflects a stance which qualitative
research inherited via the Chicago School from later German Romanticism. Faced with the disappearance of peasant culture under the impact
of industrialization, writers in the Romantic tradition undertook direct
observation of rural life. As Gouldner (1973) points out, by regarding the
marginal, the dispossessed and the lowly as worthy of study, Romanticism
implanted in the social sciences an 'open' or 'democratic' conception of
data in which nothing social falls beyond the purview of the social scientist. Alongside this democratic conception of data, however, Romanticism
also encouraged a celebratory stance towards data; one which 'wants and
appreciates the object in its concrete totality, in its uniqueness and indi-
viduality' (Gouldner, 1973: 352). Grounded in what Gouldner terms a
'collector's aesthetic', this celebratory stance can encourage a fascination
with the data themselves at the expense of the analytic process. Thus
Anselm Strauss records his irritation with students in his seminars being

'entranced by data' (1987: 162) in ways which inhibit their capacity to get on with analysis. In a critique that is partially self-directed, Lofland (1970), too, criticizes qualitative researchers for a failure of analytic nerve which discourages them from the task of transforming richly descriptive data into wider conceptual and theoretical understanding. Such failure is self-perpetuating because it inhibits the search for alternative, and potentially richer, conceptual frames. It is also, according to Lofland, abetted by the difficulties which inhere in the analysis of qualitative data. From this point of view, anxieties about computer use might not reflect reluctance to use new technology so much as an ambivalence about the analytic process itself. The computer promises to make the analysis easier, but it also forces the researcher to confront the need to embark on the analytic journey. In at least some cases, we would contend, concerns about the alleged distancing effects of the computer also embrace a reluctance to take that fateful step.

Related to this, it is interesting to note that some of the anthropologists Jackson (1990) interviewed felt embarrassed about their fieldnotes. One of them said, for example, 'Rereading them, some of them look pretty lame. How could you be so stupid? Or puerile?' Although we found nothing comparable to this in our focus group material, it is at least conceivable that some researchers are actually resistant to looking back over field materials because these remind them of their mistakes. Computers are, of course, both systematic and without feeling. Computer-based methods might ensure that particular materials are not discarded or discounted because of the researcher's negative feelings towards them.

Unintended Consequences

There have been some worries that instead of studying social settings and processes in depth, qualitative research, under the impact of the computer, might come eventually to mimic survey research, taking a broad sweep across a large number of cases. In other words, computer use might encourage qualitative researchers to trade resolution for scope, to use John Seidel's phrase. Seidel does not argue that working with large amounts of data is intrinsically wrong. His fear is that computer use will foster an illusion that large data volumes can be handled adequately. In exchanging resolution for scope, however, researchers 'will end up missing interesting and important things in the data' (1991: 109).

We sought in a number of ways to explore how far the availability of CAQDAS might have affected sample sizes. We have fairly detailed information about 15 of the projects undertaken by our respondents. In Table 3.1 projects are ranked by sample size within data collection method. Methods are ordered from those we take to be less structured to more structured approaches. We have distinguished projects which we

Table 3.1   *Projects by data collection method and sample size*

Project type	Data collection method	Size
Academic (gender)	Life history interviews	100
Academic (conversation analysis)	Unstructured interviews	10
Academic (medical sociology)	Unstructured interviews	40
Academic (medical sociology)	Unstructured interviews	56
Applied (health)	Unstructured interviews	150
Academic (education)	Semi-structured interviews	45
Applied (environmental studies)	Semi-structured interviews	50
Applied (housing)	Semi-structured interviews	50
Academic (social policy)	Semi-structured interviews	60
Academic (media)	Semi-structured interviews	100
Applied (health)	Semi-structured interviews	150
Applied (welfare)	Semi-structured interviews	150
Applied/academic (educational evaluation)	Semi-structured interviews	160
Applied (housing)	Open-ended questionnaires	156
Academic (medicine/welfare)	Open-ended questionnaires	646

considered to be academic in scope from those having a more applied focus. We have also indicated the broad substantive area within which each project was located.

These projects are not, of course, representative of any wider population. But it is worth making several comments about the distribution of sample sizes. First, the median sample size for the 15 projects is a surprisingly large 100 cases. While the smallest sample had 10 cases, the largest had 646. Academic studies (median = 56) tended to be smaller in terms of sample sizes than applied projects (median = 150). Large sample sizes are apparent for each data collection method. As one might expect, though, the general tendency is for less structured methods to be based on fewer cases than more structured methods.

We found little in the testimony of our focus group participants to suggest that packages were encouraging researchers to feel they could handle larger samples than usual in qualitative research. Instead it seems that what had led people to look into CAQDAS in the first place was that they had to deal with a large or varied amount of data. Rather than the use of large sample projects being attributed to CAQDAS, decisions about sample size more clearly reflect sponsor or peer expectations or are simply the product of the specific methodological stance taken by the researcher. 'You have to make some commitment to representativeness and you are talking about housing, the range of people's homes is enormous, number of categories, so in fact it is driven by some sense of sample size, and there are certain objectives you can make within a research project and that drives the number of interviews rather than the qualitative software . . .

before I started interviewing I knew that I was going to have so much information I would need help managing it' (FG3). Someone who gave computing and research methods advice to students and others at her institution replied to a direct question about how far computer use might be driving up sample sizes as follows: 'It's tending to be the other way round. People have done collections of large data sets and they face the risk of underreporting them. Most research projects get their funding first . . . and they say "Can you find me some [software to handle the data]?"' (FG4).

Because concern about sample sizes is often expressed as a worry about overall trends in qualitative methods, we decided to supplement our focus group data with material we hoped would give us a wider picture. To do this we downloaded from *Sociofile* abstracts in which the phrase 'depth interviews' appeared (n = 556). Depth interviewing does not of course exhaust those methods regarded in the social sciences as qualitative. There were two reasons for focusing on interviewing rather than say participant observation. First of all, we wanted to keep the analysis simple. We also reasoned, however, that, if there was a trend towards a rise in sample sizes, interview studies were likely to be sensitive to it. Abstracts not directly reporting an empirical study were excluded from the analysis, as were those which contained no specific information about sample size. Table 3.2 shows details of the distribution of sample sizes for 1991, 1992 and 1993 (the last complete year for which data are available). Three earlier years, 1977, 1983 and 1987, are shown for comparison.

The average median sample size for the years shown is 37.4 (s.d. = 13.79). Inspection of the table does not suggest a linear trend towards sample size inflation; if anything the median sample size is declining slightly. In each year, however, a small number of studies appear which have rather large sample sizes. All abstracts which revealed a sample having over 100 cases were inspected individually. It seems that in many cases these were quasi-quantitative studies. Of the 21 abstracts we inspected, eight (38 per cent) indicated a definite use of quantitative techniques such as cluster or factor analysis. In another four cases, while analytic techniques were not mentioned, descriptions of the findings were firmly couched in distributional or associational terms. (In the remaining

Table 3.2 *Sample size comparisons: selected years*

Year	Minimum sample size	Median sample size	Maximum sample size
1977	3	50	180
1983	3	40	403
1987	5	37	332
1991	1	28	575
1992	5	33	150
1993	5	35	150

cases we could not determine from the abstract how the data had been analysed.)

Finally, we decided to look at all those instances where the words 'depth interviews' appeared in an abstract which referred to journals largely devoted to reporting qualitative work. Specifically, we looked at the *Journal of Contemporary Ethnography* (and its forerunners, *Urban Life* and *Urban Life and Culture*) and at *Qualitative Sociology*. The numbers involved were not large enough to explore trends. However, the overall picture is quite consistent with the patterns already seen. Some 18 articles were identified which reported the results of empirical research and which indicated a sample size. (No information on the size of sample was available for one further case.) The median sample size was 30 with a mean of 43 (s.d. = 36.05). The smallest sample size was seven; three studies reported sample sizes of 70 or over.

One implication of our focus group data is that researchers involved in such studies based on large samples adopted software early in the hope that it would ease potential data management problems. An obvious way to test this hypothesis would be to look at studies in which software was used and to compare the sample sizes from those studies with sample sizes in a more general sample of qualitative studies. There is no very easy way to identify studies of the former type. We did, however, inspect the *Social Science Citation Index* for studies citing John Seidel's descriptive writings on ETHNOGRAPH, one of the earliest and best-known packages. We did not have the resources to track down these studies and examine them. It is interesting to note, however, that of the 163 articles we identified only about a third (35.6 per cent) were single-authored, slightly more than a quarter (29.5 per cent) had two authors and 35 per cent had three or more authors. For comparison, we took a one-in-ten sample of our depth-interview studies. Of the 56 articles we looked at, just under two-thirds (64 per cent) had only one author, 18 per cent had two authors and a further 18 per cent had three or more authors. If we make the assumption that multiple authorship is more likely in large-scale studies then this provides additional evidence that researchers needing to collect large amounts of data have been particularly attracted towards computer use to analyse their qualitative data.

In addition to exploring the impact of CAQDAS on sample size, we wondered if computer-based methods were chiefly seen as relevant to the analysis of interview data. We were aware that some packages were influenced by approaches developed for the analysis of documents (in particular, some European packages have strong links to the tradition of hermeneutic analysis). Interviews are likely to have more thematic coherence than fieldnotes and/or at least some kinds of documents. While there might well be interpretive problems, respondents are responding (if only nominally) to similar stimuli on the same kind of occasion and often under similar conditions. This tends not to be true either of fieldnotes or of documents prepared by third parties where there are processes of selection and expression which are more or less non-reviewable by the user. Is CAQDAS, then, necessarily of restricted application in the analysis of data from sources other than interviews?

One should not underestimate the value of CAQDAS as a data management device; it can take considerable effort to organize and keep track of data from multiple sources, even when it is specific to a particular case. One project, for example, involved multiple interviews concerning a particular work activity as well as independent but linked observations of a separate activity. As noted above, purely observational studies and purely document-based studies were in the minority in our sample, although field observation was sometimes a component of the mixed method studies as well. Several users reported holding fieldnotes in CAQDAS as well as interview data. Thus, 'it is just as appropriate for doing fieldnotes if you know what you are going to use your fieldnotes for . . . It is useful to put on [package] just as a marker that there are fieldnotes on this person so that when you are looking at your transcripts you know there may be other relevant material. Because things like that get lost' (FG3). In fact where mixed data sources were used, researchers seemed to entertain no inhibition about using these kinds of data alongside interview data in the package. Thus 'the way I then back up the interviews is by looking at project files, so correspondence files, project diaries which firms hold, minutes of meetings, site meetings, briefing meetings . . . that does go into the package as well. It's confirming. One thing I ask is, "how much time do you spend working on a project?" . . . and I can then back that up by looking at their time sheets' (FG5). This is a very explicit account of use for confirmation and this verificationist approach to triangulation has to assume equivalence of meaning to fulfil its logic. Thus 'really the only reason I do look at the other data is as a back-up to the interviews, so somebody says "how do you know we are telling the truth?" or "how do you know you are getting the right type of answer?" [and] I can say "well, I looked it up, information to back up the case".' Similarly, 'again, I do like [respondent just quoted], using some other, apart from my interviews, background information as justification triangulation, information about the context where respondents are working' (FG5).

As noted, six of our focus group participants were currently working on research that included a quantitative element in the research design. Although we had suspected that qualitative data analysis software might frequently be used to analyse data from free response questions on an otherwise quantitative survey instrument, we found only two such instances. Of the remaining mixed method projects, one involved repertory grid (quantified responses, quantitative analysis) alongside diaries and interviews, one a short survey used to sum up basic information about the sample which was pursued in more depth by interview, another a large longitudinal quantitative study with a significant but subsidiary use of interviews, while the remaining project was part of a series of educational evaluations which combined quantitative survey data with qualitative data from case studies. There was little evidence, in other words, of CAQDAS being used to 'mop up' messy data on projects that were otherwise statistically driven.

We found both 'basic' and applied multi-method research among the projects on which our focus group participants were working. In other words, it was not only quantitatively based projects that came with an applied focus. However, in line with other work (Caracelli and Greene, 1993), we also found little evidence that different methods were extensively integrated when the time came to analyse the data. This might have some implications for the extent to which 'conceptualizing or 'theory-building' features of CAQDAS are used. Thus, 'there are questions carrying the survey and which touch on the area [covered by qualitative methods] . . . but they are not integrated beyond that, the quality is very different really, so they are not integrated beyond that' (FG1). This despite the fact that this informant both endorsed and enjoyed working with multiple kinds of data. It should be noted that most users referred to making some basic quantification of their qualitative data (often referred to as 'content analysis') at least in the sense of counting code frequencies and the like. One statistically trained user who worked in an advisory capacity was able to identify for quantitatively oriented researchers three distinct uses to which they could put qualitative data analysis software. For researchers who 'insisted that [the data] then went into SPSS I used [text analysis package] to help me construct the sensible categorization scheme. Other people I was able to convince that it was there for their searching, for them to pursue their own lines. And the last perhaps trivial but often very welcome use was the quotable quotes to put alongside the pie charts and the statistical tables' (FG4).

In the case of a large-scale study of religious beliefs, something more elaborate was being attempted. Consideration had been given to the commensuration of the data from different sources. The analytic strategy was interesting: rather than simply looking for points of connection, the difference between the two types of data was recognized, and reflected in the use of two different packages, a statistics package and a CAQDAS package. The researchers appeared to feel that the difference between quantified and textual, discursive information about the same referent should be preserved rather than seeking integration: they represented different aspects of the phenomenon being studied. 'We don't want the qualitative to duplicate what we have already got on the quantitative – pointless' (FG4). The problem of ensuring the comparability of the data is also manifest in another, perhaps more frequent, occurrence in qualitative analysis, where new data are collected after a conceptualization has begun to be built up. Since many research designs include pilot fieldwork this is quite a common occurrence, and the issue again arises of the researcher's evolving perspective leading to different aspects of the phenomenon being perceived as relevant. This quality of perspectival emergence can, however, be 'tracked' quite effectively by annotation features allowing memoing and the use of source tags (in some cases, these automatically date an entry or a retrieval). 'Most of the other things I would do would be recording information about indexing categories and you can do that fairly easily, change an index category, you can do that on [package], 'cause you can bring up comments on a category you have created and work out how it has changed' (FG3).

In summary, CAQDAS can be used as a 'gateway' to a statistical analysis, for example through export to a statistical package or by code-frequency counting. There seems little evidence, at least in our data, that this led users to analyse qualitative data quantitatively. Nor does CAQDAS appear to appeal only to researchers with a quantitative bent, or to people who only do qualitative research. Among our sample, it appears that 'pragmatism rules', though we would add the caution that methodological eclecticism needs to keep in view problems relating to the validity of comparisons.

Conclusion

The experience of our focus group participants seems not to validate the strong claims of either proponents or critics of computer-assisted qualitative data analysis software. Users experienced difficulties and frustration in learning and using packages. With some exceptions, the computer delivered data management benefits rather than transforming analytic practice. Against this, those who, for various reasons, were uncomfortable with existing manual methods of analysis generally found the systematicity of computer-based methods helpful, and perhaps even in some situations liberating. On the other hand, users also resisted those aspects of computerized methods that seemed to them to compromise the craft elements traditionally associated with qualitative research. For the moment at any rate, we would suggest that a verdict of 'not proven' is entered against the charge that CAQDAS encourages users to mimic survey practice,[3] for example by collecting data from larger samples. As a general rule computer use does seem to lend legitimacy to qualitative research. It allows researchers both to emphasize the traditional strength of qualitative research and to counter misconceptions about qualitative data analysis.

A final point is that for some there was no craft from which to become detached. As one focus group participant who was at the beginning of her career jokingly put it, 'I have never cut and pasted'. In the future many researchers are likely to be introduced to qualitative computing as a normal part of their professional socialization. As such they might need explicitly to be taught to recognize the tactile and perceptual constraints which technology imposes. By then, hopefully, computer-based methods will more closely emulate traditional practice. Meanwhile, the teaching of qualitative analysis might also have benefited from a greater explicitness about analytic procedures.

Notes

1 Trainers testify that, worryingly often, participants on CAQDAS courses seek to learn how to use qualitative software despite having only a limited background in qualitative methodology (Lewins and di Gregorio, 1996).
2 While such conventions exist in quantitative research, David (1991) claims they are less well developed than they might be.
3 Unlike the Anglo-American common law, one of the glories of the Scottish legal system is that it permits this alternative to the stark bifurcation of 'guilty' or 'not guilty'.

4

Managing Data in CAQDAS

As we have seen, the starting point for qualitative analysis usually involves classifying – coding or categorizing – some sort of textual data, be they interview transcripts, a set of fieldnotes, an official report or any other kind of document. This is also the starting point for software that seeks to facilitate qualitative data analysis. Some see in this emphasis on classification – particularly where it is referred to as 'coding' – the emergence of an orthodoxy bringing unwanted homogeneity to qualitative analysis. We address this concern more thoroughly in a later chapter. Here it is necessary simply to say that our reference to classification and use of the term 'coding' implies no more than that these are the terms our respondents used in discussing this stage of qualitative analysis. Since there is a variety of approaches to qualitative analysis, some of which are underused relative to their potential, we have no desire to encourage a narrowing of what qualitative analysis might involve. Our discussion of classification and coding is empirical rather than normative.

Classification involves several steps. The researcher identifies categories or codes which relate to the data as a whole. This is often done in some kind of 'brainstorming' procedure, a rather dramatic phrase which disguises the mundane nature of what is done. The researcher reads, and rereads, the data, jotting down possible themes, some broad, some particular. If there is more than one person involved in the analysis this might be done as a group activity. Some basic cleaning-up of the list of analytic themes is then done, often in isolation from the data. The themes might be treated as points on an outline, to be assembled into a sequence of themes bound by some logic (perhaps the most obvious is the 'chronology', which tracks a process through its stages to some kind of outcome: Hammersley and Atkinson, 1983). Some themes might prove redundant, because they overlap with others or are supported by little data. Others might simply prove peripheral to the main thrust of the analysis and be dropped for this reason.

An 'analytic theme' is no more than an idea relating to the social phenomenon upon which data has been collected and which one wishes to discuss in interpreting the phenomenon. What is the relationship between a theme and a 'code' (or 'category')? It is often the case that a theme draws on several ideas, each of which is represented by a code. Sometimes a theme is fully represented by a single code. A 'code' is a summary term which expresses some essential quality of the phenomenon as reflected in the data. For efficiency's sake, codes are usually expressed in terse or abbreviated terms. They often resemble the variable labels used to identify categories of response on a survey questionnaire. Unlike the usage of the word 'code' in espionage, a code term does not seek to disguise something to represent a broader idea as explicitly as possible. Its role is to organize the text by permitting it to be divided into segments. Segments of the data are distinguished from each other by assigning the code(s) the researcher thinks apply to that segment. The data set thus loses some of its seamless quality and chronological structure. It is reorganized by the application of different codes to adjacent segments, and also by the non-coding of segments that do not relate to the themes the researcher is developing. While some segments might exactly represent the sense of the code term the researcher is using, it is more likely that the segment will represent only an aspect or shade of meaning of the code. This is helpful to the researcher because it offers an agenda of nuances within the code which can be developed in writing up. Indeed it is this which lends qualitative analysis its richness, its ability to represent social phenomena from several angles.[1]

When the initial work of coding is done, researchers move to the next stage of coding: identifying which codes apply to each segment of the data. The documents comprising the data are marked up accordingly. This is a time-consuming stage and during the course of it researchers often find that some data will contradict, and other data will add unexpected nuances to the analysis. It is then necessary to revise the codes to accommodate these features. Sometimes researchers will need to remind themselves of why they coded a particular segment in a particular way, so an 'analytic memo' is written as a record of the thinking behind assignment of that code to that segment. Qualitative researchers often refer to the cut-and-paste or 'scissors and Sellotape' procedure. This is where the coded segments of documents are literally cut up so that all the data about a particular code can be physically placed together in a stack. This sorting operation is fundamental to the place of coding in analysis, although it can be done without physically cutting up the documents (e.g., using a detailed outline).

Summing up, the role of coding in qualitative analysis is to stimulate the identification of analytic themes, to organize the data so that the strength of its support for those themes can be determined, to illustrate those themes by providing quotable material, and to support data reduction by representing its key features and identifying redundant, peripheral or irrelevant data.

We have already presented a typology of program types which suggests the various ways that software seeks to facilitate qualitative data analysis. But we can only really estimate the impact of using CAQDAS by reference to the testimony of users. This brief preamble has sought to bring out two ideas: that coding is a key part of qualitative research, and that gauging the impact of CAQDAS on the process requires attention to the adequacy of coding as an analytic procedure as well as the qualities of the software designed to assist it. We will bear this in mind as we examine the experiences of CAQDAS users in different elements of the coding process.

Familiarization: Generating an Initial Focus

CAQDAS can assist qualitative researchers at several different stages of analysis and, indeed, we have seen that users hold strong views on what might be its principal contribution: the systematic organization of data in a form suitable for retrieval. However, CAQDAS is, at least potentially, a good deal more than an electronic filing cabinet, and we have documented a proportion of our sample (admittedly, a minority) who conduct most if not all their analytic work 'within' a CAQDAS package. The effort to generate the initial focus of the analysis is conventionally organized around a set of analytic themes. We might draw an analogy with an academic book. Overall it comprises a treatment of a particular subject located in a disciplinary field. An analytic 'theme' in this analogy might equate to the topic addressed in one of its chapters. We have already mentioned that themes are often generated in a 'brainstorming' procedure (aptly discussed in Lofland and Lofland, 1984). The data are read and/or reviewed by some other means (listening to tapes, watching film/video), so that the researcher gets an idea of the range of ideas and opinions in the data. In the brainstorming session itself, the researcher writes a list, in no particular order, of topics at varying levels of generality. Other people might be involved at this stage; Lofland and Lofland suggest that getting others involved with the project or the subject will help the researcher to overcome the tendency to look at things from one particular perspective informed by one set of biographical experiences. This 'inclusive' stage, where any idea might be included (no matter how remotely related to the data), is followed by an 'exclusive' effort to compile a topic outline with some logic underlying its sequence of topics and with some consistency between points at equivalent levels of the outline. At this point some of the themes might be combined, or become subthemes, and others might be dropped as not being directly relevant. There is also usually some effort to see what kind of data or research evidence stands in support of given themes and subthemes, so that some might be dropped at this stage if insufficient evidence is available or the data are contradictory. This stage normally precedes detailed coding/classification of the data. Indeed, the outline developed at this stage often provides at least some of the coding terms which will be applied to the data. This provides one stimulus for the oscillation between data and emergent analysis which marks qualitative analysis and makes it a recursive, iterative procedure. Of course, coding is not as 'free rein' as the brainstorming procedure described above might imply: brainstorming is only one part of the progressive focusing of the analysis discussed in classic descriptions such as Geer's account of her 'first days in the field' (1964).

With this characterization of the 'familiarization' stage in mind we can consider our users' testimony to the role of CAQDAS at such a point in the analytic process. As noted, coding is unlikely to be complete at this point and those code assignments that have been made are likely to be regarded as tentative. Thus, packages which offer a speedy means of navigating (and indeed 'skipping around') the database by searching for keywords and allowing retrievals which simply 'backtrack' along the path of previous retrievals are at an advantage. But prior even to this, users commented that the work of data entry and organizing the database facilitated their getting acquainted with (or 'immersed in') the data, so that familiarization was taking place. In some cases there was an implication that the requirements for database organization obliged the researcher to be systematic (e.g., formatting all data files with a header containing standard information). Where they formerly would have 'just stuffed everything in a folder', they felt CAQDAS 'would help me to be more organized about how I went about my analysis' (FG2). As another put it, compared to previous practice 'it is much more systematic . . . [and] you can't ignore the data' (FG1).

In settling on tentative themes and exploring the data to see whether and how these themes were supported, CAQDAS encouraged users to take account of the range of data available. In that there is substantial checking of evidence for themes as codes are applied following the initial focus-defining stage, and one criterion might be the 'amount' of relevant data, the ability to check the number of mentions of a particular theme might be useful. Something like this is suggested in the following. 'I ended up with about 50 codes . . . and then I started to look at what my codes were and what they meant, then I did counts to see what sort of things were repeatedly happening and I then had to select a very small amount of data and I managed to come out with three interesting phenomena' (FG1). Here counts were used to identify recurrent emphases by respondents, resulting in three broad themes (judged suitable in extent for a Master's dissertation), upon which attention was then focused, with subsequent data analysis being devoted to the data relating to these themes – 'I was then able to just pull out those examples to work on for more analysis.' Thus, 'familiarization' can include considerable data reduction and might overlap with a substantial preliminary coding effort designed to sieve the data into broad themes, with only a subsection thereof to be developed in the analysis (and being recoded in a finer-grained way to support the final analysis). 'Breaking the data up into relevant topics so that you . . . take one topic and then form your data sets, one from each topic that you want, makes it much more manageable' (FG1). Some might feel concern that this is moving prematurely to a highly selective use of the data and that relevant material might be lost. Against this, note that CAQDAS packages usually provide the user with some control over the context that is recovered along with each 'hit', so that material that has been weeded out in identifying data relevant to given themes could be put in front of the user again. In another instance a respondent testified to the value of CAQDAS in the initial stages because annotation features could keep a record of one's thinking as one mulled over a number of themes that might apply: 'there is no way in the world we could cope [manually] . . . because you are working with so many different ideas within a section of the transcript and they all end at different places, I couldn't carry that in my head' (FG1).

Reference was also made to the idea that one's search for analytic themes should be informed by as much of the data as possible. Respondents taking this approach tended to code before settling what the final analytic themes would be, feeling they made up in serendipity and thoroughness what they might lose by selective use of the data. 'I felt that [package] was good because it forced you to look at every chunk of data and to code it . . . [It] forces you to look for negative instances and all that sort of thing, put every bit of data into your coding scheme' (FG6). This approach does not obviate making a selection and supporting only those themes that the data will bear, but it extends the theme-identification process and shifts its resolution to a later stage. Researchers were conscious that most data sets can support more than one set of analytic themes, and saw advantages to conducting the process using software because they could return to the same data set with new analytic ideas and purposes in mind. A user who was writing both policy reports and her doctoral thesis based on the same materials commented that she had realized CAQDAS would be useful because she 'wanted to go back into things over and over again, starting to make connections of my own' (FG6). A similar point applied when a group was working together to identify analytic themes. 'We were going to be looking . . . at each other's data . . . It really was going to be a "paste" job, not just the cuts and making piles, because if you looked at somebody else's pile and wanted to reorganize it then how did you keep a record of where they had it in the first place in case they didn't want it reorganized' (FG6). Such points address the concern that software rigidifies the analysis by locking users into a given set of codes and code assignments. Mechanically, recoding is easier in most packages than it is by hand. The familiarization stage might also be aided for team researchers by the 'transparency' of CAQDAS-based projects compared to manual records. Thus, 'to make it work you have to talk a lot, have to . . . be very explicit about the techniques of analysis and the categories that you are using' (FG4). Some thought this benefit was not confined to teams (where there was a peer pressure effect). Thus, 'it has made me and people I have worked with much more explicit about the way we work . . . If I had been an individual person using this I still think

I would have been more systematic and explicit to myself' (FG4). Similarly, the speed with which one can navigate the database 'enhances my abilities to really think through the material . . . You are on that "roll" mentally' (FG4).

Users were aware that CAQDAS was sometimes characterized as leading to an 'over-analysing' pathology, but felt this was only another way of describing being thorough. 'The other thing [to the idea] that it makes you much more thorough [is] if you say that in a negative way is this thing about over-analysing what you've got. I feel it's made us more thorough' (FG4). Thus where an analysis might draw on the idea that 'most' respondents expressed some view or another, with CAQDAS one could determine precisely what proportion expressed the view. Such facilities, especially in team research, encourage consistency: 'it's helped us to be more consistent in our analysis, think through what we are doing' (FG4), whereas manually 'we might have more of a tendency to go off and analyse in our own way'. Interpretations poorly grounded in the data were more likely to be exposed. Further, rather than rigidifying early analytic thoughts, CAQDAS encouraged a more tentative, emergent approach to the analysis. Thus, 'it allows you to be more flexible and try things out and scrap them or change them around without committing yourself' (FG5). In that 'familiarization' and 'coding' seem to be stages which shade into each other in our respondents' practice, we should emphasize that simply because one begins by assigning particular codes does not mean one rests with them, just as in 'manual' methods researchers have often changed their minds, reworking themes and categorization as a natural part of the sequential analysis process. 'For me a lot of the theoretical [categories] are emerging from my isolation of, let's say, Asian female [occupational group] as a category . . . I wouldn't have thought of that category but because I have got [database] categorized in that way, [Asian/other groups, male/female, target occupational group/other relevant occupational groups] I can then take that category and say "let's do some indexing, give me, search 'politics', search 'aesthetics', search 'funding"', and from those searches I will have very interesting reading potentially, maybe not, maybe lead nowhere but because . . . I've got it indexed in these particular categories I can then take those categories and grapple with and develop their importance' (FG5). Rather than rigidifying the analysis this seems to speak to a creative process which encourages the making of new connections. Of course, there is always a tension between creative flexibility and parsimonious explanation. The necessary question is whether using CAQDAS leads to a proliferation of codes.

How Many Codes?

Computers can more readily and reliably handle large volumes of data than can people, so if researchers customarily generate large numbers of codes, or could improve the quality of analysis by doing so, CAQDAS should be advantageous. However, if the number of codes exceeds the capacity of the researcher to conceptualize (or complete!) their analysis, then what appears as a benefit might be a disadvantage. In the following case the proliferation of codes led a research team to abandon CAQDAS. 'That's one of the reasons we gave up, in that we just had so many codes. There was always this feeling that "if I code that, that chunk the same, that may be the same and then again it may not be. Is it the same as that, is it really the same as that. Perhaps we ought to code it something different, we could give it another code" . . . There is always this feeling that we could use this . . . that it would be easier at the end to put, go downwards [in the number of codes] than it would be to miss things out at the beginning. So we just ended up with hundreds and hundreds and hundreds of codes!' (FG6). The group process associated with team research, and a sense of thoroughness, combined to overload the analytic process by unrestrained coding. We can contrast this with the researcher mentioned earlier who having coded 'everything' produced 'three interesting phenomena from the data'. Here the process clearly centres around data reduction. There is a first 'trawl' using a fine net of very many codes and with every single datum being coded, but to produce a coherent and well-evidenced account the researcher has to identify a far smaller number of codes as main themes.

The question is whether the initial trawl needs to be fine-grained. If it does not, then the data-handling advantage of the computer is superfluous. This researcher certainly felt that a broad first trawl with a number of codes was appropriate to the size of data sets with which she was working, contrasting this with survey-type coding. '[The data set] is big enough to get comparisons out but not too big that you lose the refinements of the codes. Because if you are coding on really really big data sets you tend to just lump a big section of data into one code, whereas this, sometimes two or three codes in a line . . . If you coded more broadly you would still have to break it down at some point' (FG1). As another user remarked, 'you can code it all, then you can refine it later, when you actually get to the point where you are really in there in understanding' (FG1). In other words, too small a set of initial codes would yield an over-generalized analysis because refinements and detail would be cut out from the start. One needed a fine-grained first coding to detect the points of detail. A small number of codes would then be identified as core themes, but one could illustrate and provide evidence for them because one had the detail from the first sweep.

This implies that the data management advantages of the computer could be useful. For instance, CAQDAS packages can streamline code assignment, make it easy to pull out instances of each code, and enable one to change code assignments easily. They also do these things systematically, making it harder to ignore discrepancies in the data. Nevertheless, users aware of these data management advantages might not always use them. A hint of guilt enters this user's comment about reverting to a manual approach under deadline pressure, raising concern that her last bout of coding was less thorough. 'I ended up the last half-dozen or so just doing manual methods, printing it off the screen and reading it. It was miles faster. I'm not sure what that does to those interviews, because I think I hadn't coded those in the same way as I coded the other ones, where there was a lot more overlap, and I tended to see their connections. So it does alter the way you code' (FG1). Note that manual methods were 'miles faster', because the coding became less refined. But it is important to remember that one does not rest with the first, fine-grained trawl (this is extensively discussed in the next section). This is a step *en route* to identifying a smaller number of codes, which will be manageable when writing up but which will have behind them the back-up afforded by the granularity of the first round of coding. '[T]here is a tendency to bring the whole lot in, can stifle you before you even start, whereas if you are selective and say "this is what I want to look at at the end of the day, this, this, this and this" then you make your four data sets with pieces from each transcript. You are still getting the quality that you want, and as long as you took everything that is relevant to what you are looking at you can then break your data up into the different areas that you want' (FG1).

There is a nuance to add here. It is not only a matter of condensing codes between first and subsequent sweeps. There has to be some coherence, some relationship between codes. A cautionary tale we encountered, to which we will return, was that of a multidisciplinary team which encountered great difficulty in settling on a common set of codes, largely due to the different, discipline-based interests (and understandings of qualitative method) of each member. The project director commented, 'it was very difficult to make them [codes] merge together because we were trying to put together too many different sorts. What we should have done . . . was code them all for "media", done that, then we should have coded for [topic 2], then we should have coded for [topic 3], but we were up against a time barrier by the time I realized, so that just blew us, really screwed us up' (FG1). Such a serial coding procedure would have been a device to impose coherence on the coding but would in turn rely upon agreement on which codes should be applied at an early stage. It is worth adding that when another respondent suggested that, if one had not performed the transcription one should code off-screen to get in touch with the data, the project director just quoted replied, 'that's not necessarily the case, it depends how complex your data sets are, there is no way in the world we could cope [manually], not the least because you are working with so many different ideas within a section of the transcription and they all end at different places, I couldn't carry that in my head' (FG1).

It has already been suggested that these issues cannot be read purely as matters to do with CAQDAS: they relate to the research environment in which CAQDAS is used. A key distinction is between contract research and postgraduate research. This can be seen in the following exchange. A contract researcher remarked, 'we did get to a stage where we said "hang on a minute, our actual focus is classroom observation, so we'll code in detail what they say about classroom observation and we'll just sort of do it in a very sketchy way, the rest of it".' Her colleague interjected, 'But then you have things like, because we were interested in appraisal and the appraisal relationship, well, that's still there even though they [respondents] are talking about management, even though they are not talking about appraisal relations you still have to bring it in' (FG6). Thus, effort to control the proliferation of codes was continually conflicting with the increasingly refined grasp of the resonances of the data, which tended to make 'everything' relevant. A doctoral researcher then commented, 'I just wonder if we are working with different definitions of proliferation, because how many codes are too many? Maybe I've got exactly the same number of codes as you and we differ because it seemed like I was usually working with quite a manageable set, but I have been building up more but I didn't experience it as a problem ... As a graduate student this is your life, as it were, right? So you don't have teaching responsibilities, you don't have admin., you don't have that kind of thing, so I was working with it very closely and I didn't experience that as a problem' (FG6). Whatever else qualitative researchers might expect of CAQDAS, time savings are a less significant boon than the enhancement of interpretive adequacy through a more systematic approach to analysis.

Defining Codes

Researchers are conscious of the need for restraint in coding. This is one obvious meaning of 'code management'. The avoidance of proliferation is, however, in constant tension with the endless refinement of codes. To an extent one does not wish to inhibit the discovery of new details and nuances, for this is one of the great strengths of qualitative method. The issue is whether each discovery merits a new code. One obvious means of managing the process is to move towards a hierarchical conceptualization of codes, which enables fine points to be safely tucked away beneath overarching (or 'meta') codes. Another would be to seek some pattern in the relationship of codes, perhaps a network or causal pathway. Given their centrality to the *practical* activity of analysis, and their ability to swamp researchers, it is worth considering how researchers derive and define codes. A sustained look at coding might also be justified by the suspicion that the mystique sometimes attached to coding means that some initiates simply have no idea how to get started.

It is hardly necessary to say that the first step is a thorough reading of the data, but there are choices to be made even here, since the first document one examines will probably receive closer scrutiny than the twentieth. Becker characterized qualitative analysis as 'sequential analysis', because of the continual oscillation between data collection and data analysis. This both means that the two elements inform each other and introduces an element of freshness and vividness to the process. This inspires in researchers a spirit of tentativeness, a feeling that all analysis is partial and that there is never one, final 'right answer'. In fact this is a helpful posture during code definition, as this contract researcher notes: 'I usually just have the transcript by me and just as I went along, read it up, OK, line so-and-so I want that and that and that . . . with [package] the thing is to keep refining the process so the more you can reduce your putting in and transcripts and coding off-screen the sooner you can get onto the screen and work, the sooner you get in touch with the data and start revising it anyway. So you might get to the end of the first transcript and think "OK, that's a total bums-up [dead end], that's not how I want it", but by the end of that first one you'll know what you do want' (FG1). The first transcript is something of a test-bed. The codes derived from it might well change and, in this researcher's practice, the refinement of codes largely takes place in the package.

As an alternative strategy, researchers might make a virtue of a brisk initial sweep, knowing that the codes and code assignments will be condensed in successive work. 'My first run-through was just line-by-line. I read this line, how many ideas in this line, and then I looked for one idea, "OK, where does that idea end", "OK, that idea ends there" and then "what other ideas are there in that line" and "that idea actually runs so many lines" and then go to the next line. You literally, you are not making judgements, you are just saying "what is that saying, what is that about". My first coding right the way through was just, you know, "they are talking about themselves" or "they are describing this" or "they are doing this", only basic codes. Describing actions or describing their talking about events . . . Content analysis' (FG1). Another participant interjected with the next stage, 'then once you've got that you can start to look at . . . the main things they are spending a lot of time talking about. Then from that you can go back to those main categories . . . and say "how are they saying it", or you can start to look [at] what you want to know' (ibid.).

The approaches we have examined above are much in line with the essential posture of grounded theory, in that ideas are derived from inspecting the data. By no means is it the only approach. Before looking at alternatives, we should note that code definition so far is something where use of the software is marginal to the process. One alternative approach is to derive codes from the research instrument, much as in quantitative analysis of survey data. '[I]t's simply sorting it by "food", "health", "relatives" . . . Those came from the questionnaire, which is very, it's a very unstructured questionnaire. So really it comes from the questions I have asked them.' There is an implication that these are too straightforward to trouble with using software at all, as the respondent goes on to say: 'the second lot of coding that I do I may not bother doing with [package], just a pile of things about food, and do the sorting into piles' (FG3). In the following, another respondent describes a similar process, with straightforward demographic codes, along with a grounded theory strategy and recognition that package-based coding might be overkill, since some codes do not pan out. 'Some of them are from facesheets . . . marital status, age . . . I started off before I had [package] and . . . sorted out all these periods in people's lives and I never used them . . . I've never used them since. Codes come from the data, as I'm reading it the code emerges' (FG3).

An analogous situation to deriving codes from research instruments is where analysis proceeds in relation to themes which have already been settled prior to fieldwork, either through theoretical interests or because the research sponsor has commissioned a study of particular issues. 'My codes don't come through an examination of the transcript, I hope they don't, because they do come from the conscious pursuit of a number of supposedly established propositions . . . I have been given a remit to look at housing satisfaction . . . In order to satisfy that remit I have had to range over everything from fear of crime to social mix . . . What I am saying is that your codes and categories have to be theoretically informed' (FG3). Software seems marginal to this approach, too. Another source was preliminary reading. 'From the people who are saying things, codes will leap out. But you recognize them from the earliest studied material, literature review, etc., you've got a pretty good starting block of codes, I find. Then the problem is actually stopping them growing, proliferating too much, because codes will come out of the initial reading before you start getting into [package] or anything like that, reading through as many texts as you need to until you feel you are saturated with codes' (FG6). But wherever this approach was mentioned it was seen as tentative, simply a start. 'My codes initially came through the literature . . . so I had built up a series of codes which I thought could apply, just a comparison really, initial first steps' (FG5).

So where does package use come in, if not in the definition of codes? This respondent relates an instance suggesting that it is in code refinement. She first refers to constructing a code hierarchy and then to selective searching. 'One of the codes I would use is "family", then I've broken it into "family breakdown", so I would use that to indicate places where people are talking about family relations. The other way I've used it [package] is, I would code something like in terms of housing investment

and then recall that and look at the way people had talked about investment, whether or not it is something I'd thought of . . . I can look at it and
say "is this a code that I've developed or is it something that has developed from the data itself?" ' (FG3). The contribution software could make
was in respect of code refinement and starting to use coded data to confirm
or refute conceptualization, which might be hypothetical in form.

Thus, another respondent, who had studied adult returners to
education, rather than seeing coding as a hierarchical process, saw it as
essentially ' "generational" . . . In my first month's work I have generated
descriptive codes and I am moving on to generating from them. Let's
think, "social risk" might be your first code, would be something to do
with public events having been a "mature student" [adult returner], like
going to the pub, right? And you might have pages and pages about this
experience, going to the pub, how when you were served drinks someone
said "that's a college boy there" and you felt excluded and you felt you
couldn't go back to that pub. So then you might code different bits of that
and move towards a more theoretical idea about "how am I going to categorize social risk, is there elements of that which isn't social risk?" So then
I might have a social risk categorization, and that might have multiple
forms . . . My codes had evolved as a way of theorizing . . . It wasn't
especially hierarchical, wasn't nesting or anything like that, not
consciously' (FG6). Apart from virtues of data management, some packages allow this evolutionary emergence of codes to be traced, by dating
iterations (automatically) and other means of constructing electronic
'audit trails'. Another participant, who described moving from 'these
great descriptive codes to more theoretical codes', explicitly dividing the
two types of code, wondered if the evolution the previous respondent had
described led to applying the new codes to new segments or simply to
reinterpreting the code names. The first participant responded that the
movement was not linear; there could be change in any part of the analysis, code scheme and data segments: 'Sometimes I'd reduce and sometimes they'd enlarge. What tends to happen is, as I work more and more
on the theoretical ones, I'd want to work on different data. Not necessarily
less, sometimes a lot more than the first one. But I kept the first one in the
data set so that I could go back and see how I had changed them. "Public
events" didn't always become "social risk", and all of "social risk" wasn't
to do with "public events", sometimes that was "gender". It might be
[that] . . . for women it was private events, for men it was public events'
(FG6). Both recognized that codes evolved but the second participant felt
less inclined to work from the data as he became more confident. 'Sometimes . . . going through some text I think "yes, what they are talking about
here is stigma" and later on, in month four or so, it seems to be strange
working with this concept of stigma and you are still working with these
waffly quotes someone has given you. In a sense I have got past that stage
and I want to be working on what I think about that . . . It's this problem

of working with the raw text all the way through, and [it's at] the point at which reduction or theoretical notes, theoretical memos start coming in that you start coding' (ibid.). This is an argument for suspending closure on a set of codes until a late stage of conceptualization, as well as for not working purely from grounded theory.

Some respondents recognized that codes were ultimately an artful construction both from work with the data and from their own perspective. The ability to trace the emergence of codes could be helpful here. 'One of the things we were interested in was [whether] people who were volunteers in victim support schemes adopted a perspective which was professional or was it a "good neighbourly" approach. Now part of that term "good neighbours" came out of the interviews . . . Later on I became more and more interested in what do you mean by "professional", what do you mean by "good neighbour", and when you go back and look at the text . . . you find the term "good neighbour" is only actually used once or twice . . . [but] the concept, the idea of being a good neighbour appears throughout it. So that somewhere it has clicked, somebody has been using that word, sums it up rather nicely . . . and somewhere else "professional" seemed to be. It came out of that [text] but it wasn't something that was a conscious topic' (FG3). As he said later, one needed to talk about the limitation of text as well as the limitations of software: 'your coding is not the text, it's the context of that'. As we have seen, most researchers find the problem is not one of generating codes but of containing them. A contract researcher construed the process by the helpful idea of 'paraphrase'; note that the constraint the particular package placed on the length of code labels is seen as a useful discipline. '[Codes] come out of the data itself, the transcripts. If I was pushed on it I would say it was a form of paraphrasing, and restriction on listing if it's only 10 characters you can use. It was a way of trying to get the essence, the codes were a way of indicating the essence of what we felt was important in the chunk of data and something we thought we would want to come back to' (FG6).

We have already seen that researchers make a distinction between descriptive and theoretical codes. A point of agreement among researchers is that one codes differently according to the analytic demands of the project: 'the kind of codes I generate now depend on what I am doing. If I am going to do a policy thing I will tend to do very descriptive, if I have to get particular answers that's what I would be looking for. But for my PhD I was going from very descriptive things like "what problems mature students have" to "how they described them" to my theoretical ideas about how they described them' (FG6). But the lack of equivalence between the level of abstraction of different codes makes for problems in writing up, which is where annotation could be helpful. 'So I had one called "managing fragmentation". Very postmodern and waffly, but it's a long way from "problems with husband or kid" . . . I reported all those [as memos], "this is the way I did it"' (ibid.). Conventionally these problems in resolving just what one meant by coding in a particular way are resolved by 'immersion' in the data. Using CAQDAS did not replace this tactic. 'I felt "yes, I need to go back to it" but I usually only need to go back to the first paragraph . . . or kind of skim through it because I knew basically what was there very, very well' (FG6).

This kind of experience is probably more common in postgraduate research, where relatively generous time limits and the singleminded pursuit of one topic produce deep immersion. In the following case a doctoral student is working on a thesis closely related to his own previous career. 'Also through my experience of thinking what influenced me to do what I did when I was working. When I started doing the coding on-screen, people were answering my questions in the same way... The wording would alter very slightly... They were actually answering my questions using almost the same words . . . It was a bit eerie, I was thinking "am I in the right interview?" and had to go back and check the source document . . . So the actual coding from that point was fairly simple, because I simply used the words they used . . . Eventually I only had 11 codes, and within each code were three subsets, so 33 codes altogether . . . It was a very high level of abstraction, very much of an overview' (FG5). He had been working with the 11 main codes but a quarter of the way through the transcripts he encountered an article 'which suggested this way of splitting each code down into three subsets and I realized that . . . the way of coding in the system was very easy for me to do . . . Just trying to be explicit and compare the same people at similar levels in the same organizations . . . I realized it would be a very powerful addition to my conclusion if I used these three subsets' (FG5). The flexibility of the coding/recoding capability of the package enabled a major change in the analysis.

The ability of the software to reorganize coding schemes obviates attempts to conceptualize a complete coding scheme prior to applying codes to data. 'These computer packages are very good, they are very powerful tools, but they don't do the thinking for you. For me, it's the creating a code, a coding system, which is the real thinking bit. It has to come from here [taps forehead], not from, the computer can help me organize it but it's me that has to do the thinking about that. The way I started off was I had quite a lot of preconceived ideas, I could see from the interviews I'd done there were certain themes . . . I'd got a set of questions that I asked and ideas came up commonly. I was trying to develop, over-ambitiously, a coding system which would take account of all that in one go before I started to do the coding, and I fiddled around and around trying to get something which adequately explained everything I wanted to include, left out the bits I wasn't interested in, had mutually exclusive and clearly defined codes' (FG5). It is worth noting that this is *not* the respondent cited earlier in respect of the same problem, trying to get a complete coding scheme before working with the data. This respondent had found CAQDAS was the way round her problem. She had abandoned the original coding scheme – 'it was too complicated, got in a complete mess, and [I] thought that I would start again and use [package's] capacity to build up as you go along, and start with something very simple . . . and that's working much more successfully . . . [Package] is helping me by letting me start on something small, then develop, so what I've been doing is looking for one theme which I can define quite clearly in my head, so it's quite easy to pick out certain paragraphs in the interviews, coding those with a general code and then going for, say, a sample of 12 interviews, going back looking for common themes within those nodes and then coding the next level down from that, and then going back and doing that again. Gradually building up small networks. [Package] is allowing me to change things around, collapse two codes into one or divide them up' (FG5). She had moved to a process of looking for the data investing meaning in a given code from one of trying to develop high-level nodes at the outset. That is, she had adopted a conventional approach to coding, which the package supported well. As another user reported, there was an incremental and manageable character to defining a general code and then segmenting it into smaller subcodes (FG5).

There were other users who had followed a similar path, from a false start with too elaborate a coding scheme, but in the following case the sophistication of the package appears to have encouraged the user in this direction. 'Initially . . . I saw the power of building a very complex indexing system right off the bat and from there going through and attaching documents and raw data to this complex indexing system . . . [which] allowed me to develop these very abstract theoretical models which I felt it would be easy enough for me to go through and just simply find all the data and hook it up to that. And that wasn't happening [laughter]. I went through a very serious process of concern for a while . . . Now I approach [package] very much [using] a two-pronged approach, a means of bringing up purely descriptive information. I have been able to break down given interviews and have them indexed in a number of different spaces and areas . . . I don't have to remember the nature of the data as a totality but rather as having been indexed at a number of different places . . . Now I have got that information in a number of different nodes and from there you have the possibility of all kinds of really interesting things emerging. Because once you have got that level . . . you feel very much in touch with your data, you feel very much that you have reviewed it . . . and you feel confident about moving on in the theoretical side and building that indexing system . . . where you are actually building analysis from that' (FG5).

Another frequently encountered problem was working with data which addressed the *negation* of the selected code. A researcher on a health promotion project had been 'asking people about health and it's not a rigid prompt as it were . . . do you code all this stuff as "they are *not* talking about health"? I get really confused about that, and in [package] you could code all that because it is so easy to chuck codes in and take them out and put them back in again' (FG3). Coping with unprompted but possibly useful responses was a simpler matter, assisted by automated recoding. Of course, recoding is feasible manually but where volumes of data are high this involves a great deal of labour. 'Once we had discovered that a new category was emerging from some transcripts we thought . . . maybe this would be a better way of coding it than what we'd used before, so that meant going back over them. Adding the code wasn't such a pain because we hadn't got that many marked up, we'd only got about five cases. Had we got all 165 it would have been a real pain' (FG4). Researchers are naturally concerned that CAQDAS should not interfere with accepted procedures and the established canons of validity in the field, nor with creative insight. It is worth saying that the mechanical difficulty sometimes associated with manual methods can also impose on satisfactory procedures and canons of adequacy.

Using a Codebook

In survey research the codebook serves several purposes which help to organize the data at a basic level. The assignment of variable labels is broadly analogous to the coding process in qualitative research. It enables the division of the data into fundamental categorical units, which are related in some way. It also forms a record of the criteria used in defining those fundamental units. The issues are similar to those raised when qualitative researchers write *aides mémoire* about the meaning of a particular code. Third, the codebook might indicate the frequency of occurrence of particular codes. CAQDAS packages can generally provide such basic counts, although this facility is not required for all kinds of qualitative analysis. The contribution of such information is essentially one of data reduction, part of the sifting process by which themes are refined, as in this earlier-quoted example: 'I have been through the data and I coded everything . . . and then I started to look at what my codes were and what they mean, then I did counts to see what sort of things were repeatedly happening, and from that I then had to select a very small amount of data and I managed to come out with three interesting phenomena' (FG1). Clearly the process of data 'reduction' has an element of refinement to it, that is, an element of *changing the meaning* associated with the initial coding of the data. This is where the parallel between coding survey data and coding qualitative data breaks down. Once set, it is likely that the meaning of variables in survey research will not greatly change. It is this that makes it sensible to compile a codebook in the first place. It presumes a static and stable coding scheme. By contrast, the meaning of qualitative data is rather more transitory and flexible. It might change following further data collection, which might suggest new lines of analysis and/or add new data having the same effect.

Surveys are generally 'one-shot' research designs, so that once the questionnaires are all in, further data are unlikely to be added. It might be why our respondents seldom spoke in terms of compiling codebooks and were much more intent on ways by which coding could be annotated and could be revised to reflect newly recognized interests. For the codebook to play a role in qualitative analysis it has to be flexible, to accommodate the iterative character of the analytic process. '[Y]ou get your content out, then you can really look at that . . . the area you want, then start to do your thinking and refining . . . It's the same as with cut-and-paste, isn't it, you've got to somehow narrow it down to get the pile smaller and how you want them' (FG1). CAQDAS, especially the explicitly 'theory-building' packages, puts emphasis on creative work with the coding scheme, inviting revisions and offering technical procedures making it easier to revise. A researcher who began with a codebook approach described her shifting procedure. 'I started off with this idea that I can make my index and it's so complicated, and now I've made it is as simple as possible . . . You can take one thing, family, instead of having to cut loads and loads of strips of paper and hope you don't lose them, you can do very complex combinations; you can quote it in lots of different ways and it's all in the one place. You don't have to have boxes and boxes of things waiting; you can use it to look at family breakdown in the context of something else' (FG3).

Thus, the similarity between the quantitative and qualitative coding process is somewhat shallow and, while a comparison can be made, the codebook might not be the definitive document that it is in a survey. The codebook stage turns out only to be a preliminary in qualitative analysis. '[Y]ou can play with the data, that's the promise of it, you aren't limited, do what you like with it . . . go back and start again, recode things, sort it in all sorts of different ways with the promise that exciting connections would emerge . . . The coding is the price you pay for it . . . but after that it all becomes great fun' (FG6). The implication is that code assignment is both laborious and, in a sense, always incomplete and available for revision, subject to the analyst's creativity and imagination. The coding process was often construed as one of increasing specificity: 'I go through for general issues first and then subdivide them' (FG4). Perhaps reflecting the kinds of things susceptible to numerical or ordinal responses, the quantitative coding process tended to rest with the broader or 'general' issues, and analytic effort was devoted to examining relationships observable between codes at this level. However, there is a further function of codebooks: their role as a form of collective memory, a record of agreement (and discussion) on the meaning of given codes. They might further provide an 'audit trail' of the development of the code definition. We have suggested that even the most painstaking manual project is constrained by the unwieldy nature of the data in performing checks on consistent coding, and it is unusual for a research team to have the time to keep a paper record of its emergent coding scheme. Several CAQDAS packages offer features which assist such procedures.

The analogy between quantitative and qualitative coding can misleadingly obscure distinct differences in the place of coding in the analytic process; the suggestion is that once coding is completed in a questionnaire-based study the grounds for the analysis are largely set, but this can not be said of qualitative analysis. 'When you feed your numbers into the computer in quantitative it makes the connections for you, it does the calculations and you put all those twos together and all those fives together or whatever . . . What people think if you look at it [qualitative analysis] in the same way, is the feeling that the computer ought to be able to put those codes together and tell me what's coming out at the end of it, because I've done the coding and all I do with the quantitative is do the coding and then the computer tells me, makes the connection, and then I'll think about the answers. And of course it won't make the connections because the computer can't make connections between words' (FG6). One user even talked about the desirability of 'reversing' the analogy, to examine how quantitative analysis could be made more like qualitative analysis, an approach which challenges the idea of imposing order or equivalence of meaning by way of the codebook. 'I've gone backwards and forwards between large-scale quantitative projects and ethnographically oriented projects and my interest is in subverting the software that is used for quantitative analysis in order to make it more like qualitative analysis rather than the other way round, which is what most people seem to be interested in . . . I became the director of one of [the projects in a large, funded programme] where we actually tried very hard to work quantitative data in ways which were more phenomenologically resonant, shall we say . . . So I am not very interested in using these packages in order to code or index . . . certainly not to test hypotheses. I am much more interested in how they can facilitate what ordinarily could have been done manually, as we call using our minds as well as our hands, as a kind of support to doing the things I would do anyway. Which is why I like . . . packages that you can make "open", even though they are not written in that kind of way. I am very much interested in a style of approach which starts out with sociological ideas rather than [assuming that] there are "findings" in the data' (FG4). It appears that the role played by classification of data is substantially different in qualitative and quantitative research and that it is unusual for researchers to operate with a definitive codebook. How, then, do qualitative researchers go about accommodating the flexibility they want to bring to code definition and code assignment? And how does CAQDAS help? We shall consider elements of the process which relate to these questions in the next two sections.

Analytic Memos

We earlier noted that the idea of the analytic memo was developed by Glaser and Strauss (1967) in the course of their formalization of the 'grounded theory' analytic process. The idea of writing notes to oneself and to colleagues to assist the coding process is straightforward enough, though it has several elements. It can be used to support discussion and debate about the meaning of codes/categories. Once such discussion has resulted in agreement about the meaning of codes, it can be used to ensure their consistent application. It can be used to record the development of codes/categories, and thus provide 'audit trails' which might be useful in assessing conceptualization or even in monitoring the input of different research workers. In their original work Glaser and Strauss emphasized the iterative character of qualitative analysis, as work at each stage of conceptualization involved a further interrogation of the data, so that analysis amounted to an extended series of (increasingly 'damped') oscillations between the data and the conceptual framework which was emerging. The analytic memo helps to constrain the tendency of this process to lead to indulgence in conceptual development without end. It also meets the researcher's anxiety that subtle nuances might be lost, but by the same token it retains detail which might cloud the analysis or delay the final version. At a psychological level, the function of the analytic memo might even be to provide some sort of repository for the more fine-grained matter so that the researcher can get on with creating the big picture secure in the feeling that the nitty-gritty is still available somewhere. But note that the analytic memo is not confined to points of detail; some comprise a commentary on major conceptualization and are drawn on profitably in the final analysis.

Analytic memos have a preliminary use in supporting discussion about the meaning of codes. Even in small teams, multiple perspectives cause problems and any device to encourage agreement is welcome. '[W]e have very difficult problems of negotiation because there are three of us working in the group, we also have the collective information that goes on between ourselves and I'm interested in [certain topics], my colleague is a [in a different branch of respondent's discipline] on conservation, our research assistant [is in a different discipline] and interested in [another different discipline]. OK, it's horrendous!' (FG1). The researcher went on to discuss a 'fairly long negotiation' over what broad themes were to be examined in the data, culminating in a set of categories being agreed. However, each member then took responsibility for particular codes and transcripts and after working independently assigning the codes and 'saturating' them with data the team found gross divergences from the initially agreed codes. '[T]he transcript had evolved into something completely different, and lots of notes and lots of ideas and intellectually it's fascinating but in terms of coding the thing it's impossible' (FG1). The analytic memo is clearly not a panacea; the project ran into problems despite producing 'lots of notes'. The package the team was using did not (in the then-current version) permit memos to be linked to the data which had prompted them. In earlier projects team members had simply written notes in the margins of the transcript: messy, but capable of being attended to in the analysis, provided the writing outline included details of where to find relevant memos. In this project, CAQDAS actually interfered with memoing. '[T]he way we worked before this contract is to write in interpretations on the transcripts themselves, things about concepts, in the process of writing. As one does. And that is what I think [team member] found it more difficult than I did to shift from' (FG1). The team abandoned the package and the analysis was completed manually, in a deadline rush, by the project director on her own.

This should not be attributed wholly to the lack of a memo facility, or to CAQDAS in general. The team had real problems adjusting to standardized coding and to the mechanical procedures the package used. As a result, they got stuck on coding and this delayed the creative phase, when codes are actively combined, and particular search combinations are used. 'When we have worked up to now [i.e. manually] we have done a lot of creative work and writing. We write group reports, we write papers, we write memos to each other, and what it did was to stall that' (FG1). The issue arises of the distinction between codes and memos. Some researchers sought to construct very fine-grained codes to accommodate nuances specific to a single datum. We suspect this would have been a point at which an analytic memo indicating the nuance could more effectively have been used, preserving the broad general code rather than requiring a derivative subcode. 'When you get to transcripts of interviews between appraisers and appraisees [in a public sector organization] that you actually are . . . observing, you also want to get into things like tone of voice and what was actually happening in the room at the time. Body language starts to become very important, so whoever was actually conducting the . . . fieldwork wanted to feed that in as well . . . We needed to add that because you could start using codes that perhaps you had used in the [research] interview . . . and then somebody says "I thought these were all positive feelings" and you say "if you actually watch them this is very sarcastic". How [do] you actually get that into your coding?' Co-worker: 'We still have those disagreements . . . but it was actually getting it into the coding . . . that was taking the time' (FG6). Asked if they were memoing, the response was that they were not, although they did write down definitions of codes. Both were aware of the memoing idea, and the fact that it was not used was attributed to CAQDAS. 'Looking at [current] version [of package], if it had been there we would have used it' (FG6).

Responding to another participant who wondered 'whether eventually we will end up transferring memoed, coded transcripts, rather than transcripts themselves, so you can have those memos on', she continued:

'when we were looking at [current] version before we came here today we were actually thinking if we had that memo version whoever was doing the interview would actually write the memo. So you'd be able to, when we were checking out each other's . . . looking at the code sets, you'd be able to think what somebody else's thinking was. And that would have been quite useful and maybe we would have been able to work much better as a team' (FG6). This team had seriously pursued checks on validity. For instance, they coded a subsample of their colleagues' transcripts and then compared code assignments. They also set aside time to discuss coding, both code assignments and code definitions. But 'if we had had a proper memo system whereby we'd actually written down how we had come to that conclusion . . . the way our thinking worked, that would have helped a lot.' Co-worker: 'I mean, all we had really was a list of codes and what they meant to us.' Researcher: 'And the conversations we had at various times' (FG6).

An example of the 'audit' use can also be given. 'I have coded the interviews, handed them over to my colleague and he has said "OK, fair enough" and I decided to make sure he understood my indexing [so] I have given him a transcript of the index. Then we will see whether . . . [laughter] . . . I haven't got it back, that was a few weeks ago [laughter]. Trying to get the right answers' (FG3). The 'colleague' was in fact the respondent's boss. Here a memo is provided to explain the coding. Note that in many CAQDAS packages one can annotate each code assignment, with the memo appearing whenever the coded segment is printed, in which case the project director could have a running commentary on every code application. Of course, this kind of auditing can be done in the interests of data reliability as well as project management: 'we are interested to see, if someone codes something up and you use someone else [for analysis] that you understand what the code was meant to be, and then see what level of consistency the group has achieved' (FG1). Such checks are well discussed in the literature and widely regarded as good practice, but they also take time. They become expendable in the context of research with deadlines, as this respondent suggests. Interviewer: 'Did you explicitly introduce memos into the analytic process?' Respondent: 'Not on screen, no.' Interviewer: 'But on paper?' Respondent: 'On paper. Not for every code, as I got more – everything was like this pyramid that at the end [were] these three key chapters, and so the memos got smaller and smaller. So some memos I started with lots of things and they kind of disappeared as I thought "right, you know, come back to that one when I've got a job" ' (FG6). The researcher knew she could not sustain the detail she felt inclined to produce. Note that her memoing was not within the package. This was because the version she was using had no memo feature.

If the power of the computer is to help researchers cope with deadline pressure while being as systematic as they aspire to be, memo features need to be easily entered while in other program operations, and display of the memo should appear alongside relevant data whenever that data is examined. The flexibility that packages can offer can help researchers in unexpected ways. Thus, while the ability to recode data is a feature of some importance, this respondent used a memoing feature to negotiate a radical change of coding, in effect devising a 'workaround'. 'The way I coped with lots of coded changes there [in package], was that my [category system] got completely unmanageable and I ended up with chopping it all up and abandoning the [category system] completely. So I ended up with notes here, there and everywhere, and a few lines in between. So that is more flexible, it allows you to change your mind a bit more' (FG4). Discussing another package she emphasized a different kind of flexibility and a different nuance of the 'audit trail', which enabled her to organize a set of connected ideas without first coding all the data. 'With [textbase manager] I tended to read it through on the screen and then use the hypertext to go into the text and move across different files. I don't have to pre-structure what I am looking for that way, I can just go to highlight a particular sentence if I like . . . and then with their . . . "backtrack" facility you can go through how you trail the data . . . and don't have to have any fixed coding schemes in your mind' (ibid.). It can be added that, having looked at the 'trail', or connections between data segments examined in a particular session, a memo could be written indicating the connections which lay behind the selection of given segments.

This respondent's procedure suggests something of a rejoinder to the concern that CAQDAS might rigidify or over-formalize qualitative analysis, at least in respect of software with strong hypertext features. 'It's more how I would do it without a software package. It compares quite favourably with the reading through and wandering around and maybe not having any fixed idea of how the concepts are related in advance. It's just, a trail of thoughts gets going. It's only afterwards that you can find why those ideas tended to be related . . . It speeds up and lets my mind speed up slightly, moving in between files and keeping a track of where I've been whilst I'm reading it' (FG4). Here the simple provision of a means of tracking the segments examined in a session enables a broad searching strategy which seeks to profit from serendipity. A dedicated package need not be used to construct memos; a word processor might suffice. 'I might want to index and the way that I would use Word for Windows [is] using the index facility and section headings, and also to write sets of ideas about why I am calling those things *those* things, using the annotation facility, and if I change my mind I use "go to" and "search and replace" and it's incredibly quick' (FG4).

Whether it is for analytic development or audit purposes, to our minds the more explicit and interactive the process of analysis the better grounded that analysis is likely to be. It will be more easily available to third parties and more readily assessed. These contributions to analytic validity can, of course, be achieved 'manually', though our respondents uniformly felt that the time pressure of funded research militated against them. This respondent's judgement on CAQDAS extends, we feel, to the role of activities such as memoing in general: 'One of the benefits [of] using something like [packages] is that . . . to make it work you have to talk a lot, have to communicate and be very explicit about the techniques of analysis and the categories that you are using. I actually think that can strengthen the research you are doing in the end. But it is very time-consuming' (FG4). The inclusion of memo features in CAQDAS will not guarantee validity in and of itself. But it can stimulate the informal discussion needed in any collective effort at analysis.

Coding in Teams

We have already seen the business of coding in team research described as a difficult 'negotiation'. The importance of this essential building block towards analysis is often in conflict with the tedium of slowly reading and rereading the data as one divides it into coded segments. Further, no two people can approach the data with precisely the same perspective, and where teams comprise people with different disciplinary backgrounds, interests and levels of research experience there are bound to be differences of interpretation. One researcher suggested that agreeing codes hinged entirely on rapport. He had worked on research teams of three to five colleagues, and was asked about whether agreement had been achievable. 'Eventually, but for the most part working with two colleagues that I have worked with a lot and have a good relationship with them, much more difficult with people you don't know' (FG3).

The consistency brought to quantitative research by devices such as the codebook has limited application in qualitative research. It takes vigilance to 'enforce' code definitions even in solo projects and the effort can cause interpersonal troubles in research teams. 'I developed a set of qualifying codes which I was very clear about and made sense and which had been used consistently across the transcripts. X found it impossible to stick to the agreed set of codes, because she works in a way where everything becomes an intellectual challenge while she is doing it. I couldn't get her to see that we had to have the same set of codes, so the concept we started on the transcript might be something to do with [category], but the transcript had evolved into something completely different' (FG1). The three team members applied codes independently to the transcripts of the interviews they had conducted, which then had to be checked for consistency. The project director 'was confronted with three sets of transcripts . . . Some of those codes . . . actually changed in terms of their main direction, Y put them all together into one set, which was bloody awful' (FG1). The package in use limited the number of codes that could be applied to any given line, which aggravated the problems of inconsistent coding and multi-coding that were due to the different approaches of the team members. 'One of the things I kept running up against, having eventually got a second code which we agreed, kept running into the maximum set of levels because all that had to be put into three [meta-] codes, which was impossible . . . It kept happening and it's a most frustrating thing . . . We were regularly coding the lines [with] . . . eight, 10, 12 codes per line. It was just so complex' (FG1).

It has been widely suggested that CAQDAS encourages more systematic approaches to qualitative data, and it is worth noting that the project director saw the solution to these problems as being the recognition that code definition should be regarded as a discrete stage of analysis to which extra time would be devoted. 'We've learned a lot . . . What we've got to do is . . . really focus on coding as a practical exercise, and that has to be separate. What went wrong [was] trying to jump ahead of ourselves in a way because of the time constraint, and it would be much more sensible for us to have a couple of days talking together on what coding is about . . . In terms of coding, what depth we really wanted to go to at what stage' (FG1). A member of another mixed-discipline team confirmed the value of an approach which recognized that differences were inevitable and accordingly set aside time for them to be reconciled. 'The person I work with . . . with a different background, we have discussed it and looked at the interviews and sort of agreed "yes, that is a sensible way. These questions, can you do this, can you find out this from using this coding?" So we have to sit down with the transcript, I have indexed one, and we both compare how we index the transcripts, and discuss it, and possibly use it as part of the right interpretation' (FG3). Achieving code agreement is not simply a matter of designating a distinct stage of the project for the negotiation but of taking an even-handed perspective. This latter element might, of course, depend on the nature of power relations in the team (construed in broad terms: sponsors might have considerable influence here, by dictating the topics they want to see covered in the analysis). As this respondent noted, 'the important thing is how strict your coding is. As you say, [if they are] much more general [codes], sharing it with a team member is much easier. But if you have a very definite idea with coding, that's different' (FG3).

Even the code categories that researchers know must be included (e.g. because they reflect the sponsor's interest) have to be fitted to the data. The business of interpretation is inescapable. It is a subtle affair involving delicate shades of meaning. 'Most coding is a combination of things and how a word that you can use can capture the delicacy or subtlety of the different concepts involved in it' (FG3). Another researcher spoke of the 'limitation of the text' in contrast to the limitations of software: 'your coding is not the text, it's the context of that, what's going on, body language also' (FG3). The need to search for the term that best captures the dimensions of meaning suggested by the data means that false starts are inevitable. CAQDAS cannot ameliorate interpersonal problems but it does make it possible to change coding selectively or globally with less effort than manually. Then at least more time is available for negotiation, so that the pros and cons of particular choices can be unravelled in detail, a considerable effort which increases the likelihood of gaining agreement because those involved are able to explore every nuance and implication. 'Negotiating codes ... all those sorts of things, were very, very time-consuming. We had the first code set and then it was a case of going through and looking at that and thinking "this isn't quite what we want" and going through and doing it again. When there are three people involved it just seemed to take an awful lot of time, didn't it?' Co-worker 2: 'Yes, we would have been better if we had had three computers but we didn't, we had one ... So you are limited in the time you can actually spend doing it' (FG6). Apart from problems posed by resources, the team had also to negotiate the project director's scepticism about CAQDAS. Interviewer: 'Presumably he was, you were expending an enormous number of hours reconciling each other's coding categories?' 'Yes, he was, yes, and all he could see coming out of it [package] was long lists of code words, and basically [he was] saying "what are you going to do with this at the end?" and "you are just going to have code words" and seeing the code words as *being* the analysis [laughter]' (FG6). Where project work is also used as a vehicle for learning a new technique it is important to have the support of all team members for the experiment. It is worth adding that this team was able to persuade the project director of the value of the experiment, by showing how the codes evolved: 'so it was like getting the progression of code words and showing how a code changed was more convincing because [project director] said "Oh, I wouldn't have done that"' (FG6).

The resource problems mentioned above (e.g. having one computer between three researchers) should not be underestimated. An example of what can happen when a machine is being shared comes from another research team, which discovered, when they needed to recode some data, that back-up files containing it had been deleted. 'They have all gone. This is one of the problems because there is [*sic*] three of us. Bits have been on the machine and left, and I think "forget it, we've been working so long on what we've got, try again next time"' (FG1). This was the same team which suffered from its members having different disciplinary back-grounds. Thus, the team's failure to complete the CAQDAS-based analy-sis could be attributable to the disciplinary mix, hardware availability or to difficulty with the package. In fact, it is the last of these which was emphasized by the project director, but note that the problems came to a head around the issue of coding. 'Psychologically what happened is that it took us such a huge amount of time to do the coding, then one was faced with another three months or so of having to put into [package; the version used required off-screen code assignment followed by entering codes using the keyboard], basically just floored us. So we did it in patches, became one of those tasks that you do tomorrow' (FG1). There is a rationale behind a package design which requires off-screen coding. The rationale is based on the developers' view that the importance of coding is such that it should be done with care and with a view to the context of the particular segment being coded. At least one developer has argued that on-screen coding might be so procedurally easy that code assignments might be too glib, leading to problems of superficial analysis. But the research team we have been looking at was described by its director as being under time pressure. Part of this pressure arose not from the length of the contract but from delays in agreeing codes. Already facing problems in the intellectual process of agreeing codes, the coding procedure in the package they were using no doubt contributed to their problems. But it would be wrong to attribute all their problems to this. Our respondent had not been put off CAQDAS for good and was preparing to use it again, emphasizing the advantages of systematic analysis but recognizing that the initial supposition that CAQDAS could also speed up analysis was not realistic.

These matters of group dynamics are not the only obstacles to be negotiated in coding. Respondents reported that different sorts of data were differently susceptible to coding. Having steadily coded 60 one-to-one interviews, one team had then to code transcripts of dialogues during two-person meetings (meetings between research subjects observed in the field). 'It was really when we got to looking at how to code the meeting between the appraiser and the appraisee that we started to get bogged down with it. It was much easier to code the structured interviews than it was the unstructured interviews . . . We had confrontations between the team members' (FG6). The interview schedule used in the structured interview provided some codes automatically. 'It was easier to agree codes in our semi-structured interviews . . . because you had some indication of what information you wanted in the first place from the questions you were asking, and so that was the starting point' (FG6). In contrast the field observation, in which the researcher merely observed and recorded, offered no in-built structure and, moreover, the team member conducting the observation had a privileged position in that they were aware of 'tone of voice and what was actually happening in the room at the time, body language' (ibid.). These latter attributes might affect the interpretation, although body language was not an explicit focus of the project *per se*. With team members working from transcripts at the coding stage there was a need for discussion to bring out these dimensions and then for further discussion to determine how they should be reflected in the coding. Such discussion was also necessary to establish the equivalence and consistency of coding necessary to invest faith in selective searches using the package (in most packages, searches are displayed only with the text assigned to the code, not its surrounding context). Working relations and software requirements have to be negotiated. As one researcher put it, 'we were only a two year project and the three of us had never worked together before . . . We were a totally new team to each other . . . You are all negotiating how to work together as people, never mind trying to negotiate how to work together with a package' (FG6). Thus, trust not only makes for a conducive working environment but for collaboration at each stage of the analysis.

These issues can, however, be seen through the lens of 'rigour' as well as that of 'obstacles'. The team we have been discussing contrasted the pains they had to take in agreeing codes with the tendency the solo researcher might have to leave some things implicit or to tolerate ambiguity in the data. 'When there are . . . more than one of you, you've *got* to interpret the codes and it's further going to mean saying to someone "what did you mean, what did we mean when we decided to call it that?" And I can still hear the voices of these people having transcribed them, having listened and knowing that at this point for some inexplicable reason this person had burst into tears, or having a pause in the interview' (FG6). She went on to say that each member had to bring into discussion all that they uniquely knew about each datum, and that, although this is demanding, 'I'm kind of hesitant about how far you can do team research if you don't have that . . . Because it was going to be written up as a whole we have to do this, we have to make sure we are looking at things in the same way . . . And if you are going to do that you have got to communicate between the three of you' (FG6). Granted that such discussion is vital, it can displace other elements of the work, so some teams set aside an agreed, timetabled period for coding discussions between rounds of coding by individuals. 'Maybe it's just the way our team get on, that we will sit and agonize over things for hours on end. So what we did – because there are three of us doing the analysis and we didn't want to end up being totally inconsistent – was have frequent meetings; on a daily basis we'd have half-hour coding meetings and we'd discuss the codings we'd got, discuss the relevance of, and alter everything accordingly. So it was a lot of talking going on but at the same time it didn't get messy, you didn't go so far into something' (FG4). While regular meetings with a clear agenda and careful timekeeping benefit the coding process, CAQDAS can also help by providing means to track code assignments made by different team members.

We have referred to the possible influence of sponsors on coding. It might seem an odd idea to those outside contract research. It is not so much a direct intervention in the nitty-gritty of coding to which some of our respondents testified. Rather it is a matter of a sponsor (often a government department) having a declared interest in certain broad themes. While qualitative researchers see themes 'emerging' from the data, sponsors are apt to regard research as going out to find the 'answer' to an issue they have already identified. This issue then comprises the main theme of the analysis, in the sponsor's view. Thus, discussing a two-person project where the nominal 'other half' had confined her role to getting the grant and writing up, a respondent commented, 'the analysis and coding is coming from me because it's not a [government department]-funded project, there isn't somebody from outside coming to say "somebody wants X, Y and Z". I can send them what the data tells me' (FG4). A number of our respondents referred to sponsors' tendency 'six months later [to send] somebody along and say "no, you've got completely the wrong idea" ' (FG4). If this happened and one's analysis had been carried out using CAQDAS, one respondent suggested, there was no alternative but to revert to manual methods, since such interventions usually occurred at the end when working drafts were being reviewed. The best means to avert the problem was to have close and continuous liaison with the sponsor: 'It depends on how much the researchers work with the people who actually have got the money, because a lot of projects are based on the researcher going away and doing it for two years and then you get to the end and they suddenly say "didn't you look at that?" or "you've not thought of looking at it that way!?" That is where the problem arises, if you've got a specific package where you have invested a lot of time in using, then the only thing you can do really, if it's major changes, [is to] abandon it, go back to the pieces of paper' (FG4). We have deleted the reference in this segment to two specific packages, but it is interesting to note that both offer quite sophisticated recoding facilities. It is evidence of the lag between software development and the research community's grasp of what packages can do. Presented with a last-minute demand to recode, it should certainly be no slower with a package than without, and will be a good deal less *ad hoc* (the exception might be very small data sets, but these are not characteristic of contract research).

We have characterized this 'sponsor intervention' issue as a problem largely of contract research (generally in a policy context), but one of our respondents cited four instances, some of which were 'academic' projects. She attributed cessation of package use to such interventions. 'Everybody that I know who has used [package], they've . . . done the basic analysis because they were the researcher employed on the project but then perhaps discussed that with other researchers who had other ideas about what it meant analytically and that was six months into the project and then the person who was directing the project was saying "It's not that at all" and it has been another six months' work . . . Everybody that I know who has used it on a project, four lots of people, that has been the common experience. The point at which it is set up enough for the "grown-ups" as it were, the people who were funded to do the project that they were employing this person on, at the point at which the researcher setting it up met the funded researchers . . . the whole grounds of analysis that were built up by the researcher, they wanted to change it. Then they found they couldn't [in a coded data set]. That was the point at which they abandoned it' (FG4). In these cases the divide between grantholders and researchers invariably led to the latter's CAQDAS-based analysis being abandoned. The subtext here is a move away from an analysis grounded in the data to one reflecting the prior orientation of grantholders who were themselves not immersed in the data. In other words, there is a loss of rigour. Thus, 'there was a divorce between what the researchers had done, which got abandoned. I can think of a number of projects that were based in this department where the researcher left and then the other people carried on doing what they would have made of it anyway' (FG4).

Such problems seem to have little to do with CAQDAS *per se* (although they might be affected by the research director's unfamiliarity with CAQDAS), and much to do with the organization of social research. There is a parallel with quantitative research, where project directors sometimes suffer from a lag between their knowledge of statistical procedure and the current capacities of statistics software. Banal as it might seem, perhaps it is worth saying that the solution is to reduce distance between sponsor/project directors and researchers 'on the ground'. Thus, a researcher whose project director was wholly non-computerate commented that he had not felt distanced because 'we make sure he is fully involved; although he doesn't actually use the package we have weekly meetings and we sort of air the problems we have had so that he is totally involved' (FG4). Likewise another respondent observed that the 'naive' question could stimulate new thinking, provided such queries were not all stored up for the final stages: 'I found a certain advantage in [project director] not being able to do specific bits in the packages because she would ask me questions that otherwise she might not, like "why are you doing this like that, can you not do this?" and "this means you end up with this, have you thought about that?" ' (FG4).

An issue like agreeing codes has a built-in orientation to what one can do using CAQDAS and what needs to be done in direct interaction. It is true that several developers have directed effort to teamwork within their package, and computer-supported co-operative work [CSCW] is likely to move into qualitative research just as it has into fields such as architecture. For this to take place, care needs to be taken over machine/software compatibility as well as human compatibility. A multi-site, multi-method study had set out to co-analyse a section of the data. The fieldwork was also shared between sites, with instruments designed in one being used in all, and so on. 'We are all gathering each other's data. For example, I interview not only for my own project but three others. And one of the original reasons for applying for the package was that it was something we could share and that would be the aim: know what we were doing and be supportive in the group. But it hasn't worked out that way . . . Data must come to me and all the other researchers in the same form . . . and it isn't doing that. Various people give various reasons why, computers and so on' (FG3).

This is a straightforward irritation, but time-consuming to put right. More daunting is the case where one is a subordinate in a team which has adopted a methodology derived from a discipline other than one's own and which produces qualitative data one is asked to process on unfamiliar precepts. A sociologist was working in a team including a psychologist who wanted to apply personal construct psychology in the field. The sociologist explained that he respected the approach as a clinical technique but not in the field. But he was obliged to analyse the material because it was qualitative and that was what he had been hired to do. 'Having kicked off on this and been employed to do this I have to cast around for another way of getting some formal sense from theoretical ideas which have been gathered in a qualitative way . . . Having embarked on something, tested it, found it wanting, [I needed] something to produce sense out of data collected for certain theoretical reasons in a formalized way' (FG3). The sociologist and psychologist had 'nearly come to blows' and were no longer speaking. In another study there was initially a division of labour, with our respondent responsible for survey analysis and a colleague for CAQDAS. We might characterize the situation as 'serial team research' because 'she then took herself off elsewhere' at a stage when the qualitative data had revealed something of keen interest to the government department sponsoring the work. As a result our respondent was obliged to take on the CAQDAS role 'and I went back to . . . where she had categorized it [and] I couldn't make any sense of it and had to go back to the beginning' (FG3). The initial separation of roles did not serve the team well because it discouraged collaborative work in favour of complementary work. When his colleague left, the respondent had to familiarize himself both with the qualitative data and the package, while under pressure from the sponsor's display of interest.

Subject to these sorts of problems, it is hardly surprising if the more demanding elements of CAQDAS-based qualitative analysis become squeezed by time pressure. While the tenor of our earlier discussion might suggest that coding must be the most demanding stage, this is not the case, at least if we take into account the facilities that many packages offer to support conceptualization. We have in mind such things as hypothesis-testing features, Boolean searches, and the graphical representation of relationships between codes. But if projects run into problems at the earlier stages there is a strong pressure to rest with a broadbrush retrieval of coded data. This is somewhat analogous to the 'cross-tabbing everything by everything' approach which survey researchers might do as a first sift to identify points of possible interest. The point of the analogy is that, having cross-tabbed everything by everything, the survey researcher generally homes in on those possibly interesting points and subjects them to further statistical analysis. In some qualitative projects, it appears that researchers reach the preliminary stage but do not continue with the more discriminating enquiry.

Here we would make a comment which draws on our experience of qualitative research as much as it does on the present study. We would suggest that there is a tendency in qualitative projects to devote a great deal of time to fieldwork and then to find that time for analysis is too little. This might be because of difficulties of access, although we suspect that researchers often find that 'fieldwork is fun', or at least, rather engaging. There is also the possibility that doubts about the adequacy of qualitative analysis might appear resolvable by collecting rather more data than can realistically be handled when it comes time for analysis. At any rate, it is our feeling that timetable slippage is often a consequence of such factors. Now let us suppose that CAQDAS is inserted into this scenario. A new set of procedures is added to those with which researchers are familiar. The new procedures place additional demands upon the analysis stage. Looking back over the project, researchers might well 'blame' slippage on CAQDAS. But their inclination to do so masks the contribution to delay that extended data collection might have caused. Further, because delay has squeezed analysis time, researchers are apt not to have pursued the facilities the packages offer for conceptualization, and are led to the view that CAQDAS is essentially a useful clerical device but cannot significantly contribute to analysis.

This conceptualization perhaps sheds light on our respondents' emphasis on data management as the chief value of CAQDAS. Thus, most of our respondents suggested that the forte of CAQDAS was 'mechanical' (or 'clerical') file management and could never be the creative elements of the qualitative research process. 'On the project I am working on at the moment I have to do a lot more sophisticated theorizing about a whole range of ethnographic material and again we have used [package] to code very basic categories . . . and much more what I consider to be more factual kinds of things. But actually the most interesting part of it is to do with generating what we call themes, and that is done by talking between us, and . . . making endless lists and rewriting them and bits of writing, trying to make sense of it. I don't know how I would use a package to do that' (FG4). This emphasis was particularly strong among applied researchers. It is an issue to which we will return in examining the role of CAQDAS in the later stages of analysis.

As to the fundamental business of agreeing codes in team projects, we have seen some critical comments about the place of CAQDAS in the process. In essence the criticism is that learning the package adds time to a pressured process and this is no doubt true. But packages do not take forever to learn. Once it is mastered some researchers, at least, confirm one of the mooted benefits of CAQDAS: that it encourages rigour. 'It's helped because there are three of us doing the analysis. Having to think round using the package as well helped us to be more consistent in our analysis, think through what you are doing . . . It has led to us being more consistent whereas if we hadn't we might have more of a tendency to go off and

analyse in our own way. It's more comparable' (FG4). We have characterized the problems of coding that researchers face as the product of a
concatenation of teamwork issues, the software, and indeed the inherent
complexity of qualitative data analysis itself. It is worth reminding
ourselves that working in teams also has advantages, and that these can
be mobilized by thoughtful and appropriate use of the software.

In a book on academic writing, Becker (1986) complained of the
tendency for metaphors to become stale and drained of their original
meaning. Perhaps the 'learning curve' idea is an instance. It seems increasingly simply to stand for 'obstacle'; if something cannot be grasped
quickly it must be deficient or obscurantist. We are in danger of forgetting
that pedagogically the implication was that 'little and often' was ultimately a more effective pattern for formal teaching than 'all in one dose'.
Working in teams encourages incremental learning, as members
contribute different interests and perspectives. In the extract in the paragraph above, note that 'consistency' was seen as being related to 'having
to think round using the package'. Note also that reference was made to
'us', with the group working collaboratively to understand the package.
Thus, while a considerable investment by team members was needed to
master CAQDAS, an increase in rigour was achieved.

At this point a comment can be made on our own coding process, which
was carried out with the support of two CAQDAS packages. In a first
reading of the data, some 20 codes were identified and listed. We
discussed the list, looking for hierarchical (code and subcode) relations.
Then we carried out a sweep through the data, assigning codes to
segments. In the course of doing this another 10 codes were added to the
code list. Virtually all of the new codes were subcodes, refinements of a
broader code. For instance, the generic code labelled 'coding' already had
three subcodes, but two further subcodes were added. Memos were also
written on assignments of a code to a particular datum. In several cases
these memos effectively represented subcodes, as they picked on a
particular nuance of the code brought out by that datum. We thus
concluded the initial coding sweep with a hierarchy of codes, subcodes
and sub-subcodes.

An across-the-board retrieval by code was then done, along with a count
of the 'hits' by code. The code hierarchy was used to inform an initial
writing outline. We say 'inform' carefully, because the writing outline
came to be modified as we worked with the sorted output (the results of
the across-the-board retrieval, where every segment relating to every code
was printed, so that we had print-out of segments sorted by codes in just
the way that a manual cut-and-paste procedure results in sorted clusters
of data).

Now the development of the idea about 'blaming' slippage on
CAQDAS, suggested above, in no way emerged directly from the data. No
one spoke in these terms. It emerged from (1) reading the data relating to

'teamwork problems', particularly as they related to coding (our code here was 'coding in teams'), (2) our experience of sponsored qualitative research in small teams where all members were collecting data and collaboratively analysing it, and (3) our awareness of the capabilities of the CAQDAS packages our respondents were using. Out of these we lit on a conceptualization based on the way that researchers accounted for their limited use of CAQDAS in the later stages of analysis by attributing delay to the 'learning curve' while discounting the part played by, for example, the fetishization of fieldwork, interpersonal dynamics, pressure from sponsors and so on. We were then in a position to designate a 'meta-code' binding together certain applications (to segments) of the codes mentioned above with new code assignments to which we were only sensitized as a result of this further analytic work. Selective retrievals informed by the meta-code could then be made.

Qualitative researchers are familiar with the idea that qualitative analysis is 'sequential', involving a repeated cycle between data collection and data analysis. It is implicit in this that qualitative analysis is also 'incremental'. Indeed, qualitative researchers often complain that it is not obvious when to stop, when to apply 'analytic closure'. There always seems to be more that one could squeeze from the data, and, further, it is never obvious that one has 'solved' the analytic problem, 'proved' a relationship between factors, and so on (whereas in at least some statistically based studies one can see a 'solution', for instance establishing the proportion of the population living below a defined minimum wage). For qualitative researchers engaged in contract research it might even be something of a relief to know that, whatever might be there 'in' the data, analysis has to cease by a given date because the report is due. One implication is that qualitative researchers should guard against the tendency to over-extend data collection relative to data analysis. Another is that developers might need to devote more attention to the refinement of the data management side of CAQDAS relative to sophisticated data analysis features. But the implication we want to emphasize here is that 'amortized learning' is a general feature of computer systems. A heavy initial investment yields increasing returns, but one has to remain on the scene long enough to get the benefit.

Note

1   As we indicated earlier, there have been criticisms of the term 'code' in the literature. Any term bears nuances, as anyone coding data quickly comes to appreciate. Alternative terms for 'code' include 'category' and 'classification'. It is not necessary at this point, however, to engage in the debate about the merits or demerits of the term 'code'. In two and a half years of fieldwork on qualitative researchers using CAQDAS we did not encounter a single qualitative researcher who did not understand the term.

5

Analytic Pathologies

To a degree, the topic of analytic pathologies leads us back to the issues we have been examining in relation to coding in team research. We should make clear that this is not because team research is inherently problematic but because it obliges researchers to be more explicit about their assumptions and particular understandings of qualitative research. Team research makes the research process more transparent. Working in teams might help to counteract other pathologies, such as the unchecked proliferation of codes and the contrasting problem of coding which is too 'thin' or superficial. The solo researcher, typically the higher-degree student working under relatively loose supervision, might well prolong the coding process to a point where the coding scheme is unmanageable. Equally, without the regular foil of colleagues who have to be persuaded that one's coding is adequate, the solo researcher might proceed unchecked in adopting a superficial or poorly grounded coding scheme.

In case the term 'pathologies' seems melodramatic, we will begin this section with a quote which suggests the force of researchers' feelings when work with CAQDAS goes wrong. 'Can I come back to one point, you were asking whether [name of package] has actually affected the project ... I think it has affected us detrimentally and I think it is partly because of our inexperience. But the psychological block that we have developed as a team in terms of having to go through this routine of getting the codes, getting them on the machine, put us back a lot and it killed a lot of the enthusiasm and interest that we had intrinsically in the project. The whole thing became coloured by our hatred and resentment of the bloody program and what we had to do to put the data in, and in the end we all became extremely bitter and twisted. And what happens, except another day, another week had gone because none of us could actually face sitting there for another three or five hours getting blasted codes and typing. So the mechanics of it in many ways killed quite important chunks of time, it would take up [time that we needed] to do other things ... in a way it became a block to us writing. When we have worked up to now we have done a lot of creative work and writing, we write group reports, we write papers, we write memos to each other. And what it did was to stall that because it became the whole [thing] that we had to get over before we could start on anything else. And I think we lost a good three or four months on the project' (FG1). In light of our theme about the complications in evaluating CAQDAS use which are introduced by teamwork issues, we would point out that, early in the extract, our respondent indicates that part of the fault lay with the team's inexperience. It is, nevertheless, a testimony to social researchers' tenacity that this respondent, despite the team's dire experience, had persisted with an interest in CAQDAS and planned to continue use after the end of the project in question. We simply want to register that, in discussing problems of coding, we are confronting a key stage in analysis and, along with it, a point at which undue procedural or technical problems can exacerbate the difficulties associated with classification in general.

Until recently there has been little enough detailed discussion of that general process. In common with the other elements of qualitative analysis, coding seems to have been regarded as one of the mysteries, the sophisticated special trade of researchers which can only be learned by experience in tandem with a years-long programme of reading exemplars of studies which use ethnographic methods. An implication of this neglect is that it is hard to disentangle the problems of coding in general from the problems of coding using software (we should really say 'the problems posed by the way particular packages seek to support coding'). The above excerpt came at the end of a discussion of problems which the team had in reconciling different perspectives arising from different disciplinary backgrounds. Such problems would have arisen independent of software use. But to use the package the problems had to be confronted and resolved, whereas they might well escape without resolution in a project not using CAQDAS. For instance, researchers who wished to pursue an interest peripheral to the main themes could be indulged by being allowed to write a separate section, drawing as they will on material marked up as pertaining to the main codes. Where CAQDAS is in use the need to agree code assignments is more pressing because reserving certain extracts for use in developing a marginal theme directly affects the number of 'hits' on a given code, and where selective searches using Boolean operators are to be employed one needs as many hits as possible to provide the broadest possible base for the search. Constraining the number of hits would be a particular problem in packages like HyperResearch, where the 'hypothesis test' encourages a quasi-statistical form of reasoning (the package searches for instances of particular code combinations expressing propositions and reports how many interviews, for instance, conform to the proposition). The option is to multi-code, but we have seen that there can be mechanical problems caused by limits on code levels here. Further, research audiences are unlikely to tolerate any significant degree of reuse of extracts in written reports.

Both package development and user experience help with this kind of problem, but the problem goes deeper than this. CAQDAS tends to marginalize the isolated comment, the singular observation, by making very apparent the size of the data corpus from which it stands out. Virtually all CAQDAS packages offer some facility for counting aspects of the data. This amplifies the apparent importance of themes attracting numerous hits, as does the encouragement that 'theory-building' software gives to work with the codes themselves (and in isolation from the data). We have already suggested that clerical file management, not theory building, best typified the 'average users' main use of CAQDAS. It might not only be unfamiliarity with the package that gives rise to this, but adherence to familiar approaches to analysis. For many, the derivation of broad themes based on main codes *is* the analysis. This would speak not only to issues relating to CAQDAS but to the need to address coding pathologies in the training of researchers. Thus, users thought that CAQDAS increased the importance of agreeing code definitions, and this required researchers to be more flexible and accommodating. '[T]he important thing is how strict your coding is. Much more general sharing it with a team member is much easier. But if you have a very definite idea with coding that can be a problem' (FG3).

When people are obliged to 'see eye to eye' on coding there is a need for criteria by which a putative assignment can be assessed to be made explicit. A problem that arises is how explicit should be the 'anchor' in what was actually said for the coding term which a particular researcher wants to assign. Researchers are used to paying attention to the cues that are picked up in the field itself. But let us consider a familiar problem: that research subjects might allude to, but not explicitly state, 'what they mean' (or, in the following case, 'who' they mean). 'I have one code which is called "them and us", which is when people are talking about other people and conflicts. That one definitely emerged because I thought I would be able to pick up people's comments on racism or those horrible whities round the corner or those nasty [Pakistanis] down the road. But people don't talk about "whities", they talk about "them", so a word search will come up with nothing' (FG3). The researcher will have to 'read in' the nuance to the words actually used (and if it is desired that the program should be able to pull out these instances, the word for which a euphemism is used will have to be typed into the transcript). All interpretation involves a measure of 'reading in', but the stark light of the monitor exposes this more clearly. The other side of the rigour and systematicity encouraged by CAQDAS is that singular, contentious or delicate nuances might be harder to sustain.

Team research increases the likelihood of each member having to account for their interpretation, particularly where there are collectively undertaken tasks rather than a thoroughgoing division of labour. It appears that using CAQDAS has a similar effect. Together they can take researchers some way from a tradition that emphasizes experiential ways of knowing, rapport with subjects and a sense that all interpretation is partial and incomplete. 'You do hear the voice and you do know, it is very quick, it is very easy once you start reading an interview transcript, you are back there doing it. When you are observing something sitting there you can see the room and know when you were and what was happening and the bits that you hadn't remembered, you transport yourself back into it. And so there really was this difficulty [in agreeing codes with a colleague who had not been present in the field], and . . . maybe it isn't possible' (FG6). While these features might sometimes be over-romanticized, taking account of the experiential dimension will affect the granularity of the codes, whether they are broad or 'fine-grained'.

Theoretically CAQDAS is neutral on this, accommodating several layers of hierarchical coding and considerable amounts of multi-coding in most packages. There are researchers who describe CAQDAS as supporting very fine-grained analyses, far more particular than would be possible if one relied on one's memory. The way that CAQDAS can promote the opposite is simply that the awareness that CAQDAS can handle larger data sets than can a human being might encourage researchers to collect more data than is usual in qualitative projects. Once this material is formatted in the package, researchers then discover how demanding the task of coding will be and are obliged to use broad codes. 'One of the coded interviews came out at about 100 pages, so I am not talking small, talking around a couple of hours recording with ten people which . . . took hours to code it. The biggest one, the 100 page one must have taken six or seven hours' coding, but it's big enough to get comparisons . . . but not too big that you lose the refinements of the codes. Because I think if you are coding on really really big data sets you tend to just lump a big section of data into one code, whereas this, sometimes two or three codes in a line . . . Even so, if you coded more broadly you still have to break it down at some point' (FG1).

It might also engender a feeling of impatience if the researcher is familiar with the more 'intuitive' process of manual coding. 'Huge input of data . . . even getting the transcription, putting it in, because I was taking . . . anywhere between five or ten lines, often using one term actually. I didn't want to do it in those great big lumps but then you've got to. And towards the end I was flagging, I was thinking "I wish I could just code with some description, I just wish it was transcribed and printed".' This was the respondent who indicated guilt at coding the last transcripts manually. Although faster, she worried that 'I think I hadn't coded those in the same way as I coded the other ones . . . So it does actually alter the way you code' (FG1). One could read the inconsistent application of codes testified to here as a consequence of the demanding nature of basic coding operations in the package. Another way of coping is described, critically, by this respondent: 'breaking the data up into relevant topics so that you . . . take one topic and then form your data set, you feed in so many cases with just the material on that topic. Because that way you can have several data sets, one from each topic that you want and it makes it much more manageable. I think there is a tendency to bung the whole lot in, can stifle you before you even start' (FG1). While this might resolve problems of 'too much data' it poses an obvious danger of working to a prior analytic framework rather than moving 'up' from the data in grounded theory fashion.

There is also the argument that, if one has not personally collected (or transcribed) the data, one needs a slow, deliberate and demanding coding process in order to get in touch with the data. In this case the idea was expressed as a defence of so-called 'two-step coding'. 'On one hand . . . you want this process speeded up so you can get on with it but on the other hand that is a very important part of the whole process. So I am torn, really . . . If you have done the transcription then you can code it straight into the screen much easier, but if you haven't done the transcription then you need to go through the process of coding it all off-screen to get in touch with it' (FG1). There was considerable debate about this issue, with some respondents confident that on-screen coding was most effective regardless of one's degree of acquaintance with the data. Indeed, one saw no case for work off-screen and did not believe that handling the hard copy was necessary to get a deep knowledge of the data, a habit that had been forced on her as a penniless postgraduate conscious that each printed sheet cost money. 'Some of the interviews in fact I transcribed straight onto my machine and never printed and [name of developer] had a fit: "you've got to work through paper interviews" but . . . that wasn't a facility that was actually available to me, wasn't practical and even now I don't find it as important. There is this thing that you are supposed to print things out and that will make it more real and I don't subscribe to it' (FG6).

We have already noted the problem that users have in coding for what they think subjects are saying rather than the words they actually use. This is not the only 'risk' attached to interpreting text in order to code it. Another coding complexity is whether code definitions for responses by individuals in one-to-one interviews and for responses in the course of group discussions should be treated the same way. Respondents found one-to-one interview transcripts the most straightforward to code (but note that few of our respondents were working extensively with documents, such as legal statutes) and some went on to say that such material was the best suited to analysis using CAQDAS. In group discussions there are group dynamics which complicate coding and raise doubts about whether such data should be coded, and consequently analysed, as if they were responses in individual interviews. Nevertheless, this was what researchers generally did. 'I wasn't quite sure how to deal with it, if I should try and code it for the people who were there and so on. In the end . . . I identified each person in the beginning because they give indications of who they were, what they did, where they came from, ethnographic things . . . I identified that individually for each person in the group, and then I just coded the rest of the discussion . . . the same sort of codes as individually. So that when you get a segment coming out . . . you can then relate that back to the people and ethnographic information . . . But it was different to coding up individuals. Interviews are quite straightforward with just one person. And of course you have to keep track of individuals within their groups so you don't lose them. So that was my compromise when we [were] doing it without getting codes for conversation' (FG1).

Doubt about coding group discussion data extended to doubt about coding such data as part of a CAQDAS-based project. 'That's the problem because I am less convinced that [package name] is of value in group discussions . . . The complexity of discourses and groups makes it much more difficult to get on [get coded] and with us, because we are working in depth with people then we are much more interested in the group dynamic . . . So you do need to know who is talking and how it contributes and the whole discussion just flows differently as a group, across the group. What is happening in group two is different from what is happening in group five or six . . . There are quite interesting methodological problems in dealing with groups that we haven't really got to grips with' (FG1; it might be added that the lengthy extracts required to illustrate the development of points in a group discussion are more likely to be tolerated in methodological discussions than in applied research reports or substantively oriented studies). The respondent suggests that codes developed for one group might not apply to another. This obviously challenges the normal CAQDAS approach, which is to assign codes whose development can be traced across a number of cases. There is no reason, however, why codes cannot be developed case by case. But again, if analysis is to take account of what Becker called 'quasi statistics' (and what analysis does not include reference to 'more respondents thought X' and the like?) the need to operate within cases will be a constraint.

While reducing the number of cases covered by a set of codes might pose problems if one is using CAQDAS, there are pathologies associated with allowing codes to proliferate as well. Cessation of package use was attributed to this in one case. 'I suppose ultimately . . . that's one of the reasons we gave up, in that we just had so many codes . . . There was always this feeling that if I code that . . . chunk the same as that code, that may be the same as that, and then again it may not be, is it the same as that, is it *really* the same as that? "Perhaps we ought to code it something different", "we could give it another code and then we could . . ." When we go through it there is always this feeling that "we could use this", "we could actually put them together". It would be easier at the end to put, go downwards [reduce the number of codes] than it would be to miss things out at the beginning, and so we just ended up with hundred and hundreds and hundreds of codes!' (FG6). This problem was particularly acute for contract researchers: 'The proliferation of codes comes from two directions, doesn't it, from hierarchic generating codes like "positive feelings" and all that stuff, just capturing too much. "We need three of these" and then it goes on and on. But then there's the other way, when you start saying "well, these three codes are really tapping into the single concept here, we need a code for this concept. We don't want to lose those three codes" [laughter], because you think once you've done something irreversible . . . You get codes coming from all directions. Eventually we just had to call a halt, say, "we are generating these codes but how really germane are they to what we are doing here?" . . . Quite interesting things might be going on, but we have a job to do, we have to call a halt . . . Having coded some of these [we] said we are not going to use these' (FG6). This contrasted sharply with one of our previously cited doctoral student respondents, who wondered if she and contract researchers were working with different definitions of proliferation, and suggested that the same number of codes might represent proliferation to applied researchers while for her it was a matter of documenting the movement 'from descriptive to theoretical'. As a graduate student she was free to invest all her working time in the analysis and while her coding scheme was indeed 'building up', she 'had clear in my mind what that set was, and I think [each code] is really different' (FG6).

Once again an issue which might be presented as a problem of CAQDAS appears to relate to the research environment as much as to the encouragement CAQDAS might give to code proliferation by supporting the mechanics of coding. But the very flexibility of CAQDAS does allow users to change their minds without invoking the massive clerical effort that would arise from changing coding in a manual project. We have already referred to the downside of this, where users endlessly delay analytic closure, stimulated by the encouragement that CAQDAS gives to creative 'play'. One of our respondents contrasted three packages: 'I have gone through all these packages and seen which ones are most flexible for that sort of thing . . . That's where I came unstuck with [package 1], because it takes such a long time to do the coding process, and although you can tinker with it slightly, actual major revisions are quite time-consuming. [Package 2], the way I coped with lots of coding changes there, was that my "tree" [graphic representation of coding linkages] got totally unmanageable and I ended up with chopping it all up and abandoning the tree completely. So I ended up with nodes here, there and everywhere, and a few lines in between, so that is more flexible, it allows you to change your mind a bit more' (FG4). Perhaps the desirability of 'changing your mind a bit more' is as difficult to judge as 'how many codes are too many', but, insofar as the end product of the project employing the second package to which the respondent refers is normally an elaborated tree structure we might be looking at an account of confusion rather than one of flexibility. The user goes on to remark that in her approach to qualitative analysis 'a trail of thought gets going. It's only afterwards that you can find why those ideas tended to be related, which is I don't think what the other packages [compared to a textbase manager package] encourage in any way' (FG4). She maintained that the computer could not help establish those connections, only transport one around the data set quickly, preferably leaving a 'trail' (as the package she mentioned does) of where one has been, from which connections can be drawn. But the making of connections is just what such packages aim to facilitate. In other words, for some users, at least, it might be as important to support the making of connections by offering prompts and in-built guidance through help features, as it is to design in features that let users skip around program operations and the data set.

Packages that have a relatively demanding coding process exacerbate another pathology. The qualitative methods literature abounds with warnings about the problem of going native, but we suspect that the problem of not going in deep enough is equally common. Much is made of relatively shallow fieldwork encounters, a small number of interviews/observations, with coding that focuses on ideas that come glibly to the researcher and conveniently fit her or his frame of reference. If coding is unduly tedious the user might rest with his or her first shot. 'The first trawl through the coding tends to be very, very general, "issues we are doing around disability" and so on. [You] highlight something that has been for "independence" and then discover that it is an issue around "personal care" or "privacy" and therefore needs listing. You have to be very precise about what you are doing at that stage, otherwise you end up doing revision. The temptation is that you want to do everything once rather than look at one very, very closely. I think you need to be able to take that step back and say "how much time am I going to save by being very focused in the early stages?" But possibly at the cost of not being able to have the loops of thought that you have a brainwave halfway through and you realize you need to go back [to coding] again' (FG4). It appears that the user is describing quite a profound shift in procedure, while recognizing the consequent loss of spontaneity. Instead of two or more 'passes', he suggests that the systematic, demanding coding process be done in one round, with an eye to saving time overall. It requires the user to be 'very focused' at this stage.

Later in our discussion the same respondent discussed the idea of creative play, that is, manipulating the coding scheme and examining the results, as the payoff for the tedium of coding. What is implicit here is that it might actually be easier to re-jig one's coding if one is working in a superficial manual approach where coding is more *ad hoc* and less comprehensive than accepted standards, because manual work is less reviewable. One hesitates to air such a supposition, which is tantamount to saying that if one is prepared to rest with a non-systematic and shallow analysis, then there is little doubt that manual methods are quicker and easier. But it would be hard to contradict this user's assertion in the following brief extract if a 'level playing field' comparison were being made between manual and CAQDAS methods, that is, where a systematic, fully satu-rated analysis was the objective. '[I]f I did make a mistake I could look in my coding system and [if I] didn't like it, if you do it by hand you may be reluctant to throw it away whereas if I am doing it with the computer I could easily re-jig it' (FG5). A respondent elaborated on such an instance. 'One problem I've had . . . was [that] I'd analysed several interviews, prob-ably about a quarter of the way through my data collection, and came across a paper which actually suggested an alternative way of coding the data, which . . . [I] realized it actually applied very usefully to the work I was doing and so I went back and recoded everything. And I was quite pleased that I was able to do that very easily, very quickly. In the program it wasn't a feature I was aware of until I tried to do it and . . . it didn't neces-sitate me altering the way I interviewed people at all or how I collected data or how I thought about things' (FG5). Perhaps not all 'brainwaves' need be pathological.

Some epistemological guidance is available here on the matter of whether to have one, sharply focused round of coding, or several rounds which progressively focus more sharply. The argument that all analysis is partial and incomplete reflects the non-positivist drift of the qualitative heuristic. It tends away from the positivist stance towards social reality because it takes to heart the consequences of relativism. While there certainly remains qualitative work in the positivist tradition, qualitative analysis increasingly tends towards either the naturalist or 'realist' posture (Silverman, 1985). Both of these emphasize the multiplicity of perspectives on the social world, and it is in accord with this idea that no single analy-sis can ever be definitive. If we accept that the analyst becomes more aware of the perspectives relevant to her or his subject as the work of interpret-ing data proceeds, then we must accept that coding will be both a recur-rent and a recursive process. The implication is that, no matter how 'focused' the first round of coding, it cannot and should not aspire to be the last. Thus the position put by the users we have been discussing is flatly contradicted by another team, who learned from experience that a single sweep was not feasible. Interestingly, they suggest that the package itself discouraged a single sweep (but this did assume that the technical competence of the team was such that the mechanical procedure was not so arduous as to be a disincentive to changing codes). 'We tried to do too much with the original code because we thought "right, we'll code it" but . . . what you do is you take those first codes, then you code it all again'. Colleague: 'One of the things we were trying to do was . . . formulate codes that would actually be usable across a whole [data] set, the whole case study. So when we actually used a code like "observation" we would be able to use it in the same way whether it be an appraisal interview or one of our own face-to-face [research] interviews. Things like "positive feel-ings" we ended up, you can't have "positive feelings" just as a code, because it could mean anything to anybody, we needed hierarchies of codes.' Original speaker: 'We were trying to actually make one-step [coding] where I think in [package name] things come between this because it uses several stages [in its coding operation]' (FG6).

Thus, as the effort proceeded it became clear that the broad codes first identified were too readily 'saturated' and there were intervening micro and mezzo levels or dimensions to the codes. These were manifest from several package features, including the exposure of context surrounding coded segments in segment retrievals, the invitation to 'nest' codes, and selective/global recoding facilities. Although the version of the package in use did not support memoing, such a feature also invites finer-grained coding as one gains acquaintance with the data. '[W]e were also trying to do things like, "positive feelings" we tried to make that one code, didn't we, so we started . . . getting codes like "pos feel" . . . and decided that that wasn't as good as actually having words that actually meant something, so we then used more than one code word for things' (ibid.).

It is worth reminding ourselves that, in order to code something, the researcher has to understand what the respondent (or document) is saying (or what observed actions mean). This prior act of interpretation is needed before one can search for a summary or gloss which captures the essence of what is being coded (Rosen, 1978). Studies of intercoder reliability indicate that, even in quantitative research, no matter how strictly schooled to stick with literal 'on the surface' meaning, coders of survey responses inevitably 'read in' meaning, actively engaging with the datum, thinking themselves into the circumstances of the respondent, drawing on previously coded segments of the datum, making use of meaning accumulated across cases employing culturally encrypted understandings, and so on (Tony Hak, personal communication, September 1994). This, too, suggests that it is futile to expect that one's first sense will be one's best sense, no matter how zealous, picayune or Zen-like one's attention. If software belabours or elaborates the classification process, it might well be to the benefit of the final analysis.

6

Manipulating Coding Categories

A strong spur to the development of CAQDAS was the demanding nature of retrieving data by hand. The more sophisticated the analyst's retrieval strategy the harder it was to support, given the shortcomings of paper-based filing systems. This posed a real disincentive to the development and practice of sophisticated retrieval methods and must, we suppose, have constrained the development of sensitive coding systems and fully elaborated conceptual schemata. We say 'suppose' because there is no direct testimony in the literature to this effect (though see Hammersley, 1989). However, the problem can be inferred from the many references in the methods literature to the need to plan for the practical demands of the stage where analysis is being developed through the repeat application of data to conceptual schemata. Thus, analytic procedures such as analytic induction, grounded theory, deviant case analysis or Agar's iterative schema resolution procedure (Agar and Hobbs, 1982), which require the iteration and refinement of analytic schemata, have to be seen against the practical constraints of data management (and we consider formal analytic approaches further in the next chapter). No doubt most qualitative researchers will have been acquainted with these and other systematic approaches to qualitative data analysis, but it remains moot how far such approaches are routinely prosecuted and, if they are, with what degree of accuracy and systematicity.

These are harsh words, we admit. But we would frankly question, outside a small number of exemplars, how frequently the full demands of the constant comparative project (or the few other formal approaches) have been fulfilled. It might be that the chief occasion in a researcher's career where there is full engagement with a systematic approach is in the doctoral study. Thereafter, time pressures, filing systems and, perhaps, a rising sense of professional confidence, work against the sort of procedure which requires the researcher to revise the coding scheme, recode the data, combine codes, modify codes, delete codes, write, read and act on analytic memos, seek and incorporate new data, and so on, many, many times, in order to arrive at the final analysis. We concede that the research world does include paragons and perfectionists, and that some are blessed with the resources that enable them to work rigorously at every step. But we are merely making the practical point that without the computer the procedures for systematic retrieval in the service of refining one's conceptualization are so unreasonably demanding that only the stubborn or the acknowledged experts are likely to persevere (or be in a position to do so).

Is it possible to draw a contrast between this circumstance and the situation post-CAQDAS? Technically the answer should be an obvious 'yes'. Packages offer a variety of artful means to support rich retrieval strategies. A user with basic competence in the package might test hypotheses by writing rules in propositional form (as in HyperResearch), might employ logical 'operators' to retrieve segments in semantically informative sequences (as in NUD•IST, Atlas/ti, ETHNOGRAPH and others), might list 'hits' to determine frequency, adjacency and other features of positioning (as in all CAQDAS packages), might highlight key hits on a figurative schema and automate recoding as new ideas emerge from work with such graphic displays (as in NUD•IST and Atlas/ti). Perhaps as important as any given feature is that our user might conjure up each and every segment assigned to a given code and ponder whether it truly 'belongs' with that or some other code, sifting for sense in a way that simply could not be sustained by working with paper. In short, much is possible. But is the potential being realized? We sought evidence that it was.

Outside the enthusiasms of the developers and the training workshops, we have to report only meagre evidence that users are newly investing time in working imaginatively or systematically with retrieval. Our impression might reflect both the skew of our sample to people working on applied projects and the relatively early stage of the research community's exposure to CAQDAS. Interestingly, researchers working in the European hermeneutic tradition do apparently testify to full use of the analytic features of packages such as MAX and Kwalitan; we suspect this reflects the working conditions and relative independence from policy research of academic social science in at least some European countries. Nevertheless, our broad impression suggests an underachievement in respect of a key potential for which CAQDAS is touted, and it might be helpful to offer examples of strategies for working with retrievals in a systematic way.

Retrieval of Coded Segments

The sort of thing we have in mind is not complicated, though if one attempts it 'manually' it can be very demanding. Thus, using software 'you can take one thing, "family", instead of having to cut loads of strips of paper and hope you don't lose them, you can do very complex combinations; you can code it in lots of different ways and it's all in the one place, you don't have to have boxes and boxes of things waiting, you can use it to look at "family breakdown" in the context of something else' (FG3). Similarly, 'I'm doing some qualitative analysis on women in prison and, God, I keep wishing I had it on my [package], about 55 [interviews], every single issue that I want to write about I've got to get all 55 out, divide them into mothers and non-mothers and then get the issue I want, and then get the bit [of data], it's a nightmare!' (FG1). One user simply summed up: 'the pay-off really comes when you search' (FG1). Systematicity, consistency and discovery were all cited advantages of retrievals using CAQDAS. 'Where it would have been useful in the previous project was that I wanted to go back into things over and over again, starting to make connections of my own. My own doctoral research is based on data from a previous project and it was becoming apparent when I was doing the cut-and-paste bit and thinking "Gosh, this is taking me hours and if we had had it on there in the first place I could be doing this . . . so much more quickly".'

Dividing text into segments is an essential preliminary to assigning codes. While the software supports this activity in various ways, it soon becomes obvious that segments and categories are defined, and can only be redefined, by the researcher. 'We have to split it, and go to those segments and look at them ourselves' (FG1). The researcher has to 'split' the text into segments, inspect them and assign codes. Segmentation is a basic, essential step in code retrieval, but packages are quite capable of treating each word as a segment or an entire interview as a single segment. As one user put it, it was a 'completely fatuous claim' that CAQDAS could 'analyse' data: 'it codes, it just divides things up into chunks, and that's all it does, and I think it does that quite well, but it doesn't build theories, that has to be done here [points to head]' (FG3). In fact it accentuated the importance of the user being clear about the meaning of the code: 'if you choose the wrong one then it can really alter your data and it is crucial to know why you chose it and how it's going to affect your analysis. Before you choose you must decide what you are going to say' (FG3). This last point suggests a circularity in the process. Importantly, then, segmentation and code assignment govern the quality of code retrieval, and presage analysis by configuring the data.

Manual and CAQDAS methods are similar in the practical procedure of defining segments. Both are time-consuming. Differences emerge when it comes to revising the boundaries of segments or the assignment of codes to segments. Manually this involves crossing out and generally making a mess of the transcript. This not being the case with CAQDAS there is more of an encouragement not only to reconsider initial code assignments but to ponder them and precisely specify their meaning: 'once you've got that [initial coding] then you can start to look at what people are talking about, and then from that you can go back to those main categories and . . . say "OK, how are they saying it", or you can start to look [at] what you want to know' (FG1). In this user's practice this plainly implied a process of refinement: '[Y]ou have got your own ideas of what might come out [but]

what can happen is the content codes sometimes make you shift the theoretical balance, because you begin to see data emerging [in a] different
balance from what you expected, and then your more complex codes come
from that. You've got your sheet [of codes] and then you do the thinking,
and then you start again' (FG1).

Perhaps the most basic preliminary to code retrieval is for the relevant
data to be available to sort. We came across a case in which one user
referred to not having done a retrieval across all the interviews to examine
variation in comments about sexual behaviour in a subsample of respondents having a particular characteristic. The reason offered was that the
behaviour in question had attracted extensive comment whenever it was
raised: 'in fact I've never done that [retrieval] because it would be a giant
thing taking up three days. Everything everybody says about [behaviour]
is this high [indicates stack of transcript]' (FG1). Another user asked how
many cases were involved: '150' came the reply.

'And how many of those would be likely to be [subsample who
commented on the behaviour]?'

'There wouldn't be very many.'

'If you are just going to restrict it to the pieces of narrative where they
have made that comment, you should be able to get that out in ten sheets
or less.'

'Well, the other thing is we haven't all the sheets up, that's the problem.'

There are two things going on here, and both suggest, in our view, a
misunderstanding of code retrieval. First, it emerges that the user studying sexual behaviour has assigned a single code to very extensive
segments of transcript rather than using subcodes to differentiate aspects
of the main code. A retrieval to search for the subsample commenting on
the behaviour would fail because it would produce too much print-out to
digest. This is a problem of data reduction. Second, it emerges that some
of the interview data has not been entered into the package. Software can
hardly be expected to manipulate data that is not available to it. The
second user in the dialogue rightly notes that if these basic conditions were
satisfied a properly specified retrieval would result in a reduction of data
from 150 transcripts to a few pages.

Code retrieval can be not only a creative but a playful process. This
prospect motivated users through the hard work of transcription and code
assignment. '[T]ranscribing was laborious and the coding was laborious,
but when it started to come together it was really good, and it did get your
creativity going, just the stimulation of seeing the [thing] organized and
saying "right, I can do anything with it" and you can play about' (FG1).
This sense of creative play included the stimulation of trying unaccustomed approaches to data analysis, such as going more 'micro'. While
there might on occasion be a eureka-style insight, we suspect that new
analytic angles more usually result from the painstaking process of trying
different retrievals, that is, different conjunctions of the data: 'I'll print out

a code and index category and comments to see how the index and category has developed' (FG3). Where CAQDAS is used alongside quantitative analysis, efforts at triangulation might lead the user back to the qualitative data with new angles in mind. In particular, a new set of codes might be suggested which map onto topics in the quantitative data set. '[Our project has] got three strands to it, one of which is case studies. We have also got a quantitative national survey alongside it. When we want to actually make connections . . . when things start coming out of the quantitative national survey . . . we will go back into the qualitative data to see whether we have got any confirming things there. So it's that ability to play with data, the phrase I keep using, that I will be able to go back and play with that over and over again in different ways by using the package, which would be very very time consuming when you are doing it with pencil and paper' (FG6).

To get to a point where creativity benefits could be realized a good deal of work was needed in organizing the data. For some, the facilitation of data management arising from this organizing work was the main contribution CAQDAS could provide. An idea of what is meant by using packages to manage data rather than to contribute directly to analysis is conveyed by the reference to stopping at coding ('the headings') in the initial study referred to in the following case. 'It was two and a half years [before] there was the time to be able to use a qualitative package to its fullest extent. It was built on a previous project in which the researcher merely had time to listen to the tapes twice and categorize them on a piece of paper and then they were given the money to do a project which had a lot more time and the feeling was "we can really get to grips with the transcripts, there is time to go for what we think the headings are but also what else there is", and that the qualitative package was going to provide that . . . having the time to really look at the data properly' (FG4). Users consistently emphasized that there was a price to be paid in terms of carefully organizing the data before the creativity benefits could be realized. 'Some people say quite interesting things but take three pages to say it . . . and I could encapsulate in three lines. But every time I turned up that code and I was asking it to sort I was getting the three pages again and . . . I couldn't remember what the three lines of succinct paraphrase were, so I was getting really bored' (FG6). Hearing this, another respondent exclaimed, 'It sounds to me as if you need to put more effort into the coding stage!' It was an apt remark but users have to be clear that the extra effort is worthwhile.

The benefits of package use had therefore to be clear and worthwhile, because users were very aware of time pressure. 'Go back and start again, recode things, sort it in all sorts of different ways with the promise that exciting connections would emerge . . . But coding . . . is the price you have to pay for it, the time you spend there. After that it all becomes great fun. Unfortunately I'm a contract researcher, we never have time to go back and play with it – you can fulfil the terms of your contract, produce a research report, and then you move on to your next commission' (FG6). In the following case the preliminary investment was made and it was only then that the team concluded that software-aided analysis would take too long. 'You asked me why we gave it up, and that's when it came to the stage of cutting and pasting and moving about. It was the output which absolutely staggered me, I was not really prepared for this . . . We got a pile of interview transcripts and had 88 interviews plus fieldnotes and observation from appeal hearings. When we got to the stage we said we can't code any more, we've done 50 plus [codes], and we've got to start analysing, we said "right, we'll start with something simple, have all these instances with just one code" and the print-out was about *this* thick [stretches arms]. One code of about 50-odd codes we had generated! And that's without any nesting of codes or crossing of codes [multiple sorts] and [package] allows you to use Boolean operators as well! We thought, "Jesus Christ, all that to work through, and you've got to read all through it again"' (FG6). This appears to be a case of 'so near and yet so far'. The respondent might have been best advised to press on to make use of the Boolean operators available. By using specified retrievals he would have been able to reduce their stack of print-out to the data they needed for their analysis. By remaining within an approach to analysis fastened at the data/code level ('all these instances with just one code') they missed the opportunity to get the benefit of all their hard preliminary work.

It takes time (and creative 'play') to appreciate the approaches to analysis that CAQDAS facilitates, approaches which are well grounded in qualitative epistemology but in practice 'new' to researchers because of the difficulty of operationalizing them manually. Thus we should not be surprised that, by and large, users seemed not to have capitalized upon the approach to analysis offered by specified retrievals. 'I assumed [that] somewhere some people must be using computers to take a lot of the actual physical grind out of the analysis. I was amazed when I found out that some of them actually, not exactly put together theories for you but connected things up in search ways that you could thread, I wasn't thinking about it in that sense, I was thinking about it just in terms of the physical work that it would cut down on' (FG4). Perhaps we need a reminder of the rather lax approach to which qualitative analysis is susceptible in order to appreciate systematic retrieval features: 'as a PhD student I was involved in various research projects as a research assistant, and we would do semi-structured interviews, and then the person who was looking after the project used to just put ticks by various statements, pull out those statements and that would then be his research report. And I was quite aghast at this, which is why I was looking for something to make it more rigorous, I didn't believe that was the correct method to do it but that is how the department culture had built up, that was how you analysed interview data' (FG5). So what does 'rigour' mean here? One available meaning can be dismissed: rigour could stand for simply combing through all the data (and becoming 'saturated' by getting 'immersed' in it). However, in the above example the person who 'looked after' the project was indeed reading everything – once. The respondent's concern was over the fact that there appeared to be no rationale for selecting those segments that were honoured by a tick. An element of rigour can be added by the memoing features we have already discussed but a further element is searching for and retrieving data that precisely tracks a relationship one suspects might be present. One could argue that packages subtly encourage users to do such retrievals because if they just select all the data on a given code they are likely to be inundated. Thus, 'there is such a colossal amount of it, I think it is too much. And I thought "I wonder what they are thinking about something", press the button, out comes about 8,000 sheets. I have to really home in on exactly what I want' (FG1).

However, the respondents recognized that there was a danger of over-characterizing the short-termism of researchers. Contract researchers took an ongoing interest in their work and might return to the data long after the report was submitted. 'I started off this survey as a contract researcher six years ago, and I am still analysing the same survey . . .' Second respondent: 'Are you still a contract researcher?' 'I am now a lecturer, but what [package] has meant is that because you can play about with it, look at different aspects, you can go on analysing the same data for years. I can just see things in it, it's partly because I've got the time but also because the package lets you look at different codes' (FG6). We do not want to indulge in a counsel of perfection here. We are not trying to argue that the analysis time for contract research projects must be extended or that such projects produce inferior analyses. We simply note that software beckons users with the prospect of new insights and sometimes users are not in a position to respond positively. Being unable to respond can be frustrating. 'That was the disadvantage we found, we abandoned it after a while, because it does offer those possibilities, but within one research project with limited time you don't have the opportunity to do that, and it almost became a burden because you were having to spend that set-up time' (FG6).

One way to secure the time one might need to get more out of the analytic process is to persuade sponsors that this is justified by an enhanced analysis with higher surface validity. Research sponsors might be particularly persuaded by the technicist, scientific appeal of computing-based methods. Paradoxically, this can be a turn-off to those with authority over the project who are knowledgeable about, and committed to, traditional methods. We might recall the graduate student who ran into such problems with her thesis supervisors. The 'play' aspect of creativity was at issue. The group had been discussing the credibility-enhancing appeal of CAQDAS. '[T]he arguments about rigour which might work for civil servants definitely didn't work for [my] supervisors . . . "It's not supposed to be fun, what are you doing spending all this time on a computer, you should be working" [laughter] ... I actually carried on working on computers quite a lot, as some kind of act, partially, of rebellion and just to say I think it's actually a good method, I'm going to ... use it well to justify it' (FG6). For this user the problem was not time but persuading her supervisors, and this led to some circumspection in their relationship, as she was unable to seek help or express her frustration at some of the problems she had with the software. 'I did have the time because I embarked right at the beginning of a PhD and said "this is the kind of software I am going to use", and exploring lots of the packages to learn one quite well. I had problems with all of them ... [With] every package I felt like "I could develop this package to do what I really wanted it to do". I spent more time thinking about "Oh, if I had a menu there to do that, that would be exactly right" and that was hard because I was having to convince supervisors that this package was absolutely fine, rigorous, but they were always coming against [the fact] that it didn't work' (ibid.). While contract researchers encounter time problems in using software that pushes them to take a more systematic approach, academic users also face problems which reduce the time available for analytic work with the package. In terms of retrieval these might lead to less finely grained coding and/or restrict the retrievals to the main categories and to single sorts. The effect of both would be to limit the development of category-as-category relationships and keep the analysis focused on data-to-category relationships. This tends to produce descriptive analyses which are confined to using the data to 'illustrate' a category.

There was in fact a substantial scepticism about approaches to analysis which moved beyond the 'illustrative quote' mode, at least where it involved work with software. One group approached the issue after discussing whether there was a danger that researchers would think the computer could 'do' analysis without human intervention. It was a supposition one user found puzzling: 'I've worked in both quantitative and qualitative and I've never expected computers to do any thinking. They obviously make a calculation but you've still got to think about the meaning of the quantitative stuff, as well as the qualitative, you've still got to think up the codes. Thinking is never gotten rid of by the computer and I never imagined it would be' (FG6). This sensible view is only the start of the matter, as became clear when the discussion moved to specific analytic features. Here we can see users making a distinction between code-and-retrieve packages and those with particular conceptualizing features; note that the distinction is organized around an explicit criterion of what it is realistic to expect a package to do and what is a 'fantasy'. 'It won't make the connections because the computer can't make connections between words. Some offer the potential, a certain type of fantasy that that would happen. Like HyperResearch has a hypothesis tester when you can use Boolean operators, and so you can say, my work was on mature students,

I want to look at all that have issues around child care and issues around work leave but not problems with partner, and you can feed that in, and my hypothesis is something to do with those and it will churn through all your data and codes and say "hypothesis found, false or true". Now that offers a fantasy' (FG6). It should not be thought that this one package is being singled out for the criticism that it claims something implausible. HyperResearch targets its conceptualization on this particular feature (and it is one with much appeal for those operating deductively) but the procedure is feasible in several packages which put similar emphasis on constituting retrievals so as to look for particular patterns of code assignments in text.

What is interesting is that these features, which are the first step towards making systematic retrievals, and which move attention from the data–category link to those between categories, provoke resistance. In one case, it is because the user wants to use the package for data management and little more; in another because the user is dubious of the logic behind the feature. 'I feel my use of [package 1] as being very simple, and these techniques of playing about with codes and seeing how they related to each other as a separate enterprise which it sounds as if [package 2] does, [package 3] advertises that it does, that might give you this feeling that you can use the thing to help you think, which I don't think [package 1] does for me. I don't think I've been able to use it that way, it's just a way of reducing mechanical things, it's not to alienate thinking' (FG6). This prompted the user acquainted with HyperResearch to observe that 'I used it but didn't ever report the findings 'cause I was very suspect about how it worked, it seemed so contingent on the way that you code things. Even the manual . . . says "if your hypothesis proves to be false and you don't think it should be perhaps you have coded something wrongly" [laughter] . . . I used to give this as a story in one of my lectures because they use this data set called "Cinderella complex" . . . and their test is . . . if you have got no conflict between work, no conflict at home, so you have that and that but no other comments of conflict, then your hypothesis is that you would have the complex. I found that really suspect for my stuff' (FG6). It is worth noting that the plausibility of this feature is assessed by reference to the example in the package's demo. The user sounds unconvinced about the procedure in general but, moreover, dismisses the procedure because the example does not seem to apply to her own 'stuff'. The criticism seems to hinge on its substantive inapplicability to her own data as well as the problem with the logic of hypothesis testing when applied to qualitative data. This user is clearly concerned about the weight a hypothetical logic puts on the code label which one applies to a given segment of data. She objected to the idea that if a hypothetical proposition was confounded the user should consider a change in the code, despite not being averse to carefully reviewing code assignments. 'Especially because they [developers] advocate going back and checking your codes. Checking your codes is fine but saying [that] if I made that [code assignment] into "conflict" it would prove my hypothesis worries me, especially the language of hypothesis testing. It's all very well saying "do I want to refine my theory and take account of the fact that I've got generations of codes?" but to actually say my hypothesis will matter false or true seems a bit suspect' (ibid.). To some the appeal of qualitative analysis lies in its concern for the ineffable, the shades of grey between black and white. To them, approaches to analysis which involve 'proof' or take 'and, or, not' as the essential thing about the relationship between codes and segments, are misconceived.

Thus, a similar reservation was that the hypothesis-testing approach was uncomfortably close to 'verificationism', looking for data to 'prove' a pre-existing theory rather than working 'up' from the data as in the classic grounded theory approach. One supervisor wanted to take the package away from her student: 'he used it to look for the data that backed up his theory, that he was looking for. I find that worrying' (FG4). A similar concern was raised by a user who felt a particular package encouraged him to be more rigorous and contrasted this with the verification approach: 'this is my concern with [package] methodologically speaking – that people will use [package] as a way to affirm existing categories that they have in their minds and . . . by using [package] somehow it's legitimate. Now I've got . . . a very serious problem with that approach, and as a result I have tried to become more rigorous in my thinking. The sheer fact that I am able to hold more data and to collect more data, analyse more data, allows me to be more representative?!' (FG5). The tone of the final sentence made it clear that the respondent was sceptical of the idea of 'representativeness' in respect of qualitative data.

Some put such reservations more strongly still, expressing acute scepticism about the analytic assumptions they see as embedded in the software (and in the following, the respondent went on to contrast this with word-processing packages, which she felt were as capable of useful retrievals as CAQDAS but free of such analytic assumptions). 'The packages have epistemological consequences for how one not only conceptualizes the data but what might result, and we used the packages not to produce an analysis but to look at their epistemological assumptions and how that structured the kind of analysis that resulted' (FG4). This respondent was concerned that, while one could not decide one's retrieval strategy until one had a good grasp of the software, by then it was usually too late. '[W]hich of the packages I would use would depend upon the nature of the data and what I wanted to do with it . . . You can only really begin to figure out those things about a package when you have used it for quite a long time, and for most people they have invested so much in using them that they can't then say "Oh, hell's teeth, I should never have used [package] 18 months into a two-year project." But it is usually at that stage that people realize how the package is structured, the data, and whether that is inappropriate for what they are wanting to do' (FG4). This (well-taken) observation about 'fitness for purpose' was accompanied by an example about how packages treat different database structures. 'We used them [packages] in relation to two quite different projects. One was a project where there were 70 day-diaries that were not linked at all . . . where we wanted to preserve a very individual case as an individual case, as well as to look at features in common. We had another project which [included] a set of individual interviews, joint interviews and transcriptions of meetings which fitted together . . . and we concluded that some of the packages were more appropriate for one of those than the others' (FG4). There is some support for this idea in the literature; in a comparative evaluation of two CAQDAS packages, Horney and Healy (1991) suggest that the analyses produced by the packages did differ in 'texture'.

The flexibility of packages in respect of individual data source versus whole case/all sources is an important consideration (Weitzman and Miles, 1995) and certainly affects the way that retrievals can be done, but the issue seems to be technical rather than epistemological (since there are packages which will accommodate either approach, and some which can support both). However, as one respondent implied, the user has to have considerable confidence to impose their approach on the package. 'I've had a chance to compare all the different ways [that] the different manuals tell you to do things, and I've found you can use the packages in a way they weren't meant to be used. You can use all the procedures for a completely different way of looking at your data. For example, [package] and the grounded theory approach which, after persevering for a while [I] disregarded completely and used the package in a more [code-and-retrieve] way. But most researchers, not having been given that opportunity, follow what the particular package suggests. You would have to know quite a lot about general methodology, and epistemological questions, to say "I don't want to do what [package] tells me to do here". It's things like text units, you think is a kind of mechanical procedure until you discover at the end that it is actually quite significant for the results you get' (FG4).

Before users can determine what approach they wish to take to retrieval there are several prior considerations. Informed choice assumes that several packages taking different approaches are locally available. This is not so for the great majority of users, and it is hardly surprising if users conclude that the one package available in their institution or social network is ill-suited to their analytic approach. As the respondent notes, issues like what counts as a text unit fundamentally affect the analysis that can be done. While one might debate whether these concerns are 'technical' or 'epistemological', the following extract adds further considerations to database structure and text units. 'It's very difficult to subvert that these are packages which . . . take care of all these issues, that text units are a technical decision. Well, they are not, they have enormous ramifications

... but it is only at the end of projects that ... you come to realize it, because that's the point at which you reflect on using them, the way they encourage you to set the data up or ask you to code it or encourage you to put [your] ... code into variable trees and so on. All of which at the time can seem like purely technical features of the package but aren't in terms of the analysis that results' (FG4). The problem was not so much that packages have 'assumptions' but that these were not made clear, or that qualitative analysis was characterized in terms of a single approach. '[It] is very invisible. That is what makes it more dangerous, all these things have been seen as technical decisions – text units, whether you put it in a tree or not, whether it's "coding" or "indexing", and none of these packages seems to discuss anything along these lines' (FG4).

Adopting a package too 'early' is a particular issue in teaching package use alongside qualitative methods generally. 'It is almost like limiting the way that they are seeing what qualitative analysis could be ... because they have to jump in and make decisions about using ETHNOGRAPH or NUD•IST early on, and then it can close the options down very quickly, the way that you use it. Because you are using that package, that's what qualitative research becomes to you ... [There is] somebody I have been encouraging to abandon [package], a student just starting her PhD and approached [package] quite nervously, and had quite a lot of technical problems setting it up, and whose categorizing and coding system suffered incredibly because she is trying to fit it into this program which she is not quite sure she is in control of. She thinks she has nothing in her interviews because the categories that are coming out are so boring. So we decided that she has to stop and just start doing the kind of thing you would do manually and she's being much more creative' (FG4). The general point about over-early adoption is a sound one, although there is no CAQDAS package that can suggest category names and none contain predetermined coding schemes. The case says much, however, about trade-offs between systematicity and creativity. While using a package may have inhibited the student's creativity this is less a matter of package design than of appropriate choice and of knowing when in the analytic process to start using software. Interestingly, an example was given of a package that did not come with 'concealed' assumptions or an approach to analysis that was prefigured by its procedures and features. Thus, '[package] is a free package, it's a bin that you put things in, and then you think "how do I want to use it, in what ways am I going to carry out searches, in what ways am I going to use hypertext" ' (FG4). The interesting point is that, for all its virtues, this package is an example of a 'textbase manager' rather than a 'code-and-retrieve' or 'theory-builder', i.e., a package with features intended to facilitate qualitative analysis. Its chief merit was seen as its hypertext facilities, a set of features opening up significant alternative analytic procedures. We consider hypertext approaches in the next chapter.

For those comfortable with code-based analytic approaches, the assumptions made by developers will not be wholly unfamiliar. But there are exceptions to this construction of qualitative analysis. Thus, 'I came to qualitative research through conversation analysis . . . and even coding was a suspect move to make. I guess that's why I am happy with a very open, flexible program like [textbase manager]' (FG4). The route from conversation analysis might be one from working micro-sociologically and descriptively but there are other approaches which apparently value the *ad hoc* and have problems with assigning codes. It will be remembered that one researcher had commented, 'I am not very interested in using these packages in order to code or index, or . . . certainly not to test hypotheses. I am more interested in how they can facilitate what ordinarily would have been done manually, as we call using our minds as well as our hands' (FG4). This respondent made heavy use of hypertext to move from one segment to another, rather than assigning codes. Her retrieval strategy was based on making connections by looking at the data that were thus linked. Behind this stood her view that there was a quality to the data that remained ineffable and which no code could capture. 'Because of [my] research interests I tend to flit about from subject to subject, so I code for one particular set of ideas and then I will think "I could use this to look at something completely different". So I have gone through all of these packages and seen which ones are most flexible . . . With [textbase manager] I tended to read it through on the screen and then use the hypertext to move across different files. I don't have to pre-structure what I am looking for that way, I can just go to highlight a particular sentence if I like, and the ideas will be totally unrelated to each other, and then with their "backtrack" facility you can go through how you trail the data and don't have to have any fixed coding schemes in your mind . . . It's more how I would do it without a software package . . . The sort of reading through and wandering around and maybe not having any fixed idea of how the concepts are related in advance. A trail of thought gets going. It's only afterwards that you can find why those ideas tend to be related . . . I go for [textbase manager] because it . . . lets my mind speed up slightly, move in between files and keep a track of where I've been whilst I'm reading it' (FG4). Software can do quite a bit for such a user, in the way of data management and the provision of hypertext links and source tags. What it cannot do is support a search for patterns; the data have to be coded for such retrievals to be performed. Note that the respondent does not rule out the making of such connections, but suggests they come later and outwith work with the package ('It's only afterwards that you can find why those ideas tend to be related').

It might be observed that a concern about rigidifying the meaning of a segment appears to be behind some of the critical observations about the coding requirement. There is a technical response here: most packages permit both the assignment of more than one code to a segment, and allow codes to be revised. A sense that this does not rigidify the analysis but stimulates creative retrievals, at least for some, is conveyed by the respondent who suggested that coded categories did not lead him to simply pull out quotes as instances of what someone in the occupational group thought but allowed him to perform a task analogous to cross-tabulation, tracing the occupational group's response in tandem with that of other occupational groups to various processes relevant to a particular work process. Thus, 'from those searches I will have very interesting reading potentially, maybe not, maybe lead nowhere but because . . . I've got it indexed in these particular categories I can then take those categories and look at them and grapple with and develop their importance' (FG5).

We have already made the obvious point that before one can retrieve, one has to code. An associated issue is to what extent the retrievals one wishes to perform should be taken into account during coding. We believe that this can only be done to a limited extent. During coding, attention is focused on capturing in a code the essential qualities of the data segment. How the codes thus generated are to be interrelated is a remote consideration. But once one has a code list as a result of assigning codes to all the data, it could be useful to have an interim step, working with the code list to see what associations and patterns are available with which to compose multiple sorts. This apart, users are well advised not to get ahead of themselves by thinking about retrieval patterns while still coding. This seems to have been one of the problems in the team project discussed earlier, where working with a package seriously obstructed the analysis. '[W]e agreed over a fairly long negotiation [that] what we needed to look at in our data, was where [there were] discussions about [topic of research] issues, need to look at that in [package], and need to look at what role the media played' (FG1). The next move, typified as 'a big mistake', was for each team member to take certain themes and code the data for these. The result was three very different codings of the same data set. Each member had developed their own 'analysis' through their coding and by reference to the initial discussion of how the code categories would eventually be related to each other. It was then much harder to gain agreement about the final coding, which attempted to bring together the three separately coded data sets. The purpose of supporting creative exploratory retrievals would have been better served by assigning broader codes whose meaning could more readily be used consistently by several people, bearing in mind that any problematic assignments, or codes which needed redefinition, could readily be done using automated recoding features.

As we said earlier, codes can be condensed between first and subsequent sweeps. If all the data reduction is attempted in one round of coding the effort might be too much. A distinction is made here between what might be called 'case-constant codes', to use Udo Kelle's term, and data attracting more analytically sophisticated codes. The first sweep is like the first look at a jigsaw puzzle, where the pieces that are easily categorized are retrieved and put to one side. One operates broad categories (e.g. all the blue pieces) initially and then works within those categories for a finer-grained classification (e.g. which blue pieces are 'sky' and which are 'water'). A retrieval only on the case constant codes would be somewhat unilluminating. As recoding proceeds, the types of retrieval possible might enter the picture (e.g. if we want to find the bits of 'water' which have parts of 'the boat' in them, should we have a new pile for those?). The quote we have just looked at ends with a sceptical comment about being able to work towards themes within the software. While this user plainly preferred to do this off-screen, the choice is not so stark. Packages can accommodate the activity by providing code lists, memoing, providing source tags and automated recoding (on all or part of the coded data), and, if this is a collaborative process, will keep track of who has advocated a particular configuration.

Thus, coding begins with but a dim view of how it will eventually support the retrieval process, but moves toward a point where the desired retrievals come to have more influence on the coding. There is a shading of the coding process into the retrieval process. Looking at it from the retrieval 'end', we can see instances of retrievals informing coding, as in this comment quoted earlier in discussing the process of 'defining codes': 'I would perhaps quote something like in terms of housing investment and then recall [retrieve] that and actually look at the way people had talked about investment, whether or not it is something I'd thought of. I use [package] for that. I can look at it and say "is this a code that I've developed or is it something that has developed from the data itself?" So it's quite useful in that you can go back to it ethnographically' (FG3). It is interesting that the user characterizes this process as 'ethnographic'. One certainly gets a sense of emergence (as opposed to 'forcing') from the following account of the delicate process by which two codes came to the researchers. We have met the following quote before in discussing code definition. 'One of the things we were interested in was [whether] people who were volunteers in victim support schemes adopted a perspective which was professional or was it a "good neighbourly" approach. Now part of that term "good neighbours" came out of the interviews and it wasn't a major thing . . . Later on I became more and more interested in what do you mean by "professional", what do you mean by "good neighbour", and when you go back and look at the text there is no text and you find the term "good neighbour" is only actually used once or twice by something like 54 people [but] the concept, the idea of being a good neighbour appears throughout it. So that somewhere along there it has clicked, somebody has been using that word, sums it up rather nicely and that's where that code comes from, somebody had decided, and somewhere else "professional" seemed to be. It came out of that [text] but it wasn't something that was a conscious topic and [was] talked about' (FG3). Here again we find the initial retrievals being used just as one would flip through the transcript as one traced an idea, the difference perhaps being that the retrieval can be that much more comprehensive than flipping the pages. The process of scanning initial retrievals can also have a 'history' attached to it, an account of the course of one's thinking as one works with the code and its emerging place in relation to its data segments and to other codes. Thus, 'you might code different bits of that and move towards a more theoretical idea about "how am I going to categorize social risk, is there elements of that which isn't social risk?" So then I might have a social risk categorization, and that might have multiple forms . . . I was trying to document how my codes had evolved as a way of theorizing' (FG6). Such an approach would be extremely difficult manually.

Retrieval also enters the coding process when one takes a cumulative, one code at a time approach. We have so far been discussing coding as a process where one identifies a broad set of codes which apply across the data set, and then refines these. A high-level or broad set of codes is identified and then developed by combination, division into hierarchies and so on. An alternative is 'going through looking for a code as it were, trying to identify segments of text attached to that code. And then going back and refining that code' (FG5). The retrievals are used to 'flesh out' the code before going on to the next retrieval. Another strategy by which retrieval can inform coding is to count the frequency with which given terms appear: 'I started to look at what my codes were and what they meant, then I did counts to see what sort of things were repeatedly happening and from that I then had to select a very small amount of data' (FG1). The small portion of data which was selected was then the focus of detailed analysis. The data set was subdivided and each part then treated as thematically coherent. The retrieval process was thereafter conducted separately by theme (each was a different conversational 'phenomenon'): 'breaking the data up into relevant topics so that you take one topic and then form your data sets, you feed in so many cases with just the material on that topic. That way you can have several data sets, one from each topic that you want, and it makes it much more manageable' (FG1). As this (confident) user went on to say, 'if you go through and just look at the content and then divide it up then you can work in detail, because there is no point going a whole day coding up something that is not going to be in most of the data set' (FG1). This approach might represent too heavy a reliance on the quantitative analysis of content, and too much separation of the theme-relevant data from the rest of the text, for some qualitative researchers. But, for most users, a procedure by which broad initial codings are subsequently specified by work with retrievals emerges as a standard approach: 'that first stage of coding and how you are thinking . . . comes prior to the [package] and then . . . the stage where I wanted some more complex codes I did that by pulling out data that were to do with the initial codes' (FG1). Similarly, 'I knew looking at my data and . . . the ideas I had before that, that I did have hierarchical codes, and also that

I might not be quite sure about what they were going to be at the initial stages and I might want that flexibility of being able to move things around' (FG5). Thus it is quite usual to subdivide the data as one refines the coding.

Elaborating Category Systems

If the coding process can be characterized as dividing up the data, recombining it, subdividing it, reassembling it, in the search for patterns and analytic themes, the retrieval process has something of a behind-the-scenes role. As we have seen, there are a host of retrieval strategies: retrievals of all data in a category, retrievals aimed at supporting numerical counts, hypothesis-testing retrievals testing propositional forms, retrievals by respondent characteristics, retrievals aimed at establishing formal relationships, retrievals aimed at exploring substantive relationships, retrievals using Boolean operators and those employing set logic. But this aspect of analytic procedure attracts limited coverage in the methods literature or in methods teaching. On the evidence of our sample, one strategy still predominates: retrieving all the data in a category, to be used to illustrate the category. Further, researchers raise serious reservations about doing anything more systematic than this. Once again the case of contract researchers comes forward. The following is a highly explicit account of the sponsor's heavy-handed push to take a verificationist approach. 'Reasons they don't use [package] for their categorization [is] based on policy customers and their requirements, who basically say "tell us about X, Y and Z in relation to this, particularly benefits". And they are saying that their requirements of the research is such that they have to draw up headings and do the transcripts. Although it's called qualitative research it is very much just about getting some quotes to use . . . Qualitative packages are not suitable for that because the freedom to wander round and analyse and make categories is not required by the customers. Therefore they have used [package] in the past but they are not using it now' (FG4). Asked what these researchers did use, the answer was 'charts, just charts with headings, interview transcripts down the side, what fits here, what factors are next, somebody in that column and not that column . . . They know what they want to find before they start' (ibid.).

Even in an ideal world free of sponsor and time pressures, researchers need convincing that formal retrieval strategies are consistent with the nature of qualitative data. It is as if qualitative researchers have taken to heart the criticism that such data are 'soft', lacking in reliability and external validity, subject to reflexivity, reactivity, and the relativist critique. It might also be that researchers find it most comfortable to press on with familiar techniques and, in the absence of external pressure for greater rigour, continue to produce reports of a sort that sponsors expect to read and analyses that peers and supervisors can readily validate by reference to established procedures. However, if the accepted ways of validating data collected in the field have any merit, we should be able to estimate the reliability and validity of our data, and thus be able to employ the systematic, selective retrieval strategies as well as those which feed the reader illustrative quotes. The place of retrievals in the analytic process can to some extent be inferred from the various strategies we have noted. But with the exception of the retrieving-all-data-in-a-category approach, we can say that the object of these strategies is ultimately to elaborate category systems. It might be to test a system which one has generated inductively or derived deductively, but this in itself will extend the conceptualization. In other cases, the retrieval is overtly oriented to building on the initial category system, perhaps by fleshing out a hierarchy of codes. So how do users go about elaborating the category systems upon which their conceptualization is based?

We have already encountered the researcher who performed a highly selective retrieval based on counts of frequently occurring topics in order to identify three features of talk for a conversation analysis. The steps in elaborating the category system were (1) coding by type of discourse strategy, (2) the count of frequencies of types of discourse within the interviews, (3) selection of three from the set of types, (4) checking for deviant cases where an identified discourse form was used to another purpose than that observed in other cases and (5) detailed conversation analysis of the three identified forms (done off-line). Thus, 'I managed to come out with three interesting phenomena from the data. One was how people downgrade their talk and make something less of an event than it was, and how people upgrade their talk and make something sound more than it was, and the other area that came out was sensitive issues, where they are talking about sensitive topics. From that I was able to just pull out those examples to work on for more analysis' (FG1). A similar case involved retrieval by respondent in a study where area of residence was thought to influence expressed attitude toward a development project having environmental implications. 'The [package] is [used] to identify where the people are, and then we have to split it, and go to those segments and look at them ourselves. We might dig them out and then decide the relevant ones' (FG1). In both cases the elaboration is relatively flat or shallow, involving only a small number of iterations. It is also the case that once the initial round of retrievals was done the analytic action took place off-line. There is little sign in these cases of the researcher going more 'micro' by subdividing data from the initial retrieval and performing comparative retrievals within it, although in one example there is a check for deviant cases. Nor is there any sign of a macro-level attempt, say, to wrap together the three discourse types into a more general conceptualization of discourse strategies.

We are not commenting on the quality of the analyses thus produced.

We are, however, suggesting that the sophisticated conceptual elaboration foreseen by developers who have included theory-building features in their packages elicits rather little mention among our respondents. There were signs that instead it was happening in the off-line work – 'the content codes sometimes make you shift the theoretical balance, because you begin to see data emerging from [a] different balance from what you expected, and then your more complex codes come from that. You've got your sheet and then you do the thinking, and then you start again' (FG1). Again, there is no demerit in this happening off-line, although the researcher has to do without some of the features such as hypertext and memoing that can facilitate elaboration. However, there appears to be a limited awareness of the features available to support conceptualization, and indeed a tendency to construe conceptualizing as a homogeneous and discrete activity rather than a set of procedures, several of which can be aided by software.

Indeed, a user who remarked, 'it is a very useful way to index things but the analysis and thinking is done by the user, it has to be' (FG3) proceeded to describe her own package use in terms that clearly did indicate it having an analytic role, although we would not dispute that, of course, the thinking (at every stage) is being done by the user. In this case, the software was also aiding data collection in line with Becker and Geer's 'sequential analysis' process: 'I'll print out a code and index category and comments to see how the index and category as well has developed but I'm still trying to get all my transcripts on before I go out of the field, so I have used it for some supplementary searches, it is quite interesting to see how your coding develops' (FG3). In sequential analysis, a preliminary conceptualization is used to guide further fieldwork, for example by adding new items to an interview schedule, with the resulting data then used to elaborate the preliminary conceptualization and so on. The most basic way that category schemes are elaborated is by adding new codes. 'A disadvantage and an advantage, you can create new codes as you are coding, so that can lead you completely up the garden path so you get a ridiculous situation where you are coding each person's [transcript] and then you think you have to go back and put that on other interviews' (FG3). Apart from the fact that it is hard to see a case for not coding each individual transcript, one might observe that, time-consuming as it is, adding refinement by recoding produces an analysis which more closely reflects the data and, if one embraces this basic precept of grounded theory, it is a lot easier to do using a computer than manually.

One thing that seems to inhibit the elaboration of coding systems by code revision is the granularity of the codes initially assigned. The following exchange begins with a comment on retrieval, returns to the problem of changing codes and culminates in a statement implying that, despite using broad codes that were very likely to require revision, the revision itself was then done manually. Note that we have commended the use of broad codes for the initial sift but have predicated this on the basis that inevitably these will be superseded and/or extended. 'I found the computer, once you got it transcribed and on [the machine], then . . . the coding and the . . . drawing out [retrieval] given all the codes, was quick. But that presupposes that you don't change your mind about what you want to do as you go along . . . I started off looking at one particular thing and then I suddenly think something else is more, is really interesting looking at another concept, I've not coded that . . . When you are doing your transcribing you come up with a lot of the categories. I coded on fairly broad categories . . . Once I had got all the quotes about different areas I tended to do it by hand what different people had said about this particular area' (FG4). Since it is a simple matter to retrieve by respondent (particularly in the package being discussed) the comment suggests underutilization of what the package offers. Thus, even when we find evidence of a selective retrieval it might be restricted by not fully exploiting the software.

If we do regard 'building' theory as a series of stages, with elaboration of the category system one stage within it, then we should further subdivide the elaboration process. We have already suggested that there is an issue about the breadth of coding, with a move from broad to more specific codes. Procedures like hypothesis testing (or work with closely specified propositions) do rely on relatively fine-grained codes. '[H]ypothesis testing only works if your coding categories are very narrow. We had great broad coding categories so we couldn't use it in that way. We were basically only using [package] for text retrieval, so that we were coding it and retrieving those codes and analysing that piece of data. We found it is probably easier to do that straight from the transcript . . . The next round of interviews when they use smaller coding categories, depending on how time-consuming it is, maybe use that' (FG4).

For some, the use of CAQDAS imposed little change on their way of analysing qualitative data because they were less persuaded by the idea of 'emergence', feeling that there was always an element of verification because no researcher could realistically approach a project with an entirely 'blank' mind. 'I am not entirely convinced about the idea of being creative that goes with grounded theory . . . What it does allow you to do is to be flexible and try things out and scrap them or change them around without committing yourself to doing something . . . I don't think my thinking about my data has been significantly changed by using [package] yet. I am not using it maybe as grounded theory people would expect to use it but I don't know whether I can, I don't know whether I can sit there and these ideas will just emerge out of the data. I think you always have some preconceived ideas to guide what you are looking at . . . Just using it to legitimize preconceived ideas but I think you always do that to a certain extent, so I don't have a feel of it particularly being creative' (FG5). This was met by the rejoinder that, yes, the open mind was a myth, but so was the fully worked out prior mental set. Thus, 'the creative, unknown element or maybe the open element, which is there for you to mould, is the way in which you establish these indexing systems and the creative ways in which you can potentially organize your data and just rethink relationships and say . . . "What happens if I do this, let's try this" . . . So there are those spaces that are unexplored and when we explore them something maybe pops up. Maybe something doesn't but that affirms something else . . . It doesn't necessarily enhance that, it just allows that to take place at a more proficient level. It allows you to keep track of those thoughts, ideas and developments, better than doing it on paper and writing through ideas, when you are working with files and moving things around, when you always have a paper trail of it on-line and it's fast and you can do it with a lot of data' (FG5). Getting to grips with this approach had led this user to a change in the way he classified or coded the data. 'The idea of keywords, keywords from my respondents, from books, keywords to be applied as an index node, it's something I've become more acutely aware of, i.e., my forms of categorization have changed slightly, they haven't changed from what I was thinking before, the way in which I categorize data has changed, [so] as to allow for easy facilitation into [package] store [i.e. the database]' (FG5). A similar account was given of someone who had not at the start structured the data in a way that would allow retrievals between commensurate categories, and consequently did not continue using CAQDAS. 'It comes back to [whether] you [are] willing in the middle of your research to go through and change the way you have coded this . . . to make it usable . . . If you are halfway through [the analysis] the investment just doesn't seem to be there, whereas . . . we have actively attempted to adopt the necessary structure, and made this part of the early stages' (FG5).

Looking at elaborating categorization as a series of steps we earlier drew on the distinction between case constant codes and codes assigned to represent particular analytic themes. The resulting structure of the coding scheme closely affects what retrievals might be performed. In the following, a methods advisor is discussing her colleague's doctoral project. 'I was trying to draw a tree yesterday from one of your sets of data [turning to another respondent]. The base data may actually be "these are my primary sources, these are my secondary sources, these are my primary sources on-line, these are my secondary sources on-line, these are my off-line", and you begin to make trees of that kind. What you might then do is have a broad structure in which [the] . . . thematic analysis is actually a completely separate "tree". And then maybe another tree about people, the informants and so on. Then you will have to start drawing across the lower nodes comparing a particular ethnic background in the case of [occupational group], working in the particular kind of situation, for their views, etc.' (FG5). As the extract suggests, the structure of the category system has a close effect on the retrieval pattern. This is one reason it is useful to be able to revise the category system and to automate recoding. The respondent being addressed countered with a different structure. 'An example of the base data that I've got running would be something like [occupational group 1, occupational group 2, etc.] . . . and those would all be different categories within one base data of interviews. Another base data group would be something like conferences, where people have transcribed them and I have used that as raw data. Now from there you can do analysis of given speakers and of different voices, by positioning them . . . These [occupational group members] have a particular position in my research. I have to grapple with what they are saying in relation to what [their] power is, what impact they have' (FG5). This pair of extracts illustrates the kind of thinking associated with working with 'demographic data' and type-of-sources (analogous to 'fields' in the distinction between 'cases' and 'fields'), as in the first extract, and with thematic and type-of-source data, as in the second extract.

Some users contrasted the output of CAQDAS packages and that of statistical packages in order to make the point that CAQDAS was a tool and its use an interim stage in analysis. The output of statistical software represented a report which was close to being 'the findings' while qualitative software output was an interim step. The 'outline' idea in the following represents the product of retrievals intended to elaborate the categorization. 'It is a new way of writing outlines . . . a stage prior to the writing up . . . A way in which to hold outlines, to sustain links and relationships between data and theory in the computer environment' (FG5). As such, the conceptualization in the package was always interim, 'a sort of analytic framework that can be put down and later to go back and be picked up and played with' (ibid.). An implication of the elaboration process is that 'there is never any given point where the program says "OK, you now have enough data". It's infinite. It can go on infinitely. This process of becoming self-reflexive – you can take data you have analysed and re-analyse it and reanalyse that' (FG5). Here is another test of whether the computer is 'doing the thinking'; it cannot make this crucial decision, cannot indicate closure (although it can report on such things as how much data has been coded, with precision). 'One of the crucial issues is deciding when to quit, deciding when you have got the maximum yield . . . you could carry on splitting and splitting, there is no physical limit to that. It becomes a matter of your own research criteria. [Colleague] decided that this was something they wanted to come back to. They wanted to hold the data in this form and reanalyse it in that form later. It's not a monolithic relationship' (FG5).

Thus the 'relationship' between the data, the category system, and the final analysis, was not something to be settled in one 'round' of work with the category system. Here we encounter an important hint of what might lie behind resistance to CAQDAS use in general and full exploitation of conceptualizing features in particular. The respondent in the previous extract makes play with the distinction between mechanical or practical-procedural elements of the work of analysis and those which are creative, intellectual and conceptual. Thus, if the package were merely an aid to the former, mechanical, kinds of tasks then we would expect it to do something like signal 'you have enough data' or 'you have taken the analysis as far as it will go on the data available'. Of course, the software cannot do this. Let us consider a comment from a user who encountered many difficulties – both practical and conceptual – in her use of CAQDAS. '[T]he way we worked before this contract is to write in interpretations on the transcripts themselves, things about concepts, in the process of writing as one does, that is what I think [co-worker] found more difficult than I did to shift from. So to see [package] as a mechanical process primarily rather than being an intellectually interpretive process, that was the difficulty, and I don't think we have resolved it. And we have now abandoned it and gone back to our old way of doing it' (FG1).

If we consider 'manual' qualitative analysis it is essentially a process of reading (the data) and writing (the analysis). There is an interim, organizing stage, 'cut-and-paste'. But the emphasis has always been on gaining creative insight, which 'emerges' from the data but is not wholly bound by it (this informs 'axial' and 'selective' coding as compared to 'open' coding). It is true that there are more or less systematic renderings of the interim process, and a sign of how hotly contested the role of the interim stages can be is the earlier-remarked critique by Glaser of his former colleague Strauss's reformulation of grounded theory (Glaser, 1992). But qualitative researchers have largely construed their analytic work as lying well to the inductive end of the spectrum, and as an intellectual process where the 'value added' comes from the analyst's creative insight rather than from the data. Now let us consider how this maps onto the use of software for analysis, as opposed to data management. Qualitative software takes the analytic process and subdivides it, in order to provide a set of features to support the researcher's reasoning. There is a mechanical element to these procedures: the data need to be structured 'just so', consistency of coding is necessary, the researcher needs to make particular steps in a particular sequence, and so on. There is also something of an encouragement to think deductively. Used to construing 'analysis' as a solidary ('monolithic') stage in the process, the researcher's sense of control and creativity is challenged. Looking again at the extract, our frustrated user says, 'so to see [package] as a mechanical process primarily rather than being an intellectually interpretive process, that was the difficulty, and I don't think we have resolved it'. We think this is a very apt expression of the frustration we have all experienced when confronted with recalcitrant software. But we do not agree that this package (a moderately sophisticated code-and-retrieve), or the others, in fact construes analysis as a mechanical process. Rather, they construe it as a process with more stages, involving more iterations, and involving oscillations between 'mechanical' and 'intellectual' elements, and this does decidedly contrast with the seamless feel of analysis before the computer. We need hardly add that seamlessness concealed quirky interpretations, false assumptions, the elevation of data that supported pet perspectives and a variety of other bad practices, just as it also produced the elegant insight and profound exemplars which have made it possible for qualitative research not only to survive but to inspire.

To this thought might be added the observation that students – as Strauss and Corbin recognized – are most likely to confront the relatively unsystematic procedures of qualitative analysis with its harshest challenge. Their supervisors, committees and examiners are looking for a display of 'rigour', of having moved carefully through a series of orderly steps. Once this pressure is off and the qualitative researcher is 'licensed' as a member of the community, corners might be cut. We think this might be behind the fact that, in our sample, it was postgraduate students who tended to express most enthusiasm about package use, and contract researchers and established academics who were most sceptical. The 'adepts' grow impatient with being obliged to dismember an analytic process they have learned to treat as seamless and whose steps have become so intuitive and implicit that they are no longer experienced as discrete stages at all, while novices welcome the way that packages break the process up into accessible units. Further, novices are less likely to be committed to particular schools of thought and analytic preoccupations, and less likely to read the routines for the retrieval procedure as pushing them down a particular construction of the analytic process.

We have already suggested that, insofar as qualitative researchers recognize an interim stage between the mechanical and the intellectual, the position is occupied by the cut-and-paste procedures. Here, researchers are accustomed to an interplay between the practical and the creative: 'your codes and categories have to be theoretically informed' (FG3) and 'those ideas come in some parts from reading but also very often intuitive feel, you develop the codes after that' (FG3). In CAQDAS, the recoding might be represented by identifying new boundaries of segments and assigning a new label: 'Were you still attaching those new codes, your month four codes to the same bits of text?' 'Sometimes I'd reduce and sometimes they'd enlarge . . . As I work more and more on the theoretical ones [codes], I'd want to work on different data, not necessarily less, sometimes a lot more, than the first one, but I kept the first one in the data set so that I could go back and see how I had changed it' (FG6). Again, the elaboration of the categorization was a coding stage activity. In one case a user of a package with a feature for graphically representing the coding scheme had been unable to use the feature because it was not available in the version of the package at her university. Instead, 'for me it's the creation of codes, a coding system, which is the real thinking bit . . . I had quite a lot of preconceived ideas, I could see from the interviews I'd done there were certain themes that each interview fell into. I'd got a set of questions that I asked and ideas came up commonly, and I was trying to develop, over-ambitiously, a coding system which would take account of all of that in one go before I started to do the coding, and I fiddled around trying to get something which adequately explained everything I wanted to include, left out the bits I wasn't interested in, had mutually exclusive and clearly defined codes' (FG5). Such 'fiddling around' can be facilitated by CAQDAS, but, despite intending to use a package at subsequent stages, the user put great effort into refining the coding scheme off-line. Such testimony might account for our impression that the elaboration of category systems is largely happening during the coding stage rather than the later, analytic stages which have been the focus of the developers' efforts in providing features to support elaboration. It is not the same work but it appears to be the main point at which categorization is elaborated.

We noted above the case of a researcher who had tried to construct an elaborate category system prior to coding. This researcher was in fact defeated by the effort and changed tack by working within her theory-building package. 'I decided it was too complicated, got in a complete mess, and thought that I would start again and use [package's] capacity to build up as you go along, and start with something very simple. And that's working much more successfully . . . [Package] is helping me by letting me start on something small, then develop. So what I've been doing is looking for one theme which . . . I can define clearly in my head, so it's quite easy to pick out certain paragraphs in the interviews, coding those with a general code and then going for, say, a sample of 12 interviews, going back looking for common themes, and then coding the next level down from that, and then going back and doing that again, and gradually building up small networks, and [package] is allowing me to change things around, collapse two codes into one, or divide them up' (FG5). We also identified a case where a measure of explicit technophobia inhibited the full exploitation of a quite straightforward code-and-retrieve package. Again, the elaboration effort was construed and acted on purely as a coding-stage activity. 'I use the very basic sort [procedure] to begin with and that's all. It is partly because I am used to it but partly [the] coward's way out, daren't risk if things go wrong. But also some of the things are fairly subtle and complicated and I think it would take so long to organize the material that I might as well have done it manually anyway' (FG3).

Thus, users are doing with software what they are used to doing manually (and draw the conclusion that the software is largely a device for clerical data management). The rhetoric of package documentation in some cases encourages this approach. The key methods literature – virtually all written pre-CAQDAS – devotes considerable attention to coding. It has little to say about visualizing categorical relationships, because this is hard to do without electronic graphic displays, little to say about formally specified retrievals, and issues of internal and external validity are treated by reference back to fieldwork/data collection considerations rather than to procedures involving, for example, quantification for the purpose of content analysis, or systematic cross-corpus checks on the patterns of key terms used.

Yet these are the features and procedures upon which developers set considerable store as the means by which their packages aid conceptualization and even theory building. These claims encounter substantial resistance at the same time as the features are little used, even by people well acquainted with CAQDAS. Here is a dialogue on these lines. '[T]he process of building theory is the process of making connections between different things that people say. [Package] can't make those connections. It can't say "this chunk of transcript about family relations obviously links into economic difficulties with sending money to your relatives" . . . It seems obvious to me but it can't make that connection. "You can relate to different levels up and down [the coding hierarchy] and do matrix searches." "But, OK, matrices are quite crude, and what is interesting about what people say is looking at things which don't apparently fit in with [your coding system]. For instance, I'm poor because I send all my money to relatives, so family relations and poverty are connected, and then people who don't fit into that, and how you can adjust your theory. So your matrix might say the same but your contextual understanding of why people said what they said, and whether they are exceptions or whether you have to cue your code in to them, that's all a very different process from building matrices"' (FG3). Matrices might indeed be a convenient device for organizing data, and merely a step towards a heuristic, but the notable thing about the extract is that (apart from the familiar undertone that 'computers can't think') the winnowing, case-comparative and deviant case analysis discussed are all readily done by CAQDAS, and indeed do not require software as highly developed as the package the researcher was using.

Another user with experience of a theory-building package picked up the theme. 'I can spend an afternoon just playing with it, put together codes, combine this one with this one and see what I get, but . . . as I've gone through I've been aware I have to put it together to contextualise information . . . I would go through and write memos, "so and so has said this, how does that relate to other situations, what happens when they are in different financial circumstances" . . . You can do this node-builder exercise and combine codes. I've looked at it and said, can you do it in [package] by combining these codes and excluding something else, but the bottom line comes from who does it – you have to' (FG3). Again we encounter the red herring about computers thinking, but we also hear a description of a specified retrieval in the service of elaborating the category system ('combining these codes and excluding something else'). In fact, this user's conclusion was that 'the theory building comes from you, [package] can help it'. Remarkably enough, it seems that there are those who have been led by rumour to suppose that there are indeed 'thinking' packages. 'I must have, in the last year, talked to a dozen people who have said I've heard there are packages that can theorize. There seem to be both relatively inexperienced researchers, and some quite senior academics, who have got the impression via second-hand reporting . . . that there are packages that do it all for you: "So you drop the stuff in one end, and it comes out the other, almost completely written for you" ' (FG4). We might dismiss the problem as being merely a matter of terminology, were it not for our impression that features beyond code-and-retrieve are largely being ignored. 'Theory' is a contentious term, as this comment on hypothesis-testing features suggests. 'I could use it . . . not to develop theory but to test certain types of propositions about the fact that people might find polar evaluations, the whole concept of polarity being central to personal construct theory. Trying to look for ways in which people's evaluations involve plausible poles and constraints would be a way of using this, but again that isn't building a theory. That is, "testing", using theoretical framework to explore data or demonstration of whether people's evaluations [are] bipolar, and I don't think that is theory build-ing at all' (FG3). There are many who would not agree, feeling that such 'testing' is a part of building theory.

   We can approach this matter of building theory from a different perspec-tive: those who have entertained great expectations and been led to the view that, while these are not met, something useful is available which is essentially a suite of various means to elaborate category systems. 'I heard that [package] was based on grounded theory, notions of theory build-ing . . . For me it was very important to maintain a certain link between a field, a real grounded, real world aspect through which theory has been built and upon which theory has been applied. Using the software was a way to pull these two worlds together. The reality of it is that the capaci-ties of theory building are not what I had initially envisaged . . . Certain things can be achieved, and other things can't, and certain other things can be achieved that I didn't expect' (FG5). Of particular appeal was the package's approach to the data indexing system. The refinement of theor-etical bases within grounded theory was well served by having an index-ing system one could manipulate. Once there was a fully coded data set, with data being coded under several different codes, attention naturally shifted to the indexing system. This user felt that once he had described each interview in a number of different categories he did not have to worry about that interview any longer and 'you feel very in touch with your data, you feel very much that you have reviewed it, you have seen it, it's a very physical experience, you are very close to it. As well, you feel confident about building that indexing system into an increasingly theor-etical system' (FG5). The extract suggests that simply wishing to bring a set of formal conceptualizing features to bear does not imply any weaken-ing of the emphasis on grounding the conceptualization in the data. Before this respondent embarked on the elaboration of the category system using various formal retrieval strategies he had assiduously coded each item of data. Indeed, there had been a coding-based elaboration of the category system in that process. Again, analysis on this model is a series of steps, rather than a discrete and somewhat opaque act of 'writing up'.

7

Computer Analysis and Qualitative Research: New Directions

In this chapter we step away from our empirical material. Specifically we look at what are to date less commonly used approaches, a variety of formal analytic methods, as well as analytic approaches based on hyper-text. While they differ radically from each other, each is a good example of how the computer facilitates novel means for the analysis of qualitative data.

Formal Analytic Methods

Qualitative Comparative Analysis (QCA), an analytic method proposed by Ragin (1987), is based on Boolean algebra, the algebra of sets and logic. This is not a field traditionally associated with qualitative research. (Indeed, early applications of the field were mostly in electrical engineering, in the design of logic circuits like those found in a computer.) However, Boolean concepts and terminology have become increasingly familiar to qualitative researchers as computer software for qualitative data analysis became more widespread. Many programs, for example, allow the analyst to search textual material using the standard Boolean operators AND, OR, NOT.

QCA provides a simple, compact, if somewhat restricted, way of analysing patterns of causation in a small to moderate number of cases. (The method is also known as qualitative configuration analysis: Huber and García, 1991.) Suppose you are interested in worker resistance to plant closures in manufacturing industry. Detailed examination of qualitative case materials such as documents, media reports and interviews might suggest that resistance was linked in some way to the availability of various institutional supports (Rothstein, 1986). Table 7.1 shows hypo-thetical data which associate the presence or absence of worker resistance in particular cases with four conditions. These are: (a) the early involve-ment of national trade union officials following the announcement of the closure (designated as ETU in the table), (b) a plant location within a monoindustrial region (MIN), (c) high local support for a party or parties of the left (LPS), (d) the availability of funds for regional development (RDF). Each row of the table represents a particular case. The last column of the row shows the output variable, worker resistance. A code of 1 is used to indicate that resistance occurred. A 0 indicates the absence of resistance. The row as a whole can be read as indicating the combination of the four conditions associated with the outcome for that case. Again, in each instance, presence is indicated by a 1, absence by a 0.

Unlike the data matrix in quantitative research, where the analytic focus is on variables displayed in the *columns* of the table, it is the *rows* in the table which are important here. What is being examined for each row is the *configuration* of causes associated with the presence or absence of the outcome for that case (Ragin, 1994: 112). As Ragin points out, focusing on configurations of conditions and outcomes has a number of implications. First, it allows for the possibility that different combinations of conditions can generate the same general outcome. Second, contradictory patterns of causation can be accommodated. In combination with some variables, a particular condition might generate a positive outcome; with some other variables a negative one. Third, it is possible to eliminate irrelevant causes. As shown below, the pattern of configurations might allow you to conclude that the presence of a particular condition is not essential to the production of the outcome under consideration.

QCA proceeds by means of 'Boolean minimization'. While this procedure can be carried out by hand, it rapidly becomes tedious for anything other than a small number of cases. Computer programs, such as QCA and AQUAD, are now available which implement the necessary procedures (Drass, 1992; Huber and García, 1991). The first step in the process is to produce a 'truth table'. A truth table lists 'the various combinations of independent variables that appear in a data set along with their corresponding values [*sic*] on the dependent variable. Configurations appear only once in a truth table, regardless of their frequency of occurrence in the data' (Drass, 1992: 6). A truth table having been constructed, the configurations within it are then simplified. (A clear exposition of the principles involved is given in Ragin, 1987; see also Ragin, 1994: Chapter 5. The method for simplifying configurations is based on a well-established procedure known as the Quine-McCluskey algorithm.)

Table 7.1 *Worker resistance to plant closures (hypothetical data)*

Case	ETU	MIN	LPS	RDF	Resistance
A	0	0	1	1	1
B	1	0	1	0	0
C	0	1	1	1	0
...					
n	1	0	0	1	1

Briefly, and non-technically, the computer systematically compares each configuration in the truth table with all the other configurations. The aim of this procedure is to simplify the truth table by removing configurations through combination. The rule for doing this is as follows (Ragin, 1994: 125):

> If two rows of a truth table differ on only one causal condition yet result in the same outcome, then the causal condition that distinguishes the two rows can be considered irrelevant and can be removed to create a simpler combination of causal conditions (a simpler term).

To take an example, suppose in considering configurations in Table 7.1 you had two cases. (Upper-case letters indicate the presence of a condition, lower-case letters that it is absent. The dot [·] between the terms signifies an AND relation.)

CASE I: ETH·MIN·LPS·rdf = RESISTANCE
CASE J: ETH·min·LPS·rdf = RESISTANCE

In Case I, worker resistance occurs in the presence of the early involvement of national trade union officials, where the plant is located in a monoindustrial region, where there is local support for a left party or parties and where regional development funds are unavailable. In Case J, worker resistance occurs in the presence of the early involvement of national trade union officials and local support for a left party or parties. It also occurs in a plant not located in a monoindustrial region and where regional development funds are unavailable. Notice resistance occurs when the plant is located in a monoindustrial region in one case but not in the other. Clearly, therefore, it is not necessary for a plant to have a monoindustrial location for resistance to occur. As a result, we can combine the two configurations by excluding location in a monoindustrial region as a condition. This yields:

ETH·LPS·rdf = RESISTANCE

In other words, resistance occurs in the presence of early involvement by trade union officials, local support for a left party or parties and the absence of regional development funds. As Ragin comments (1994: 124):

> [This] simplification strategy follows the logic of an experiment. Only one condition at a time is allowed to vary (the 'experimental' condition). If varying this condition has no discernible impact on the outcome, it can be eliminated as an outcome.

Using the procedure outlined above one attempts to combine as many rows of the truth table as possible. These can be simplified further in a further process of minimization. This produces a Boolean expression which contains only the logically essential 'prime implicants'.

QCA has a number of strengths. As Ragin (1987) stresses, it is a holistic strategy designed to produce complex yet intelligible formulations; the procedure, moreover, is an inherently inductive one which proceeds in a methodical stepwise manner. QCA 'maximizes causal complexity', as Coverdill et al. (1994: 57) put it. Traditional multivariate methods emphasize goodness-of-fit or variance explained as criteria of analytic potency (Lieberson, 1985). By contrast QCA seeks to recover the complexity of particular situations by recognizing the conjunctural and context-specific character of causation. Unlike much qualitative analysis, the method forces researchers to select cases and variables in a systematic manner. This reduces the likelihood that 'inconvenient' cases will be dropped from the analysis or data forced into inappropriate theoretical moulds.

While acknowledging the 'tremendous potential of QCA', Amenta and Poulsen comment that it is a 'deceptively simple approach' (1994: 34; see also Griffin et al., 1991). One way in which the simplicity of QCA is deceptive is in the specification of input conditions. The first problem that arises is how to choose candidates for inclusion as input conditions. Amenta and Poulsen point out that

> Combinations of dichotomous variables grow exponentially from a base of two, and thus a large number of independent conditions makes QCA unwieldy and decreases the likelihood that any given combination will have an empirical referent or will be theoretically interpretable. Moreover, the larger the number of independent conditions, the more likely that each possible combination with a case in it will have only that one case. (1994: 23)

According to Amenta and Poulsen, a number of strategies for identifying suitable input conditions can be envisaged, none of which is entirely satisfactory. One might, for example, attempt a 'comprehensive approach' in which all existing theories, hypotheses and explanations are scoured for likely variables that might be included in an analysis. Such an approach is cumbersome and likely to produce a hodge-podge of possible conditions lacking in theoretical substance. Alternatively, one might take a more selective tack based on specific theoretical perspectives or on factors suggested as potentially significant in existing variable-oriented research. Both these approaches, however, run the risk of ignoring potentially important variables. Nor do they provide clues as to which input conditions might be fruitfully combined. This leaves two further possibilities. One of these Amenta and Poulsen refer to as the 'second look' approach. Starting off with variables which existing quantitative research suggests are promising, the analyst looks again at variables rejected by this approach but which might be promising on theoretical grounds. The objection to this is obvious: the procedure is effectively an *ad hoc* one. Finally, Amenta and Poulsen advocate a 'conjunctural theory' approach which starts from the examination of theories which explicitly specify possible causal combinations for particular outcomes. It is not entirely clear, however, where these theories come from or how they relate to existing bodies of theory and data.

A second problem relating to the selection of input conditions is how they are to be defined and measured. QCA requires dichotomous input variables. If the original data sources are qualitative in character – interviews, documents and the like – what kinds of prior data reduction need to be carried out in order to select relevant input conditions? If source data are quantitative, how are ordinal or interval-level data to be handled? Moreover the method assumes that the way in which input variables are defined has no impact on the overall configuration of conditions and outputs produced by the analysis (Coverdill et al., 1994). Coverdill and his colleagues make a further point. Used as a tool for historical or comparative research, QCA has tended to be applied to sets of 'local' cases which are bounded and fairly easily delineated: revolutions in Latin America, for instance. Perhaps for that reason, issues to do with sample variability have been little discussed by its proponents. In consequence, as Coverdill et al. put it, 'Unless advocates of QCA can develop something akin to an analogue of the central-limit theorem for prime implicants, QCA is vulnerable to the charge that it capitalises on chance and may well produce wildly different results across samples' (1994: 90).

Assessments of this kind view QCA largely from the perspective of quantitative research. From a qualitative perspective Weitzman and Miles (1995) have reviewed the computer program developed by Drass and Ragin (Drass, 1992) to carry out QCA. They note that the version reviewed would not be easily accessible to someone who was unfamiliar with the concepts lying behind the method. However, usefully, they reanalyse data from an existing qualitative study. A matrix display of the kind described by Miles and Huberman (1994), showing factors affecting the implementation of an educational innovation, was recoded into a form suitable for entry into the program. Minimizing the truth table suggested a pattern not seen in the original visual scanning of the data. Even so, QCA is potentially at some disadvantage when judged against more conventional qualitative approaches. Firestone (1993) notes that the method does not easily handle process. Furthermore, as he goes on to point out, in QCA:

> the definitions of the situation and belief systems of those studied are at best reduced to simplified categories if not entirely ignored in favor of conceptually neat variables developed by the research. For highly analytic efforts at theory development, these losses may be minor. Yet they are some of the major reasons why people turn to qualitative research . . . [I]t remains to be seen whether this extremely formal approach can be included as part of a more traditional qualitative study or whether it tends to drive that part of the work out. (Firestone, 1993: 21)

One further issue needs to be borne in mind. QCA clearly has the potential to be used beyond the historical and cross-national contexts originally envisaged by Ragin. One thinks, following the example of classical analytic induction as employed by Lindesmith and Cressey, of fields like criminology. In such instances, however, the issue of data protection becomes important. Care might be needed when arraying individual-level case material in a data matrix or truth table. Even with the use of presence–absence dichotomies, some identification of individuals might be possible.

Hicks (1994) suggests that QCA has affinities with what he calls 'neo-analytic induction'. In using this term, Hicks recasts Robinson's distinction between analytic induction *as described* and analytic induction *in practice* as a distinction between 'classical analytic induction' and 'neo-analytic induction'. Neo-analytic induction extends classical analytic induction in three ways. First, like analytic induction in practice, neo-analytic induction does not look simply at cases where the phenomenon to be described is present; cases having negative outcomes as well as positive ones are examined. Second, rather than working with a succession of single cases, successive multiple-case comparisons are made. Finally, while neo-analytic induction aspires like classical analytic induction to universal solutions, it is willing to accept 'reasonable' theoretical closure some way short of that goal. Its aims are directed to the development of theory rather than theory testing.

It will be remembered that classical analytic induction involves a stepwise interplay of definition, hypothesis and data. An alternative to the kind of Boolean methods just described uses artificial intelligence techniques to recreate that interplay in a computer-supported form. Hesse-Biber and her colleagues (1991) have developed HyperResearch, a program on which our respondents' views were noted earlier. It is explicitly designed to allow a process of cycling back and forth between theory and data in order to aid the refinement of definitions and the formulation and reformulation of hypotheses. The vehicle for doing this is an expert system that allows the analyst to develop a set of production rules governing the subsequent computer-generated inspection of cases. The analyst starts by specifying sets of codes which have already been attached to segments of data. (These are in present versions of the program text segments. Future versions promise to support analysis of graphical, audio and video materials.) These codes might be related to one another in simple or complex ways using the Boolean operators, AND, OR, NOT. Production rules have an IF–THEN form. A rule can be established such that if a specified configuration of codes is found in a particular case, then a particular conclusion can be added to the rule-base. In this way, as Mangabeira (1995: 133) puts it, 'the creation of production rules describes the inference of one or more new codes, which were not derived directly from the data but inferred from the presence or absence of certain codes in the case being analyzed'.

Hesse-Biber et al. provide an example of how the production rule system might be used to analyse data from a study of eating disorders among college-age women. A rule might take the form:

For a given case,
IF code A is present
AND code B is present
AND code C is present
THEN ADD code D.

Or, to use the specific instance given by Hesse-Biber et al.: if a case has been coded 'mother is critical of daughter's body image' and also coded 'mother and daughter relationship strained' and coded 'daughter is experiencing weight loss' as well, then the code 'mother's negative influence on daughter's self image' is added to that case. Sets of rules and conclusions can be chained together to produce further and more complex chains of implication. For each chain of inference, a terminal rule or goal is specified. This goal can be thought of as a hypothesis about the nature of the inferred relationships in the data.

The program can be run against a full or partial set of cases to test the hypothesis embodied in the production rules. The program applies the rule-set to each case. If the codes specified by each rule are found in the case, the rule is fired (i.e. invoked) to add the new rule to the rule-base. If all the rules in the set fire successfully, the goal is reached and the hypothesis is said to be supported. A rule evaluates to false (or fails) if the codes specified in that rule are found to be absent from that case. If a rule fails, subsequent rules are evaluated until no further rules are available for that case. The program reports for each case the success or failure of each rule and whether or not the terminal rule or goal – the hypothesis – has been reached. Thus the rule given above would fail in a particular case if the code 'mother and daughter relationship strained' had not been applied to that case. A hypothesis based on the relationship of that rule to a series of other rules would be said not to have been supported. Hypothesis testing in HyperResearch is not a once-for-all event. Instead it can be considered as having a diagnostic character. Where and how rules fail can be used to assess the adequacy of coding, identify negative cases and/or evaluate the researcher's theoretical assumptions. From this can be initiated a process of code refinement and hypothesis reformulation in the manner of classical analytic induction.

There are some weaknesses in all of this. First of all, the prospect of 'proving' a hypothesis might tempt researchers into relaxing coding definitions or making rules so slack that they cannot fail to fire. One of our focus group participants, for example, expressed unease at a colleague who, as she put it, 'used [the program] to look for data that backed up his theory'. Second, the hypothesis-testing procedure in HyperResearch is open to logical objections (Richards and Richards, 1994; Kelle and Bird,

1995) of the kind Robinson advanced against analytic induction. A crucial issue here is the relationship between codes and text. Typically in qualitative analysis codes are not, as Kelle and Bird (1995: 23) put it, 'precisely defined Boolean facts'. In other words, they represent topics of interest to the researcher and which are present in the text rather than the presence or absence of a particular causal condition. From this point of view, adding a goal to the hypothesis is to subsume clusters of codes under an overarching search term (Richards and Richards, 1994). In consequence, and echoing Robinson, one has no means of identifying situations where the conditions specified in the production rules hold, but the goal is not met.

Even commentators who have adopted this view nevertheless welcome the heuristic benefits of a system which allows rapid and recurrent traffic between coded text and conceptual statements embodied in precisely specified sets of if-then rules. Furthermore, Hesse-Biber et al. stress the importance of directional coding rather than what they call 'coding for content'. To take the example they use, a code such as 'Self-image' is unhelpful when testing a hypothesis. It might in one case be applied in an instance where the respondent's self-image is positive and in another case where self-image is negative. Instead codes such as 'Positive self-image' and 'Negative self-image' should be applied explicitly. Hesse-Biber et al. also imply that researchers should think in terms of setting 'significance levels' for accepting or rejecting hypotheses. By this they do not, of course, mean the specification of a critical region under a sampling distribution in the manner of statistical hypothesis testing. Rather what they seem to have in mind is that researchers should pre-specify, presumably in a conservative manner, the number of cases for which a goal has to have been reached before a hypothesis is judged to be satisfied.

Mangabeira argues that embodying chains of analytic reasoning in production rule form tends to produce theoretical statements which have an ideal-typical form. (Interestingly, this echoes Turner's (1953) comment that Chicago School sociologists who used analytic induction frequently resorted to ideal-typical formulations when they tried to deal with complex and multifaceted situations rather than attempts to explain individual behaviour.) According to Mangabeira (1995: 137), 'If we think about HyperResearch results as ideal-types, the objective of the program can be understood as aiming towards the creation of provisional theoretical models.' The wording might be ambiguous here. Logically, a model cannot be a type; but it is not at all far-fetched to see the goal of a set of production rules as an ideal-typical construction. Once abstracted from empirical material, this construction stands over and against that material. Or, as Mangabeira goes on:

> The strength of the model is that it is to be compared over and over again with the empirical data. In this process, the model is refined and in this way gains greater levels of abstraction and explanatory power about social situations.

Finally, once arrived at a reasonably sustainable conclusion, the researcher can present it as a mental construct, as an abstraction which might orient future research about a certain sociological question. (1995: 137)

Expert Systems

The computer, while masquerading as technologically sophisticated, can be regarded as having a rather 'primitive' theory of knowledge (Lee and Fielding, 1991). Gerson (1984) points out that developments in artificial intelligence can be harnessed to aid the analysis of qualitative data, a possibility he characterized metaphorically as involving the transition from computer as clerk to computer as research assistant. Expert systems – a branch of artificial intelligence, the computer science specialism that seeks to emulate human cognitive processes – encapsulate the knowledge held by an expert in a particular field or domain. Such systems, which are also known as knowledge-based systems, have a variety of uses in qualitative research. Carley (1988) has developed a two-stage process for explicating the network of concepts and conceptual relationships within a verbal protocol. Coding a large number of protocols is tedious, time-consuming and prone to error. Coding assistants can be employed, but they rarely have sufficient background social knowledge to make fully explicit the definitions, connections and implications to be found within a protocol. Provided this knowledge has been made explicit for some of the data, it can be embodied within an expert system. In the first stage of the procedure Carley describes, assistants code protocols with the aid of a coding program, CODEF. An expert system, SKI, is then used to diagnose and correct errors and omissions in the initial coding produced by CODEF.

Fischer and Finkelstein (1991) have demonstrated the utility of computer-based formal methods for the description of fluid and socially intricate behaviour. Substantively their work is based on Fischer's (1991) study of arranged marriages in urban Pakistan. The arrangement of such marriages is a complex matter which involves a variety of interested parties and a pattern of preferences that shifts over time. Fischer and Finkelstein describe how, using a formal programming language, it was possible to develop an expert system which modelled this complex field of behaviour. Guided by recurrent periods of fieldwork, a set of production rules for the expert system was developed. This system predicted 'good' and 'bad' marriage choices. It also helped to broaden and deepen existing theoretical formulations as well as highlighting patterned deviations from customary practice. A further anthropological application of this kind can be found in the work of Kippen, who used an expert system to develop a formal model of the musical structures which underlie North Indian tabla drumming. The ability of the system to predict 'correct and aesthetically acceptable . . . pieces of music' (1988: 318) could then be tested on local musicians, comments from whom could be used to refine and develop the basic model. As Fischer and Finkelstein (1991) point out, gaps in a formal model which are revealed by consulting local informants in this way drive the search for new data by helping to target the researcher's efforts onto gaps in the existing knowledge base.

An important development in the application of artificial intelligence is provided by Yuen and Richards (1994). They describe a method of knowledge representation for the process of constructing grounded theory. Their approach is a hybrid one combining the use of fuzzy set theory and semantic networks. According to Yuen and Richards, the categories and relations within a theory can be represented as a semantic network in which theoretical categories form the nodes and the relations between categories the links. In qualitative research, data take the form of unstructured text. The relevance of a given segment of text to a theoretical category is therefore variable. To put this another way, the mapping of a theoretical category onto a data segment has a fuzzy character which needs to be represented by means of an ordinal ranking. This done, it is possible to develop a variety of indices which measure the extent to which categories overlap, include each other, or refer in common to a particular data segment. Overlap in particular is important because it shows the extent to which a category is relationally connected to other categories. Theoretical statements take the form of pairs of categories with a specified relation between them. Rank ordering the indices allows for the identification of such statements. These can be further elaborated into a semantic network which provides a theoretical representation of the data. It is also possible to derive an overall index of 'centredness'. Yuen and Richards suggest that by ranking categories in terms of their centredness a semantic network can be further transformed into a system of polar co-ordinates. The usefulness of this transformation is that it provides a graphical means for the identification of the core category among the set of theoretical statements, an important notion within grounded theory.

Hypertext

Writing in 1991 we identified hypertext as 'a potentially exciting development in the field of qualitative research, but one whose potential is only just beginning to be realized' (Fielding and Lee, 1991: 118). Although the concept of hypertext actually predates computers, the sense we were expressing was of something exotic, something novel. Today, any one of the millions of people who has used the World Wide Web will be familiar with how hypertext works. On the Web, one views 'pages' of text on a computer screen. Some of the words and phrases in the text are distinguished from surrounding text, perhaps through the use of colour or by being underlined or shown in bold. Clicking with the mouse on such a piece of text sends the user to another document which is linked electronically to the clicked word or phrase in the original document. Because the Web incorporates two technologies, hypertext and the Internet, one can 'jump' in this way to a document residing on a computer thousands of miles away. However, the principle of jumping from place to place and text to text can operate just as easily on a set of texts located on a single machine.

A number of existing qualitative analysis packages have at least some hypertext features, allowing one to jump, for example, from an item in a code list to the original source text. Some qualitative researchers have also experimented with fully fledged hypertext systems (Cordingley, 1991; Fischer, 1994; Weaver and Atkinson, 1995b). The attraction of such systems derives from the fact that

> In general, social scientists performing qualitative analysis are looking for insights which can then be systematically checked against evidence. They value flexible tools which can be used in a variety of ways – tools which can accommodate individual differences in analytic style *and* the changing needs of analysis as it progresses. They want tools which support analysis, but leave the analyst firmly in charge. (Cordingley, 1991: 165)

Hypertext allows information to be organized and linked in an associative non-linear way. Users can move rapidly and flexibly between information sources of various kinds. In a hypertext system one can organize and order text in multiple ways.

In their discussion of the potential of hypertext for qualitative analysis, Weaver and Atkinson (1995b) begin with the concept of a 'hyperspace'. Hyperspace is a geometric space defined by many dimensions. Weaver and Atkinson suggest that the human mind can be conceived of as a hyperspace characterized by associative networks. Within such networks nodes comprising information, concepts or ideas are 'structured by ordered, labelled relations or links' (1995b: 114). (Nodes can be defined broadly in terms of their form, and can include text, diagrams and audio-visual material: Fischer, 1994: 109.) From this point of view, hypertext might be thought of as multidimensional text. Since nodes and links form the basis for its structure, a hypertext database is organized in a way similar to the way in which knowledge is organized in the human mind. Thus, unlike traditional print media, where information is organized in a unidimensional, linear way, hypertext systems complement the human thinking process.

Weaver and Atkinson do not only identify an homology between hypertext and the structure of human cognition. They see the dynamic, associative and non-linear character of hypertext as being close to the heuristic and iterative processes typical of qualitative research. This view derives from their understanding of qualitative research as a process of reading, writing and thinking. In qualitative analysis, reading and writing are dialectically related since the assimilation and interpretation of field data are typically accomplished through the writing of an analytic commentary, typically in memo form. Indeed, it is this 'interaction between reading and writing that constitutes analysis' (1995b: 117). An important aspect of all this is that the related processes of reading and writing take place on-line since the analyst interacts with text appearing on a computer screen rather than in hard-copy form. Movement between data and the analytic commentary upon it is thus accomplished in an easy and flexible way. Hypertext tools allow commentary to be added to data as that commentary is formulated but in a way that ensures that the original context is not lost. Data can easily be re-examined and existing interpretations modified as analysis proceeds. Weaver and Atkinson argue that hypertext methods fit well with a grounded theory approach. Whatever else it might be, grounded theory – in the classical sense of the term – embodies a data management strategy. That strategy combines a tough-minded reluctance to collect more data than are theoretically necessary with an expansive concern to seek theoretically relevant data wherever they might be. The tools for doing this – memoing, theoretical saturation and theoretical sampling – depend on links, associations and trails which are difficult to maintain. Hypertext provides a technical means for doing so.

A further advantage of hypertext, according to Weaver and Atkinson, is that it provides facilities for data display (Miles and Huberman, 1994). Charts can be produced showing links and nodes and the relations between them, and such charts can be linked back electronically to the data. Unlike other strategies, the use of a hypertext approach does not depend on extensive prior familiarity with the data. Preliminary browsing through the data produces initial ideas and hypotheses, the identification and recording of which forms a basis for analytic development. This might have implications for team projects. Different analysts can choose different starting points and can navigate through material in their own way. Moreover, as Cordingley points out, since a trail of links reflects the chain of decisions which produced them, hypertext is to an extent self-documenting. Nevertheless, Cordingley cautions that there needs to be some level of agreement between team members. In particular, the team has to have some shared understanding about the formation and labelling of links. Without this, what Cordingley calls 'hybrid links' become possible. In other words, a network of links might be created which lacks internal logical consistency.

How in practice is the analysis of a qualitative data set accomplished using hypertext tools? Weaver and Atkinson (1995a, 1995b) describe in some detail the use of the commercial hypertext program GUIDE to reanalyse fieldnotes from Julius Roth's (1963) study of a TB hospital.[1] GUIDE allows the user to attach 'buttons' of different kinds to specific locations within a document. (This terminology reflects the particular

package Weaver and Atkinson used. In some other contexts, the Macintosh program, HyperCard, for example, the term 'button' might be
misleading. Here, a linkable text string is often described as being 'hot
text'.) For example, a 'note button' allows one to 'pop-up' a small window
by clicking on a relevant piece of text. This window can contain supplementary information about the text being clicked. 'Expansion buttons'
allow material in the text to be hidden or displayed, so that the amount of
detail available to the analyst can be varied. 'Reference buttons' provide a
means of 'jumping' to a different position in the same document or to relevant information in a different document. The availability of buttons is
denoted by the format of the text (underlined, bold, italicized), and by the
shape of the cursor which changes when passing over a particular kind of
button.

Weaver and Atkinson (1995a; 1995b) describe in some detail how they
went about analysing their data using a hypertext strategy. Starting with
an initial analytic question to do with how infective agents were perceived
in the hospital Roth studied, they began to browse the data documents.
From this they derived a list of relevant keywords appearing in the data.
Segments of text containing keywords were then identified using the
search facility in the program. Segments once found were subsequently
pasted into a new document which functioned as an analytic memo. (As
Weaver and Atkinson point out, while convenient, it is not strictly necessary to copy found text to a new document. One could simply list the
keywords in the document and link back from them to the original source.
Cordingley [1991] points out that not *having to* make multiple copies of
data is actually an important advantage of hypertext.) Later Weaver and
Atkinson hit on the idea of including analytic notes concerning data
segments within an expansion button. The expansion material rather than
the original keyword could then be linked to relevant memos. By linking
data to memo and memo to data in this way, according to Weaver and
Atkinson, analysts avoid what they describe as the 'culture of fragmentation' (1995a: 155; 1995b) in qualitative analysis. As Atkinson and others
have elaborated elsewhere,

> It is, after all, part of the rationale of ethnographic and similar approaches that
> the anthropologist, sociologist, historian, psychologist or whoever, recognizes
> the complexity of social inter-relatedness. We recognize the over-determination
> of culture, in that there are multiple, densely coded influences among and
> between different domains and institutions. It is therefore part of the attraction
> of hypertext solutions that a sense of dense interconnectedness is preserved,
> enhanced even, while linearity is discarded. (Coffey et al., 1996: §8.5)

Weaver and Atkinson point to a number of difficulties they encountered. First of all, establishing hypertext links can be a lengthy process. As
Fischer (1994: 109) comments, 'Little about hypertext is automatic': linking

must be done explicitly by the analyst. In mitigation, though, Fischer points out that much of this work is actually done in the ordinary course of working with the data; the linking process in many respects is functionally equivalent to the work of note taking and indexing that would be done anyway. Second, a hypertext consists of many objects linked in complicated ways. Because of this, 'cognitive overheads are high' (Cordingley, 1991: 175). It might not always be easy to remember relevant analytic categories when linking data to memos. It can also be difficult to remember what links are available or might be relevant. A third problem is that of becoming 'lost in hyperspace'. It is easy to become side-tracked in the analytic process precisely because of the associative character of the links. Thus, one might start with a particular task in mind but notice another possible line of enquiry which is then pursued to the detriment of the original purpose. In some cases, being side-tracked in this way actually capitalizes on the potential for spontaneity that hypertext allows. In other cases, it might simply lead one down an unproductive dead alley.

Weaver and Atkinson suggest some possible solutions to these problems. One is to focus the analysis. Either one can concentrate on a particular topic and follow through the links associated with it, or one might focus on a segment of text and explore all the material linked to it. Neither strategy is intrinsically preferable to the other, though each might be appropriate at a different stage of an analysis. To avoid cognitive overload and the problem of being lost in hyperspace, Weaver and Atkinson stress the need for the analyst to be systematic in the naming of links. They also found it useful to keep a diagrammatic representation of the link structure for the hypertext being analysed. Such a diagram can, of course, be linked back into the hypertext itself, and function much as a table of contents might.

Recall that hypertext is multidimensional. One is not confined by the two-dimensional and finite size of the printed page. Material – text, graphic, audio and video – can be juxtaposed, compared, contrasted and explored if need be at a variety of resolutions. (For a hypothetical example, see Hagaman, 1995.) There is an obvious contrast, therefore, between hypertext and conventional printed text organized in a linear way. In fact, the multidimensional character of hypertext provides an opportunity to blur traditional distinctions between 'analysis' and 'publication'. Indeed, according to Weaver and Atkinson (1995b: 153), 'Hypertext challenges the final stage of qualitative research – the ethnographic monograph itself.' As they point out, the final stage of writing up one's results involves the production of a conventional linear document. With hypertext, this last stage is truncated since there is no need to knead the material into its final linear form. To do so, in any case, is to forgo precisely those advantages inherent in the concept of hypertext. When it is presented in hypertext form the reader does not simply consume the ethnography, but interacts with it. For example, references and cross-references can be followed with ease. This increases the likelihood that such information will be used while ensuring that the holistic character of the analysis is retained. In all of this readers need not be bound by the analyst's interpretation of the material. By being able to browse the hypertext in their own way, 'readers can easily obtain the knowledge necessary to be critical of the grounds of a statement' (1995b: 155). In this way, and in contrast to conventional printed text, hypertext empowers the reader. Furthermore, because hypertext maintains a 'sense of complexity, intertextuality and non-linearity' the use of the technology is compatible with those approaches, increasingly popular in the social sciences, which draw their inspiration from postmodernism (Coffey and Atkinson, 1996).

The implications of this partly depend on how the term 'reader' is defined. The use of hypertext, and beyond that multimedia approaches, facilitates 'untutored use'. Although we do not use the term 'untutored' in a pejorative way, nevertheless we suspect that there is an issue about what background one might need to produce meaningful interpretations from a hypertext resource. In other words, hypertext might make it feasible for anyone to create the appearance of an ethnographic text, but a text which its creator finds impossible to explain or defend. If we understand correctly, it is the originating ethnographer who chooses items for expansion and reference and who specifies links through the hypertext database. However, it is precisely this which might subvert the very polyvocality implicit in hypertext. Faced with an apparently smooth and user-friendly resource offering all manner of subsidiary and supporting information, the naive user might feel that it contains 'all there is to know' about the topic at hand. A resource seen by its architects as encouraging a sophisticated appreciation of the very contingency of social knowledge will instead be received and used as watertight, supremely – and ironically – authoritative. Alternatively, the tendency of hypertext to blur distinctions between 'data', 'analysis', 'interpretation' and so on might for some be simply a recipe for confusion and indecision produced by a maze of links and connections going nowhere in particular. On the other hand, opening a text to multiple readings potentially increases its 'contestability'. In this situation, we suspect much discussion will revolve around the character and completeness of the linking strategies used. To this extent multiple use of a hypertext corpus might actually direct attention towards criteria of methodological adequacy in a way its surface appearance, however apparently postmodern, de-emphasizes.

The more inclusive one's definition of the reader, if it includes for example members of the general public, the more accessible the hypertext needs to be. The need to publish hypertexts electronically can involve a lack of transferability (Cordingley, 1991). Normally, with hypertext systems one can import and export data. However, the knowledge embodied in the data by the links is difficult to transfer between systems and between media. All of this 'works counter to the democratisation of computer developments by inhibiting the spread of their "ownership", especially into the user community' (Cordingley, 1991: 176). One implication of all this might be that hypertext should not be discussed in isolation from dissemination technologies such as the World Wide Web, and other forms of electronic publishing. Similar considerations affect the use of hypertext and traditional print technologies. Only some kinds of information within a hypertext, the data, for example, transfer easily to hard copy. Other information – the trails between documents or the information in 'pop-up' windows – is hard to produce in printed form (Weaver and Atkinson, 1995b). Cordingley records that in her work with hypertext attempts to review the analysis in hard copy form were so time-consuming and so frustrating that they were usually abandoned. Difficulties with hard-copy representation effectively meant that validation and verification of findings had to be accomplished on-line or with the co-operation of the original analyst. Cordingley also points out that in assessing hypertext materials, users bring reading strategies from printed forms to the hypertext material. Thus, for example, even where no specific structure is implied, readers still tend to read diagrammatic representations of link structures from left to right and from top to bottom.

Weaver and Atkinson argue that hypertext's empowerment of the reader does not disempower the author, since material the author does not wish readers to see can be removed from the hypertext. This evidently runs counter to the very openness that hypertexts facilitate. In any event, neither readers nor authors might be entirely free in the matter. Coffey and Atkinson (1996) point to possible copyright difficulties surrounding the inclusion in a hypertext of already published material. There might also need to be careful consideration of the legal conditions, under both copyright and data protection law, that might govern how research participants allow representations of themselves to appear, especially within publicly accessible hypertexts. One possible consequence here is that more widely available hypertexts might be largely restricted to relatively innocuous rather than 'sensitive' topics. (On publication issues in sensitive research, see Lee, 1993: Chapter 10.)

The possibilities opened up by hypertext are intriguing and exciting. How far these possibilities are embraced by qualitative researchers remains to be seen, although it is likely that hypertext will have less appeal in those areas, such as applied social research, where research goals are more narrowly defined than in traditional ethnographic research. Policy makers who dislike academics' alleged fondness for answers beginning 'On the one hand . . .' are likely to be even less enamoured of responses beginning 'On the first hand . . .'. Anthropologists might be more readily attracted than sociologists to the postmodern implications of hypertext. As Atkinson has noted in another context (1992: 40), to date at least, sociology has been less affected by the postmodern critique than anthropology. Because, he suggests, sociology has traditionally been rather less self-assured and rather more fragmented and contested than anthropology, the advent of postmodernism generated less of a sense of crisis for sociologists than for anthropologists.

In this context we wish to address some remarks to an emerging critique informed both by analytic work using hypertext and by postmodernism. This critique suggests that computer-based methods have encouraged the development of an orthodox view which associates qualitative analysis largely with the use of coding techniques. According to this view, the orthodox position is driven by an assumed affinity between computer-based approaches and grounded theory, and involves the intrusion into qualitative research of a procedure – coding – more typical of quantitative work in social research.

In their article 'Qualitative data analysis: technologies and representations', Coffey et al. (1996) note that the ethnographic enterprise, especially but not exclusively in anthropology, has become fragmented. Traditional methods and styles of data collection, analysis and reportage are no longer seen as unproblematic. In all of this is felt the impact of contemporary cultural perspectives, such as poststructuralism, postmodernism, feminism and postcolonialism, through which 'runs a discursive turn, treating as central but problematic the relations of language, knowledge and power' (1996: §1.3). Coffey et al. go on to suggest that one strand of contemporary computing, that involving the use of hypertext software and hypermedia, is well adapted to the diverse range of representational strategies opened up by contemporary critiques. However, they contrast both the theoretical ferment they describe and the exciting potential of hypertext with what they describe as a 'centripetal tendency'. What is represented by this tendency is

> a convergence, endorsed by some qualitative researchers and methodologists, towards a single ideal-type of data collection storage and analysis. That model combines computing techniques with methodological perspectives claimed to be associated with 'grounded theory'. One can detect a trend towards a homogenization, and the emergence of a new form of orthodoxy, especially at the level of data management. We note that the use of microcomputing strategies for qualitative data handling has become widespread, and this includes an almost globalizing process within the research community. The presuppositions and procedures that are inscribed in contemporary software for qualitative data analysis are implicitly driving a renewed orthodoxy that is being adopted in a large number of research sites around the world. (1996: §1.4)

We do not disagree with Coffey et al.'s characterization of the current state of ethnography, at least within anthropology. Nor would we dissent from their assessment of the analytic possibilities opened up for qualitative researchers by hypertext and hypermedia. However, neither of these arguments, we believe, depends on a contrast with an assumed orthodoxy. Put bluntly, their characterization of the current state of qualitative computing is a red herring. We suspect that Coffey et al. are led to their position less by an examination of the current state of qualitative research – we show in fact that their generalizations are empirically suspect – and more by a desire to dramatize the contrast between older and newer approaches to qualitative analysis. The writings that first describe the potential use of software for qualitative analysis were rather modest in their claims. We suspect that the earliest CAQDAS programs were seen by their developers as providing an 'enhancing' technology. In other words, by largely taking away the drudgery of handling qualitative data, computer-based methods promised a better or at least an easier way of doing things. (Couching matters in this way also had the strategic benefit of not alienating a social audience that, while likely to be dissatisfied with the burdens of manual analysis, was generally regarded as being conservative in methodological terms and likely to be suspicious of technology.) Coffey et al., on the other hand, point towards the potential of a 'transformative technology', hypertext, that provides a means of doing things *differently* rather than simply better. One might hypothesize that, while the discourses surrounding enhancing technologies will tend to stress continuity and compatibility with what has gone before, the discourses surrounding transformative technologies will stress their radical, disjunctive character. It is partly for this reason, we suspect, that Coffey et al. place so much emphasis on orthodoxy. We also suspect that criticizing a supposed orthodoxy is congruent with the tendency for many of the newer theoretical positions Coffey et al. identify to define themselves in counter-hegemonic ways.

The notion of an orthodoxy implies that a healthy plurality of approaches is being replaced by some kind of dominant discourse which suppresses variation and homogenizes practice. The first point to make about this is that claims to this effect, or indeed counter-claims, must inevitably be conjectural. The data which would allow us to make comparisons between past and present in relation to qualitative data analysis are simply not there. We can, however, contrast what we believe to be the situation in qualitative research with other fields where computers have increasingly begun to be used. Kling and Iacono (1988) describe how the growing use of computers in a number of areas has been driven by what they term 'computerization movements'. Computerization movements can be regarded as social movements in the sense articulated by Blumer (1969): 'collective enterprises to establish a new order of life'. Kling and Iacono suggest that computerization movements share a number of key ideological beliefs. Broadly speaking these are (a) that there is a need to remain at the cutting edge of technological development if a particular area of social life is to develop, (b) that computerization has only beneficial consequences, and (c) that it is the resistance of users which provides the primary barrier to further computerization. There is little doubt that many of those involved in CAQDAS are enthusiastic about the possibilities opened up by the application of new technologies to qualitative research. We would contend, however, that it is difficult to discern in the literature on computer methods in qualitative research anything like sentiments of the kind Kling and Iacono identify. The late Renata Tesch, who did perhaps more than anyone else to popularize CAQDAS, stresses in her 1990 book the heterogeneity of the qualitative research tradition. Far from propagating an orthodoxy, developers, popularizers and commentators have often stressed the need for epistemological awareness and debate in relation to software use. This is explicit, for example, in the introductions and contributions to two widely used edited collections of articles on CAQDAS (Fielding and Lee, 1991; Kelle, 1995).

One can also note that software tools for approaches not based on coding are less invisible (and are perhaps less novel: Heise, 1991) than Coffey et al. suggest. Coffey and Atkinson (1996) have suggested that text retrieval programs might be more useful for discourse analytic purposes than so-called 'code-and-retrieve' packages. Weitzman and Miles (1995), who provide detailed comparative reviews of software programs potentially useful for qualitative analysis, describe a range of software types, including text retrievers, textbase managers and conceptual network builders, different from code-and-retrieve packages. Moreover, developers of CAQDAS programs have increasingly included facilities for proximity searching, which might be useful for narrative analysis, and for 'autocoding' which could be adapted to some kinds of semiotic analysis. The provision of new features in CAQDAS programs reflects the generally close relationship between users and developers characteristic of the field, and the general willingness of developers to incorporate features desired by users even if these do not always accord with the epistemological preferences of the developer. Since packages increasingly support procedures, routines and features which are new to qualitative analysis or make procedures possible that were not practicable without the power of the computer, it is less and less plausible either to argue that the software is merely an aid to code-and-retrieve or to argue that code-and-retrieve is the *sine qua non* of qualitative analysis. For example, besides code-based procedures and hypermedia approaches, qualitative researchers have available to them software resources based on production rule systems (Heather and Lee, 1995). The application to case data of techniques such as Boolean minimization also depends on software solutions (Ragin, 1995).

Coffey et al. point out that procedures for coding and retrieving segments of text from fieldnotes or interview transcripts are common in qualitative data analysis software packages. For them, the injunction to code data implied by the software is an aspect of the alleged orthodoxy they want to reject in part because they see it as 'akin to standardized survey or experimental design procedures' (Coffey et al., 1996: §7). Dey has made a similar point by commenting that, 'Although "coding" has

become an accepted term for categorizing data, it has misleading connotations and is somewhat inappropriate for qualitative analysis' (1993: 58).
He goes on to point out that in everyday parlance the word 'code' refers
to ciphers and can also be applied to sets of legal statutes. These usages
might be relevant to coding procedures in quantitative research, where
numbers are allocated to responses as a way of locating a respondent's
utterances within fixed categories. They are not, in Dey's view, appropriate when applied to qualitative research.

A number of observations can be made here. First of all, it is certainly
the case that if one consults the *Oxford English Dictionary*, legal statutes and
ciphers are both given as meanings for the word 'code'. The *OED* also
makes it clear, however, that the term has been widely used in scientific
disciplines over the last 30 years in a sense more akin to that used in qualitative research. Dey also forgets that there are two verbs that derive from
the noun 'code'. One is 'to code', the other is 'to codify'; it is the latter
which embodies the legal connotations surrounding the word 'code'.
Second, coding is for many qualitative researchers an important strategy
which they would use irrespective of the availability of software. This is
perhaps evidenced by a striking feature of the history of CAQDAS already
mentioned. Many of the early programs emerged more or less simultaneously from developers who were unaware that others were doing the
same thing. The significance of this is that developers generally saw themselves as computerizing their own analytic methods, with little thought
that these methods were unusual. A similar point can be made about the
recurrent reinvention of approaches based on word processing for amal-
gamating text passages on similar topics into separate files.

Third, one needs to be careful not to confuse the different functions of
coding (Richards and Richards, 1995; Seidel and Kelle, 1995). On the one
hand, coding can be thought of as an indexing device, a mnemonic providing a pointer to the presence of a particular topic at a particular position
within a text. It can also, on the other hand, be seen as a representational
device. From this point of view, codes are categories the meaning of which
derives from their relations to other codes and to an emerging theoretical
schema. In practice, of course, these two functions, as Seidel and Kelle
point out, can rarely be separated. Not to separate them analytically when
discussing computer-based methods risks eliding program features,
analytic procedures and methodological approaches. One can take this
point further by noting that writers critical of the role of coding in qualitative research tend not to address themselves to what analysts do with
the material they have coded. They are thus blind to the fact that while
there are similarities between coding in the *survey* research tradition and
coding procedures in qualitative research, the goal of each is different.

Lazarsfeld and Barton (1951) who first codified procedures for coding
open-ended survey questions suggest that a good system for qualitative
classification should have four characteristics. First of all, it should be

'articulate'. The classification system should have a structure of categories and subcategories such that the analyst can move quickly from the general to the specific and back again. The second characteristic Lazarsfeld and Barton identify is that of logical correctness. This is the principle well known in survey research that the categories in a classification scheme should be exhaustive and mutually exclusive. In other words, there should be only one place to put an item in a given classification schema. Third, a classification should be adapted 'to the structure of the situation' in the sense that a recasting of the preliminary categories should be done on the basis of a broad conceptual focus deriving from the purposes of the study. Finally, the classification must be 'adapted to the respondent's frame of reference' in that it should 'present as clearly as possible the respondent's own definition of the situation' (1951: 157). The point here is that classification in survey research is a precursor to measurement. In other words, categories need to be formed in order to translate them into nominal, ordinal or interval scales. Such scales can be operated on to produce either multidimensional classifications through reduction of the attribute space or, by means of additive procedures, to develop quantitative indices (Lazarsfeld and Barton, 1951). Classification systems used by qualitative researchers might display the features Lazarsfeld and Barton identify as desiderata; however, they need not. Indeed, we would argue that the quite explicit rules which govern the coding of open-ended survey responses are only rarely invoked in qualitative practice. Those who developed new approaches to the analysis of qualitative data in the 1960s recognized an affinity with Lazarsfeld and Barton's methods (Becker and Geer, 1960; Glaser and Strauss, 1967; Strauss, 1987). In each case, however, rejected in these new approaches was the goal Lazarsfeld and Barton had of transforming qualitative materials into scales or indices. Instead, what was sought were procedures that would give qualitative analysis a degree of rigour while retaining an essentially non-quantitative mode of analysis.

To say all of this is not to say that coding is the only, the best, or even the preferred method for the analysis of qualitative data. Indeed, as should be clear from previous discussion, we see coding as a procedure in qualitative research, and the advent of approaches such as narrative analysis as historically contingent, reflecting in part the impact of a new technology, the tape recorder. This, by making possible the production of precise transcriptions of field data, stimulated new problems of data management. Instead of insisting on a particular model of analysis, we ourselves see computer-based methods as permitting, if we can use a somewhat inelegant term, the multi-tooling of qualitative researchers, making available to them more or less at will a wide range of different analytic strategies.

Coffey et al. (1996) argue that 'aspects of grounded theory have been over-emphasized in the development and use of qualitative data analysis software, while other approaches have been neglected in comparison'. Before accepting this position too readily it might be useful to explore in a more critical way what we might mean by the term 'grounded theory'. When qualitative researchers are challenged to describe their approach, reference to 'grounded theory' probably has the highest recognition value. The very looseness and variety of schooling in the approach means, however, that the tag might well mean something different to each researcher. A detailed examination of work claiming the label might deviate sharply from what Glaser and Strauss had in mind (and, of course, their own work has developed substantially, and their approaches have diverged). There are, in fact, several logical possibilities: (1) work that is done in a qualitative vein bears little resemblance to grounded theory procedures but lays claim to do so for purposes of legitimation; (2) the influence and application of the original grounded theory procedures is limited to a far smaller group than claim the label; (3) significant methodological developments outside grounded theory have not been applied to, or brought into line with, the original tenets of grounded theory (i.e. the original inspiration has grown stale and out of touch with research practice); (4) subsequent formulations by the authors of grounded theory following publication of the original work have not been systematically taken to heart by those claiming to work in the grounded theory tradition. Although we are not in a position to develop a fully comprehensive analysis, it is possible to identify in the literature at least some of the possibilities we have listed. Both Locke (1996) and Hood (1996) have examined recent published work putatively based on grounded theory methodology. They observe that such work frequently has characteristics at variance with the method as originally developed. Authors, for example, rarely make reference to theoretical sampling, a procedure classically regarded as indispensable to the method. Analytic procedures which do not form part of the grounded theory repertoire are sometimes used, while the term 'grounded theory' itself is sometimes invoked in ways which suggest that its primary purpose is to legitimize an inductive approach.

Even if we assume that the notion of grounded theory is used in a consistent and defensible way in the literature, can we go on, as Coffey et al. do, to see grounded theory as underpinning computer-assisted qualitative data analysis? In suggesting an association between computer-based methods and grounded theory, Coffey et al. cite with approval Marrku Lonkila's (1995) work examining the influence grounded theory has had on developers of CAQDAS programs. However, there are difficulties with Lonkila's analysis. First of all, it is perhaps those developers of the programs Lonkila identifies as being most explicitly influenced by grounded theory, NUD•IST and Atlas/ti, who have been least enamoured of an over-reliance on coding as an analytic procedure (Richards and Richards, 1994; Muhr, 1996). Second, Lonkila's analysis is methodologically problematic in that he asserts the influence of grounded theory but then looks for evidence only of that influence. It is perhaps appropriate in this context to examine the early literature on CAQDAS. This is where one might expect to see intellectual influences most clearly. Interestingly, some of that literature was produced by anthropologists who early turned to mainframe programs for managing fieldnotes and for whom grounded theory was not a model (Podolefsky and McCarty, 1983). In sociology, on the other hand, one can find, for example, Seidel and Clark describing the development of ETHNOGRAPH thus: 'Our research practices are strongly informed by grounded theory methodology' (1984:12). While this might support Lonkila's contention, it is interesting to note that they also cite as an influence the analytic methods described by Spradley (1979) and mention the approaches to qualitative analysis taken by Lofland and Lofland (1984) and Becker et al. (1961). In a similar way, Drass (1980) and Agar (1983) invoke grounded theory as an influence but also see the computer as aiding the generation of quasi-statistics, an approach that one does not expect to find in 'pure' grounded theory methodology. More recently, in their article describing HyperResearch, one can find Hesse-Biber et al. (1991) equating analytic induction with the constant comparative method at the heart of grounded theory, an equation not everyone would accept, despite the similarities in the two approaches. We take all of this to mean that there can be very real difficulties in attempting to identify clearly influences on software development.

It seems to us preferable to examine the practice of researchers themselves in order to explore the relationship between grounded theory and computer-assisted qualitative analysis. (As a general point we can observe that much of the literature on research practice is based on assertion. There is actually relatively little empirical study of how researchers behave in practice.) To identify research studies where it was likely a computer had been used to analyse qualitative data, we inspected the *Social Science Citation Index* for studies citing John Seidel's descriptive writings on ETHNO-GRAPH (Seidel and Clark, 1984; Seidel, 1985, 1988). In all we found 163 studies which reported empirical findings. Of these studies 50, or 30.7 per cent, cited a work associated with the grounded theory tradition; *70 per cent did not*. (Works we took as being associated with grounded theory were: Glaser and Strauss, 1967; Glaser, 1978; Strauss, 1987; Strauss and Corbin, 1990.) Table 7.2 shows methods texts cited in those articles which did *not* cite a work in the grounded theory tradition.

From this we conclude that grounded theory is an important, but by no means ubiquitous, influence on studies where there is a strong likelihood that computer-based analysis has been used. Users of qualitative data analysis software apparently draw on a range of methodological inspiration. Admittedly, almost all of the studies considered here take what Coffey et al. describe as a realist approach to the representation of social reality. However as we indicated earlier, users seem not to hesitate to abandon software which does not meet their needs or which seems to be at variance with their epistemological presuppositions. The implication of all this for our understanding of CAQDAS is that we must not allow the

Table 7.2   *Seidel citations: methods books cited by those NOT citing works associated with grounded theory*

Title	No.
Miles and Huberman, *Qualitative Data Analysis* (1994)	14
Patton, *Qualitative Evaluation Methods* (1980)	13
Lincoln and Guba, *Naturalistic Inquiry* (1985)	12
Spradley, *The Ethnographic Interview* (1979)	11
Lofland and Lofland, *Analyzing Social Settings* (1984)	7
Bogdan and Biklen, *Qualitative Research in Education* (1992)	6
Tesch, *Qualitative Research* (1990)	4
Fetterman, *Ethnography Step by Step* (1989)	4

easily declared assertions of affiliation to a grounded theory approach to prefigure our understanding of what CAQDAS can (or should) do to support qualitative analysis. We should neither assume that qualitative research only involves grounded theory nor that CAQDAS supports only a grounded theory approach. There are other viable approaches to qualitative analysis, and indeed the practice of qualitative researchers might be rigorous without their explicitly employing any of the several approaches blessed with a memorable 'label' and a school of avowed followers.

Conclusion

It is not clear how some of the developments we have sketched here will affect routine analytic practice in qualitative research over the longer term. Our suspicion is that there will be both a good deal of experimentation with different approaches and tools, as well as a tendency for programs to find particular niches within specific analytic traditions. We need to be careful not to succumb to technological determinism. The influences on qualitative analytic practice are many and various, a topic we take up in the next and final chapter.

Note

1   Roth has made copies of his field data available to a number of researchers, and they have been used for teaching purposes in a number of contexts. Rendered into machine-readable form Roth's material provided Weaver and Atkinson with a readily available source of data. Since they had not collected the data, Weaver and Atkinson reasoned that pre-existing or emerging analytic commitments were less likely to hinder their methodological purposes.

8

The Evolution of Qualitative Data Analysis

Our working title for this concluding chapter was 'The Future of Qualitative Analysis'. A reluctance to claim anything so presumptuous as privileged foresight led us to a new title. But it is worth saying a little about that title, too. To write in terms of 'evolution' is to invoke notions of a steady, incremental progress towards a 'higher state'. There is reason to qualify such an organic analogy. For one thing, scrutiny of our discipline's intellectual history suggests that thinking on analytic adequacy has as much a cyclical character marked by eternal recurrence of established themes as it does a stepwise, accumulative and progressive character. For another thing, the gathering pace of technological development suggests that progress is anything but steady. We will argue that, while technological developments undoubtedly contribute to change in approaches to analysis, they are one influence among many, perhaps the chief of which are terribly humdrum matters of funding. Further, the significant technological developments that qualitative research is currently undergoing are not taking qualitative analysis to new destinations but causing it to revisit old debates, indeed, debates so old that many researchers are unaware that the field has already been there before.

Social researchers and methodologists currently face a substantial learning curve as they confront new information technologies. Moreover, the entity we conveniently refer to as a 'discipline' is in fact riven in many accustomed, and several unaccustomed, ways. We might list here the emergent schools of thought from Denzin's high interpretivism through to the cookbook pragmatism of the texts which demystify qualitative analysis for use in fields like management or nursing. But our list would never be complete and would, no doubt, offend everyone. That brings us to the first point we need to make in pondering the way things are going. For, while we do foresee a considerable scope for experiment, innovation and, indeed, confusion, in the face of the new technologies, we believe that the field will work much as its best intellectual histories tell us it has always done. These histories debunk the idea that social research is chiefly guided by a coolly intellectual agenda in which theory is carefully applied in empirical research whose results lead to refinement of theory, and the research community works together with a sense of collective endeavour and cumulative knowledge. Things are more diffuse and uncoordinated than that. We further believe that the evidence from the present period of methodological innovation suggests some pronounced consistencies with earlier periods of development in qualitative method as well as demonstrating the transformative potential of the new technologies (Lee, 1995b). While methodological techniques might change in response to new enabling technologies we are not yet in the midst of a revolution. Things are more stable than that.

What, for example, do new methodological procedures and possibilities tell us about the way that social research will be informed by theory? In a review of Platt's historical account of research methods Tim May points out that, for theory to be shown to guide research practice, two conditions must be satisfied: it must be shown that research practitioners hold theoretical commitments independent of their research and it must be shown how such beliefs translate into research practice (May, 1996). Yet such self-conscious accounts have to date been rare, largely confined to *Festschrift* writings and thus documenting chiefly the thoughts of the eminent, and then often in the rosy, homologizing glow of hindsight. It might be that a new genre of first-person accounts of the qualitative research process, often written in the spirit of a 'reflexive' concern to locate analysis in the context of the individual researcher who has produced it, will shed new light on the matter. It remains open to question whether the bulk of social research is in fact theoretically guided rather than driven by the catalogue of pragmatic considerations Platt ably documents, such as the availability of funding from particular sources (Platt, 1996). Sometimes the opportunities presented by the world outside the academy are so quirky one could not possibly anticipate them. To take an entertaining example, Edward Gross recounted to Platt in an interview a conversation in which a colonel justified United States Air Force investment in sociological research on the grounds that if the USA lost its next war the air force could at least tell those investigating the failure that they had consulted all the experts, *even the sociologists*. Similarly, social researchers coined the evocative term 'dustbowl empiricism' to tag the origin of the federal Division of Program Surveys in the US Department of Agriculture's attempt to gauge the problems farmers faced in the Depression. To make the connection with the data in the present study, our respondents gave ample testimony to the exigencies of the social research environment in which sponsors and their interests featured strongly. As May comments, 'even if practitioners held [theoretical commitments] they would need to be fully committed to and conscious of them, to implement them with consistency in appropriate contexts and to select their methods without giving due thought to, or indeed encountering impediments from, practical constraints' (May, 1996: 150). There is, in short, a lot more driving social research than a dispassionate desire to apply, test and refine theory, and this has always been so.

It is in fact more plausible to argue that theory is led by practice, just as analysis is moulded by the methodological procedures that make some aspects of the social world available as 'data' while concealing others. As Platt puts it, 'research methods may on the level of theory, when theory is consciously involved at all, reflect intellectual *bricolage* or *post hoc* justifications rather than the consistent working through of carefully chosen fundamental assumptions' (Platt, 1996: 275). If this is so, the new equipment that we can apply to our practice might indeed presage a new period of theoretical development. The question is whether what results will actually be 'new'.

This brings us to our point about the cyclical nature of methodological 'development'. In nature, cycles occur where there are regularities in the environment which exert an enduring influence. We might consider the quantitative/qualitative dichotomy in social research methods in this vein. For some years it has been a mark of the progressive methodologist to grant that every method has its place in the scheme of things; we now seldom encounter in the published literature gung-ho statements of the superiority of this or that method (true, that kind of thing happens to students hauled before thesis/dissertation 'committees' and at conferences, but not in the literature, where people are on their best behaviour). Indeed, there is a familiar theme in the literature that begins from the premise that the distinction between quantitative and qualitative is false or unhelpful. We have to ask, though, if there were nothing to it why do we have special terms in our vocabulary with which to make the distinction? At a trivial level, of course, there must be a distinction. Working with numbers is different from working with words. The question is whether what one finds by working with numbers is more useful than what one finds by working with words. Those who believe the methods can be complementary premise their view on the fact that what one finds is different. It is worth thinking in the abstract about what this difference amounts to, apart from the different tokens (words, numbers) that are manipulated.

We would argue that an essential difference lies in the formality of the procedures associated with the two traditions. Here a distinction needs to be made between formalism, the drive to construct algebraic expressions of axiomatic knowledge, and formalization, the effort to codify methodological procedures. We have in mind formalization. As quantitative methods have developed, statistical tests and procedures have been refined. It has always been possible, within the confines of the statistics (but not necessarily their application), to identify a 'right answer'. (We would acknowledge, though, that codification does not imply consensus, an example being debate over the value of significance testing.) Precision is a virtue and has imparted to the quantitative curriculum an implicitly normative, formal character: follow these procedures and there will be no doubting your analysis. In contrast, efforts to codify qualitative analysis have not had the impetus lent by the refinement of statistics (refinements not tied to the development of social science but to the development of the mathematics and statistics disciplines). Formalizing influences have been restricted, until recently, to attempts to standardize fieldwork procedures, that is, they have operated at the level of data collection. Even in the most widely recognized statement of qualitative analysis procedure, grounded theory, the substance of the effort is oriented to fieldwork, with iterations of the analysis leading the researcher continually back to the field for confirmation, disconfirmation and the discovery of new nuances. Yet there have always been some who have been dissatisfied with the idea that the process of discovery is never-ending and have sought to make the end object of qualitative enquiry the statement of formal conditions which capture, for example, cause and effect relationships. This is the case with recent work by mathematical sociologists modelling behaviour on the basis of ethnographic data (e.g. Abell, 1988) and has been an influence on one branch of qualitative software (Heise, 1991). Increasingly, the technology is there to permit that kind of analysis (see, e.g., our earlier discussion of QCA). Yet in the meantime – and perhaps as much a result of making the best of what one has got as to do with a real preference – strong analytic traditions have grown up which repudiate the formalizing project, distrust abstraction and celebrate subjectivism.

For example, Gubrium and Holstein (1997) frame research methods as a 'set of idioms' where alternate approaches are seen as vocabularies for conveying social realities. Language-based approaches such as this take heavy account of relativism and implicitly reduce and restrict the common ground between different analytic postures. They emphasize the different ways that the same empirical phenomena might be construed, and do not see any one approach as making a greater or lesser contribution. For some adherents of approaches such as naturalism (Gubrium and Holstein use the term in the sense associated with Douglas's (1976) critical account), ethnomethodology, 'emotionalism' (that approach which ponders the existential nuances of qualitative research for researcher and researched) and postmodernism, there is little sense of a cumulative analytic project, and the approaches stand separately. This is not, in fact, Gubrium and Holstein's position, as they examine the risks and rewards of the different approaches and seek a 'renewed language of inquiry that accommodates both traditional and contemporary concerns'. However, the increasing diversity of analytic traditions offers an impression of increasingly separate if equal development. Thus, where methodology had been marked by a bipolar distinction between quantitative and qualitative, and a professional practice marked by conflict and competition between the two, we are now at a point where qualitative methodology itself harbours analytic orientations which are more distinct and engender dispute just as deep as any between, say, Znaniecki and Lundberg. Such divisions are heartfelt because they affect every stage of the research process. They affect what we do in the field and how we do it, and they affect how we analyse as well as the analyses we produce. These practical commitments colour our attitudes to new technology and what we want to do with it. Yet they have not come from technological developments but from experience of the theory and practice of qualitative research. For instance, the rise of subjectivism and postmodernism was stimulated by trends in philosophy, and much of the new interest in 'emotionalism' emerged from applied studies in medical settings. The new technologies might offer the means to so develop the potential of the increasingly divergent qualitative traditions that they have little else in common than that they do not work with numbers. But the new technologies did not put these qualitative traditions there in the first place.

One of the early speculations of commentators on the potential of CAQDAS was that it might lead to a convergence of approaches, a 'generic theory of qualitative method'. Those who felt that common conventions had always benefited quantitative methodology saw this as promising, while others were alarmed that creative differences might be driven out. Few would now see in CAQDAS such a potential. We might contrast just two renderings of CAQDAS. One is the QCA software developed by Drass (1989) for the practice of Qualitative Comparative Analysis, a procedure whose roots lie in the formal procedures of analytic induction. The other is the freewheeling hypertext-linking approach of Atkinson and his colleagues (Weaver and Atkinson, 1995a, 1995b; Coffey et al., 1996). The former is concerned with causal analysis, regarding it as the highest challenge for qualitative method. The other celebrates the role of serendipity and the multiple meanings that can be discovered when data are addressed as text. The QCA approach operates on precepts that value the formal and honour modernist conceptions of data as factual information about the real world. The Atkinsonian approach makes of analysis a delicate, equivocal thing and embraces postmodernist conceptions of data as infinitely contested interpretations of situated social worlds. There is no prospect of convergence here. Yet both approaches have been advanced beyond what would have been possible without CAQDAS. The logic-based manipulation of numerous cases in QCA could not be done practically without the help of the computer, and the ability of hypertext to navigate the text in a trice, making and cancelling links, and in such a way that newcomers can quickly achieve competence, could not be achieved using paper-based procedures. Taking this example of the relationship between qualitative analysis and CAQDAS, it is not that new procedures have been made available but that procedures whose logical foundation is long-established are newly practical.

Further, these procedures are increasingly practised. They are less and less the province of a few enthusiasts. Growth in awareness and use of software to facilitate qualitative data analysis is not only attested by sales

figures of the sort we noted earlier. Another indication of growing awareness was the emergence in 1997 of a proposed study based in a business
school and concerned to establish the market for qualitative data analysis
software. Interestingly the initial question this research addressed was
whether different segments of the market could be identified, 'like textual,
graphical, speech analysis'. Another sign of the growth of use was that
qualitative software was reviewed in the computing press (Walsh and
Lavalli, 1997), having formerly been solely discussed in academic publications. A further sign of the increasing use of CAQDAS is its penetration
into new disciplines and into the social science methods curriculum,
including input at the undergraduate level. In light of these developments
in qualitative software, are there other new developments in social science
IT which might lead to a new kind of relationship between qualitative
analysis and its enabling technology?

We can address the question of new developments by considering both
refinements of CAQDAS as it stands and developments in associated or
adjacent technologies. CAQDAS is still not 'big business', and any technology which relies chiefly on academic and applied research applications
is unlikely ever to become so. The present state of the market might be
characterized as the 'winnowing out' stage. Following the initial burst of
development by academics, varying degrees of commercial orientation
have seen some packages maintain a steady pace of refinement and
upgrades, while others have not been developed after their initial release.
As these packages obsolesce their use declines, and some developers have
by now left the market. For a very few, development of their software now
represents their principal livelihood. A major stimulus to change was the
advent of the Windows operating system, which caused a shake-out of
those willing to keep up with its programming and development requirements.

While the move to Windows involved a response to externally driven
change, other changes to CAQDAS represent the response of developers
to requests from users for particular features. This has always been a
characteristic of the CAQDAS scene. Among recent innovations have been
the provision of facilities to move CAQDAS projects around via the Internet and to lodge projects on websites, the inclusion of graphic analytic
facilities, more automated coding, a move to provide full suites of Boolean
operators, as well as better-designed interfaces. Like other software,
CAQDAS is increasingly dependent on mouse-driven graphical user
interfaces. One might feel that present preoccupations indicate entry to a
stage of refinement rather than one of radical change.

An example current during 1997 is that of adding a formatted text
feature to CAQDAS. This would preserve the format of text imported
from various word-processor packages and allow code assignments to
move around with text as projects were moved between packages. It
would also be useful in dealing with accents and non-standard symbols.

However, to do this the amount of code written would have to be very large, to accommodate all versions of all word processors, or there would have to be a large number of niche versions of the CAQDAS package, each tailored to a particular version of a particular word processor. A relatively limited market would not support the development costs currently needed to provide a feature of such modest general utility. It is not, however, the case that a limitation of the technology necessarily obstructs the analytic work of those who desire such a feature. The loss of formatting which presents the problem arises from the use of ASCII text. ASCII conversion allows software packages to read each other's output, but the price is the loss of formatting. The problem can be fixed by the expedient of using two copies of the data. The ASCII version is placed in the CAQDAS package and the formatted version in a defined directory. Search software can generally locate files by using a known phrase. When users want to see text in its formatted form they highlight a phrase copy to the clipboard and open the search software. The text will then appear in full context. Thus, the problem can be solved by using two pieces of software. Developments in object programming suggest that, in the mid-term future, text converter objects and formatting filters will provide a single package solution. Those who have the need now can make use of an effective workaround.

The users' wish list is becoming shorter and shorter. What are the present technical problems and technological prospects for qualitative research? One particularly arduous element of qualitative research is the transcription of data. There are two technological developments of interest here. One is the use of voice recognition software which converts speech to text. Aids to conventional transcription are limited to tape recorders with foot controls to start, stop and replay adjustable lengths of speech. A considerable effort is required to check transcript accuracy, and there is a host of associated problems (for example, transcription secretaries have sensibilities which might be offended by features such as swearing and jargon which are routine in much dialogue). So the attraction of transcription software is considerable. While the field is developing rapidly, so far dictation software has not proved an acceptable substitute for a human transcriber. Problems of accuracy, disambiguation and hardware resource remain. What is worth noting, however, is that this is all about substituting one means of doing something for another. There is no implication for analysis here other than, eventually, that it might take place more quickly.

Another transcription development is 'direct transcription software', where speech is recorded on a CD-ROM. Software is then used which enables the application of codes not to text but to the sound segments themselves (an example being KIT, a package developed at Aarhus University). Thus, when a search on a given code results in a hit the researcher is able to listen to the actual data rather than read them as text.

Unlike voice recognition software, this technological development does represent a significant departure from conventional practice and one which might have an analytic implication. It seems to us that the act of interpreting the spoken word might be different to the act of interpreting the written word, and that purely auditory methods of inspecting text might lead to relatively superficial interpretations. When we consider other information-rich, ideologically tinged forms of discourse, such as political speech-making in legislative chambers, it is noticeable that politicians and commentators make heavy use of transcripts and the like. Thus, comment might be withheld until the political figure or commentator has seen 'the full text', and legislatures facilitate this by producing elaborate, verbatim records of their proceedings. Although software tied to a CD-ROM allows repeated playback of coded segments (and segments-in-context), it seems likely that recourse might still be made to text for detailed analysis. This further suggests that direct transcription software might be particularly useful either for relatively superficial or narrow analytic work, such as making a first high-level 'pass' through the data as a preliminary to coding it, or for very detailed work involving the fine-grained examination of paralinguistic features of speech. It is often said that computers are making us a more 'visual' species, but whether they are also making us more 'auditory' is debatable. We would, however, emphasize that the matter awaits comparative research and that the possible difference between accounts based on text and accounts based on direct transcription software will only be relative, a matter of degree. The question will be how much researchers value the measure of additional purchase they might get on the data by working with text as compared to the efficiency of working directly with audio. If relatively little 'variance' is lost then direct transcription software might hold considerable promise by speeding up at least some kinds of analysis.

Of course, our gaze need not only be directed at CAQDAS in respect of IT developments which might affect qualitative research. There has for several years been increasing interest in the use of the Internet for research. Many readers will have received questionnaires via the Internet but there have also been experiments with the use of the Internet to collect qualitative data and, as we have noted, CAQDAS developers are already enabling qualitative researchers to take advantage of the Internet by providing facilities to lodge projects on websites for team research or the presentation of working papers and the like. Among the issues that are raised by the use of the Internet for social science research are the commercialization of Internet working, the commodification of information, the application of standards, the control of encryption, and the development of new protocols. Although advances in computing and other technologies confront researchers with a new array of tools, the real impetus behind the changes in qualitative analysis is not to be found here but in the growth and subdivision of schools of analytic thought. This growth, so apparent over the last 15 years, did not wait for new technology, and does not rely on new technology now. It is even possible to see some enduring commonalities between opposing approaches to analysis which might counterdict the potential for divergence we discussed above. Coffey et al. (1996) assert that particular practical procedures are tied to particular analytic approaches. They see an affinity between coding (or, to use an older term, indexing) and grounded theory, and between hyperlinking (or, to use an older term, cross-referencing) and postmodernist analysis. However, as Kelle (1997) points out, a consideration of hermeneutics (specifically, the long history of biblical exegesis) reveals that the techniques of indexing and cross-referencing are used simultaneously by all of those involved in the interpretation of these texts, 'whether they take into account or not the polyvocality of biblical authors, their intentions and their diverse cultural backgrounds'. Differences in analytic approach are not, then, inscribed in technique or in technology.

It is perhaps more profitable to look to the research environment for stimulus to and reinforcement of, different analytic approaches. As we proceeded with our work on user experiences we came to appreciate that the substantial willingness of our respondents to participate fully in our research was due not just to their willingness to discuss an unfamiliar technology. Rather, it was the fact that, in the main, none had ever been asked about their working experience as researchers, their practice of the techniques of fieldwork, other than as part of informal social discourse. (The notable exception here , of course, was those who also taught methods of fieldwork and the practices of data analysis; even here accounts elicited by students were seldom so particular to the practice of the individual.) Many of our 'computer-related' topics needed to be informed by reference to more fundamental matters of research *praxis*. Out of their descriptions we began to add complexity to our understanding of the way people creatively draw on the 'capital letter' strategies (Symbolic Interactionism, Conversation Analysis, Grounded Theory) that we tend to associate with the work of particular researchers and research groups. The practice and product of qualitative data analysis is constantly being interpreted and understood *de novo* in the working world of the social researcher. Technology transforms, but it is not the only agent of transformation.

References

Abell, Peter (1988) 'The "structuration" of action: inference and comparative narratives', in Nigel G. Fielding (ed.), *Actions and Structure: Research Methods and Social Theory*. London: Sage.

Adorno, T.W., Frenkel-Brunwik, Else, Levinson, Daniel J. and Sanford, R. Nevitt (1950) *The Authoritarian Personality*. New York: Harper.

Agar, Michael (1983) 'Microcomputers as field tools', *Computers in the Humanities*, 17: 19–26.

Agar, Michael (1991) 'The right brain strikes back', in Nigel G. Fielding and Raymond M. Lee (eds), *Using Computers in Qualitative Research*. London: Sage.

Agar, Michael, and Hobbs, J.R. (1982) 'Interpreting discourse: coherence and the analysis of ethnographic interviews', *Discourse Processes*, 5: 1–32.

Alasuutari, Pertti (1995) *Researching Culture: Qualitative Method and Cultural Studies*. London: Sage.

Amenta, Edwin, and Poulsen, Jane D. (1994) 'Where to begin: a survey of five approaches to selecting independent variables for Qualitative Comparative Analysis', *Sociological Methods and Research*, 23: 22–53.

Association of American Marketing (1937) *The Technique of Marketing Research*. New York: McGraw-Hill.

Atkinson, Paul (1992) *Understanding Ethnographic Texts*. Thousand Oaks, CA: Sage.

Bechhofer, Frank (1981) 'Substantive dogs and methodological tails: a question of fit', *Sociology*, 15: 495–504.

Bechhofer, Frank (1996) 'Quantitative research in British sociology: has it changed since 1981?', *Sociology*, 30: 583–91.

Becker, Howard S. (1958) 'Problems of inference and proof in participant observation', *American Sociological Review*, 23: 652–7.

Becker, Howard S. (1986) *Writing for Social Scientists: How to Start or Finish Your Thesis, Book or Article*. Chicago: University of Chicago Press.

Becker, Howard S. and Geer, Blanche (1960) 'Participant observation: the analysis of qualitative field data', in Richard N. Adams and Jack J. Preiss (eds), *Human Organization Research*. Homewood, IL: Dorsey Press.

Becker, Howard S., Geer, Blanche, Hughes, Everett C. and Strauss, Anselm L. (1961) *Boys in White: Student Culture in Medical School*. Chicago: University of Chicago Press.

Becker, Howard S., Gordon, Andrew C. and LeBailly, Robert K. (1984) 'Fieldwork with the computer: criteria for assessing systems', *Qualitative Sociology*, 7: 16–33.

Bernard, H. Russell (1994) *Research Methods in Anthropology: Qualitative and Quantitative Approaches*. Thousand Oaks, CA: Sage.

Bloor, Michael J. (1978) 'On the analysis of observational data: a discussion of the worth and uses of inductive techniques and respondent validation', *Sociology*, 12: 545–52.

Bloor, Michael J. (1983) 'Notes on member validation', in Robert M. Emerson (ed.), *Contemporary Field Research: A Collection of Readings*. Prospect Heights, IL: Waveland Press.

Blumer, Herbert (1969) 'Social movements', in Barry McLaughlin (ed.), *Studies in Social Movements: A Social Psychological Perspective*. New York: Free Press.

Bogdan, Robert C. and Biklen, Sari Knopp (1992) *Qualitative Research in Education: An Intro-duction to Theory and Methods*. Boston: Allyn and Bacon.

Brent, Edward E., Jr and Anderson, Robert E. (1990) *Computer Applications in the Social Sciences*. Philadelphia, PA: Temple University Press.

Bryman, Alan and Burgess, Robert G. (1994a) *Analyzing Qualitative Data*. London: Routledge.

Bryman, Alan and Burgess, Robert G. (1994b) 'Developments in qualitative data analysis: an introduction', in Alan Bryman and Robert G. Burgess (eds), *Analyzing Qualitative Data*. London: Routledge.

Bucher, Rue, Fritz, Charles E. and Quarantelli, E.L. (1956) 'Tape recorded research: some field and data processing problems', *Public Opinion Quarterly*, 20: 427–39.

Bulmer, Martin (1980) 'Why don't sociologists make more use of official statistics?', *Sociology*, 14: 502–23.

Bulmer, Martin (1984) *The Chicago School of Sociology: Institutionalization, Diversity, and the Rise of Sociological Research*. Chicago: University of Chicago Press.

Bulmer, Martin, Sykes, Wendy, McKennell, Aubrey and Schonhardt-Bailey, Cheryl (1993) 'The profession of social research', in Wendy Sykes, Martin Bulmer and Marleen Schwerzel (eds), *Directory of Social Research Organisations in the United Kingdom*. London: Mansell.

Burke, Kenneth (1969) *The Grammar of Motives*. Berkeley, CA: University of California Press.

Caracelli, Valerie J. and Greene, Jennifer C. (1993) 'Data analysis strategies for mixed-method evaluation designs', *Educational Evaluation and Policy Analysis*, 15: 195–207.

Carley, Kathleen (1988) 'Formalizing the social expert's knowledge', *Sociological Methods and Research*, 17: 165–232.

Chapoulie, Jean-Michel (1987) 'Everett C. Hughes and the development of fieldwork in sociology', *Urban Life*, 15: 259–98.

Coffey, Amanda and Atkinson, Paul (1996) *Making Sense of Qualitative Data: Complementary Research Strategies*. Thousand Oaks, CA: Sage.

Coffey, A., Holbrook, B. and Atkinson, P. (1996) 'Qualitative data analysis: technologies and representations', *Sociological Research Online* 1: http://www.socresonline.org.uk/socresonline/1/1/4.html.

Colby, Benjamin N., Kennedy, Sayuri and Milanesi, Louis (1991) 'Content analysis, cultural grammars and computers', *Qualitative Sociology*, 14: 373–84.

Cole, Stephen (1983) 'The hierarchy of the sciences?', *American Journal of Sociology*, 89: 111–39.

Conrad, Peter and Reinharz, Shulamit (1984) 'Computers and qualitative data: editors' intro-ductory essay', *Qualitative Sociology*, 7: 3–15.

Converse, Jean M. (1987) *Survey Research in the United States: Roots and Emergence 1890–1960*. Berkeley, CA: University of California Press.

Cordingley, Elizabeth (Betsy) S. (1991) 'The upside and downside of hypertext tools: the KANT example', in Nigel G. Fielding and Raymond M. Lee (eds), *Using Computers in Qualitative Research*. London: Sage.

Coverdill, James E., Finlay, William and Martin, Jack K. (1994) 'Labor management in the Southern textile industry: comparing qualitative, quantitative and qualitative comparative analysis', *Sociological Methods and Research*, 23: 54–85.

Cressey, Donald R. (1953) *Other People's Money*. New York: Free Press.

David, Martin (1991) 'The science of data sharing: documentation', in Joan E. Sieber (ed.), *Sharing Social Science Data: Advantages and Challenges*. Newbury Park, CA: Sage.

Denzin, Norman K. (1970) *The Research Act in Sociology*. London: Butterworths.

Denzin, Norman K. and Lincoln, Yvonna G. (eds) (1994) *Handbook of Qualitative Research*. Thousand Oaks, CA: Sage.

Dey, Ian (1993) *Qualitative Data Analysis: A User-Friendly Guide for Social Scientists*. London: Routledge.

Dey, Ian (1995) 'Reducing fragmentation in qualitative research', in Udo Kelle (ed.), *Computer-Aided Qualitative Data Analysis: Theory, Methods and Practice*. London: Sage.

Douglas, Jack D. (1976) *Investigative Social Research*. Beverly Hills, CA: Sage.

Drass, Kriss A. (1980) 'The analysis of qualitative data: a computer program', *Urban Life*, 9: 322–53.

Drass, Kriss (1989) 'Text-analysis and text-analysis software: a comparison of assumptions', in Grant Blank, James L. McCartney and Edward Brent (eds), *New Technology in Sociology: Practical Applications in Research and Work*. New Brunswick, NJ: Transaction.

Drass, Kriss A. (1992) *QCA3: Qualitative Comparative Analysis*. Evanston, IL: Center for Urban Affairs and Policy Research.

Eco, Umberto (1976) *A Theory of Semiotics*. Bloomington, IN: Indiana University Press.

Ellen, R.F. (1984) *Ethnographic Research: A Guide to General Conduct*. London: Academic Press.

Emerson, Robert M., Fretz, Rachel I. and Shaw, Linda L. 1995. *Writing Ethnographic Fieldnotes*. Chicago: University of Chicago Press.

Feldman, Martha S. (1995) *Strategies for Interpreting Qualitative Data*. Thousand Oaks, CA: Sage.

Fetterman, David M. (1989) *Ethnography Step by Step*. Newbury Park, CA: Sage.

Fielding, Nigel G. (ed.) (1988) *Actions and Structure: Research Methods and Social Theory*. London: Sage.

Fielding, Nigel G. (1993) 'Qualitative interviewing', in Nigel Gilbert (ed.), *Researching Social Life*. Sage: London.

Fielding, Nigel G. and Lee, Raymond M. (eds) (1991) *Using Computers in Qualitative Research*. London: Sage.

Firestone, W A. (1993) 'Alternative arguments for generalizing from data as applied to qualitative research', *Educational Researcher*, 22: 16–23.

Fischer, Michael D. (1991) 'Marriage and power in an urban Punjabi community in Pakistan: tradition and transition', in H. Donnan and P. Werbner (eds), *Economy and Culture in Pakistan: Migrants and Cities in a Muslim Society*. London: Macmillan.

Fischer, Michael D. (1994) *Applications in Computing for Social Anthropologists*. London: Routledge.

Fischer, Michael D. (1995) 'Using computers in ethnographic fieldwork', in Raymond M. Lee (ed.), *Information Technology for the Social Scientist*. London: UCL Press.

Fischer, Michael D. and Finkelstein, Anthony (1991) 'Social knowledge representation: a case study', in Nigel G. Fielding and Raymond M. Lee (eds), *Using Computers in Qualitative Research*. London: Sage.

Fisher, Mike (1995) 'Desktop tools for the social scientist', in Raymond M. Lee (ed.), *Information Technology for the Social Scientist*. London: UCL Press.

Fisher, Mike (1997) *Qualitative Computing: Using Software for Qualitative Data Analysis*. Aldershot: Avebury.

Geer, Blanche (1964) 'First days in the field', in Phillip E. Hammond (ed.), *Sociologists at Work: Essays on the Craft of Social Research*. New York: Basic Books.

George, Annie and Jaswal, Surinder (1993) 'An example of searching for words using GOfer', *Cultural Anthropology Methods*, 5(3): 12.

Gerson, Elihu M. (1984) 'Qualitative Research and the Computer', *Qualitative Sociology*, 7: 61–74.

Glaser, Barney (1965) 'The constant comparative analysis of qualitative analysis', *Social Problems*, 12: 436–45.

Glaser, Barney G. (1978) *Theoretical Sensitivity*. Mill Valley, CA: Sociology Press.

Glaser, Barney G. (1992) *Emergence vs Forcing: Basics of Grounded Theory Analysis*. Mill Valley, CA: Sociology Press.

Glaser, Barney G. and Strauss, Anselm L. (1967) *The Discovery of Grounded Theory*. Chicago: Aldine.

Gouldner, Alvin W. (1973) *For Sociology: Renewal and Critique in Sociology Today*. Harmondsworth: Penguin.

Griffin, Larry J. (1993) 'Narrative, event-structure analysis, and causal interpretation in historical sociology', *American Journal of Sociology*, 98: 1094–133.

Griffin, Larry J., Botsko, Christopher, Wahl, Anna-Maria and Issac, Larry W. (1991)

'Theoretical generality, case particularity: qualitative comparative analysis of trade union growth and decline', *International Journal of Comparative Sociology*, 32: 110–36.

Gubrium, Jaber F. and Holstein, J. (1997) *The New Language of Qualitative Method*. Oxford: Oxford University Press.

Guetzkow, Harold (1950) 'Unitizing and categorizing problems in coding qualitative data', *Journal of Clinical Psychology*, 16: 47–58.

Hagaman, Dianne DiPaola (1995) 'Connecting cultures: Balinese character and the computer', in Susan Leigh Star (ed.), *The Cultures of Computing*. Oxford: Blackwell Publishers/Sociological Review. pp. 85–102.

Hammersley, Martyn (1989) *The Dilemma of Qualitative Method: Herbert Blumer and the Chicago Tradition*. London: Routledge.

Hammersley, Martyn and Atkinson, Paul (1983) *Ethnography: Principles in Practice*. London: Tavistock.

Hammersley, Martyn and Atkinson, Paul (1995) *Ethnography: Principles in Practice* (2nd edn). London: Routledge.

Hansen, Anders (1995) 'Using information technology to analyze newspaper content', in Raymond M. Lee (ed.), *Information Technology for the Social Scientist*. London: UCL Press.

Heath, Christian and Luff, Paul (1993) 'Explicating face-to-face interaction', in Nigel Gilbert (ed.), *Researching Social Life*. London: Sage.

Heather, Noel and Lee, Raymond M. (1995) 'Expert systems for the social scientist', in Raymond M. Lee (ed.), *Information Technology for the Social Scientist*. London: UCL Press.

Heise, David R. (1991) 'Event structure analysis: a qualitative model of quantitative research', in Nigel G. Fielding and Raymond M. Lee (eds), *Using Computers in Qualitative Research*. London: Sage.

Hesse-Biber, Sharlene, Dupuis, Paul and Kinder, T. Scott (1991) 'HyperResearch: a computer program for the analysis of qualitative data with an emphasis on hypothesis testing and multimedia analysis', *Qualitative Sociology*, 14: 289–306.

Hicks, Alexander (1994) 'Qualitative comparative analysis and analytical induction: the case for the emergence of the social security state', *Sociological Methods and Research*, 23: 86–113.

Hood, Jane C. (1996) 'The lost art of theoretical sampling.' Paper given at the Fourth International Social Science Methodology Conference, University of Essex.

Horney, M.A. and Healy, D. (1991) 'Hypertext and database tools for qualitative research.' Paper presented at American Educational Research Association Conference, Chicago.

Huber, Günter L. and García, Carlos Marcelo (1991) 'Computer assistance for testing hypotheses about qualitative data: the software package AQUAD 3.0', *Qualitative Sociology*, 14: 325–48.

Huberman, A. Michael and Miles, Matthew B. (1994) 'Data management and analysis methods', in Norman K. Denzin and Yvonna G. Lincoln (eds), *Handbook of Qualitative Research*. Thousand Oaks, CA: Sage.

Hydén, Lars-Christer (1995) 'Illness, time and narrative', in D.J. Trakas (ed.), *Apsro Seminar II: Issues in Research Perspectives and Methodology from the Behavioural Sciences*. Athens: Institute of Child Health.

Hyman, Herbert H. and Sheatsley, Paul B. (1954) '*The Authoritarian Personality*: a methodological critique', in Richard Christie and Marie Jahoda (eds), *Studies in the Scope and Method of 'The Authoritarian Personality': Continuities in Social Research*. Glencoe, IL: Free Press.

Jackson, Jean E. (1990) ' "I am a fieldnote": fieldnotes as a symbol of professional identity', in Roger Sanjek (ed.), *Fieldnotes: The Makings of Anthropology*. Ithaca, NY: Cornell University Press.

Jonassen, David H., Beissner, Kathleen and Yacci, Michael (1993) *Structural Knowledge: Techniques for Representing, Conveying and Acquiring Structural Knowledge*. Hillsdale, NJ: Lawrence Erlbaum.

Kelle, Udo (ed.) (1995) *Computer-aided Qualitative Data Analysis: Theory, Methods and Practice*. London: Sage.

Kelle, Udo (1997) 'Theory building in qualitative research and computer programs for the management of textual data', *Sociological Research Online* 2: http://www.socresonline. org.uk/socresonline/2/2/1.html.

Kelle, Udo and Bird, Katherine (1995) 'An overview of current trends in computer-aided qualitative data analysis.' Paper given at Softstat'95 Conference, Heidelberg.

Kidder, Louise H. (1981) 'Qualitative research and quasi-experimental frameworks', in Marilyn B. Brewer and Barry E. Collins (eds), *Scientific Inquiry and the Social Sciences*. San Francisco: Jossey-Bass.

Kippen, J. (1988) 'On the uses of computers in anthropological research', *Current Anthropology*, 29: 317–20.

Kling, Rob and Iacono, Suzanne (1988) 'The mobilization of support for computerization: the role of computerization movements', *Social Problems*, 35: 226–43.

Kluckhohn, Clyde (1945) 'The personal document in anthropological science', in Committee on Appraisal of Research (ed.), *The Use of Personal Documents in History, Anthropology and Sociology*. New York: Social Science Research Council.

Knafl, Kathleen A. and Webster, Denise C. (1988) 'Managing and analysing qualitative data: a description of tasks, techniques and materials', *Western Journal of Nursing Research*, 10: 195–218.

Lazarsfeld, Paul F. and Barton, Allen H. (1951) 'Qualitative measurement in the social sciences: classification, typologies and indices', in Daniel Lerner and Harold D. Lasswell (eds), *The Policy Sciences: Recent Developments in Scope and Method*. Stanford, CA: Stanford University Press.

Lee, Raymond M. (1992) ' "Nobody said it had to be easy": postgraduate field research in Northern Ireland', in Robert G. Burgess (ed.), *Studies in Qualitative Methodology, Volume 3: Learning about Fieldwork*. Greenwich, CT: JAI Press.

Lee, Raymond M. (1993) *Doing Research on Sensitive Topics*. London: Sage.

Lee, Raymond M. (1994) *Mixed and Matched: Interreligious Courtship and Marriage in Northern Ireland*. Lanham, MD: University Press of America.

Lee, Raymond M. (1995a) 'Estimating the number of CAQDAS-aware researchers in the United Kingdom using a capture–recapture method', unpublished manuscript.

Lee, Raymond M. (ed.) (1995b) *Information Technology for the Social Scientist*. London: UCL Press.

Lee, Raymond M. and Fielding, Nigel G. (1991) 'Computing for qualitative research: options, problems, potential', in Nigel G. Fielding and Raymond M. Lee (eds), *Using Computers in Qualitative Research*. London: Sage.

Lee, Raymond M. and Fielding, Nigel G. (1995) 'Users' experiences of qualitative data analysis software', in Udo Kelle (ed.), *Computer-aided Qualitative Data Analysis: Theory, Methods and Practice*. London: Sage.

Levine, H.G. (1985) 'Principles of data storage and retrieval for use in qualitative evaluations', *Educational Evaluation and Policy Analysis*, 7: 169–86.

Lewins, Ann and di Gregorio, Sylvana (1996) 'Putting the cart before the horse: teaching computer programs for qualitative analysis to the novice qualitative researcher.' Paper given at the Fourth International Social Science Methodology Conference, University of Essex.

Lieberson, Stanley (1985) *Making It Count: The Improvement of Social Research and Theory*. Berkeley, CA: University of California Press.

Lincoln, Yvonna S. and Guba, Egon G. (1985) *Naturalistic Inquiry*. Beverly Hills, CA: Sage.

Lindesmith, Alfred (1968) *Addiction and Opiates*. Chicago: Aldine.

Locke, Karen (1996) 'Rewriting *The Discovery of Grounded Theory* after 25 years?', *Journal of Management Inquiry*, 5: 239–45.

Lofland, John (1970) 'Interactionist imagery and analytic interruptus', in Tamotsu Shibutani (ed.), *Human Nature and Collective Behavior: Papers in Honor of Herbert Blumer*. Englewood Cliffs, NJ: Prentice-Hall.

Lofland, John and Lofland, Lyn H. (1984) *Analyzing Social Settings: A Guide to Qualitative Observation and Analysis* (2nd edn). Belmont, CA: Wadsworth.

Lofland, John and Lofland, Lyn H. (1995) *Analyzing Social Settings: A Guide to Qualitative Observation and Analysis* (3rd edn). Belmont, CA: Wadsworth.

Lonkila, Marrku (1995) 'Grounded theory as an emerging paradigm for computer-assisted qualitative data analysis', in Udo Kelle (ed.), *Computer-aided Qualitative Data Analysis: Theory, Methods and Practice*. London: Sage. pp. 41–51.

Lutkehaus, Nancy (1990) 'Refractions of reality: on the use of other ethnographers' field-notes', in Roger Sanjek (ed.), *Fieldnotes: the Makings of Anthropology*. Ithaca, NY: Cornell University Press.

Mangabeira, Wilma (1995) 'Computer assistance, qualitative analysis and model building', in Raymond M. Lee (ed.), *Information Technology for the Social Scientist*. London: UCL Press.

Manning, Peter K. (1982) 'Analytic induction', in Robert B. Smith and Peter K. Manning (eds), *A Handbook of Social Science Methods, Volume 2: Qualitative Methods*. Cambridge, MA: Ballinger.

Manning, Peter K. (1987) *Semiotics and Fieldwork*. Beverly Hills, CA: Sage.

Manning, Peter K. (1988) 'Semiotics and social theory: the analysis of organizational beliefs', in Nigel G. Fielding (ed.), *Actions and Structure: Research Methods and Social Theory*. London: Sage.

Manning, Peter K. and Cullum-Swan, Betsy (1994) 'Narrative, content and semiotic analysis', in Norman K. Denzin and Yvonna G. Lincoln (eds), *Handbook of Qualitative Research*. Thousand Oaks, CA: Sage.

May, Tim (1996) 'When theory fails? The history of American sociological research methods', *History of the Human Sciences*, 10: 147–56.

Merton, Robert K. (1968) *Social Theory and Social Structure*. New York: Free Press.

Miles, Matthew B. (1983) 'Qualitative data as an attractive nuisance: the problem of analysis', in John van Maanen (ed.), *Qualitative Methodology*. Beverly Hills, CA: Sage.

Miles, Matthew and Huberman, A. Michael (1984) *Qualitative Data Analysis: A Sourcebook of New Methods*. Beverly Hills, CA: Sage.

Miles, Matthew B. and Huberman, A. Michael (1994) *Qualitative Data Analysis: An Expanded Sourcebook*. Thousand Oaks, CA: Sage.

Mills, C. Wright (1959) *The Sociological Imagination*. New York: Oxford University Press.

Mishler, Elliot G. (1986) *Research Interviewing: Context and Narrative*. Cambridge, MA: Harvard University Press.

Muhr, Thomas (1996) 'What AND, NOT and OR can and can't do: the pros and cons of Boolean retrieval techniques for qualitative research.' Paper given at the Fourth International Social Science Methodology Conference, University of Essex.

Palmer, Vivien M. (1928) *Field Studies in Sociology: A Students' Manual*. Chicago: Chicago University Press.

Patton, Michael Quinn (1980) *Qualitative Evaluation Methods*. Beverly Hills, CA: Sage.

Pfaffenberger, Bryan (1988) *Microcomputer Applications in Qualitative Research*. Newbury Park, CA: Sage.

Platt, Jennifer (1983) 'The development of the "participant observation" method in sociology: origin myth and history', *Journal of the History of the Behavioral Sciences*, 19: 379–93.

Platt, Jennifer (1996) *A History of Sociological Research Methods in America 1920–1960*. Cambridge: Cambridge University Press.

Podolefsky, A. and McCarty, C. (1983) 'Topical sorting: a technique for computer assisted qualitative data analysis', *American Anthropologist*, 85: 886–90.

Psathas, George (1995) *Conversation Analysis: The Study of Talk-in-Interaction*. Thousand Oaks, CA: Sage.

Ragin, Charles C. (1987) *The Comparative Method: Moving beyond Qualitative and Quantitative Strategies*. Berkeley, CA: University of California Press.

Ragin, Charles C. (1994) *Constructing Social Research*. Thousand Oaks, CA: Pine Forge Press.

Ragin, Charles C. (1995) 'Using qualitative comparative analysis to study configurations', in Udo Kelle (ed.), in *Computer-aided Qualitative Data Analysis: Theory, Methods and Practice*. London: Sage. pp. 177–89.

Ragin, Charles C. and Becker, Howard S. (1989) 'How the microcomputer is changing our analytic habits', in Grant Blank, James L. McCartney and Edward Brent (eds), *New Technology in Sociology: Practical Applications in Research and Work*. New Brunswick, NJ: Transaction.

Richards, Tom and Richards, Lyn (1994) 'Using computers in qualitative analysis', in Norman K. Denzin and Yvonna G. Lincoln (eds), *Handbook of Qualitative Research*. Thousand Oaks, CA: Sage.

Richards, Tom and Richards, Lyn (1995) 'Using hierarchical categories in qualitative data analysis', in Udo Kelle (ed.), *Computer-aided Qualitative Data Analysis: Theory, Methods and Practice*. London: Sage.

Riesman, David (1979) 'Ethical and practical dilemmas of fieldwork in academic settings: a personal memoir', in Robert K. Merton, James S. Coleman and Peter H. Rossi (eds), *Qualitative and Quantitative Social Research: Papers in Honor of Paul F. Lazarsfeld*. New York: Free Press.

Riesman, David and Watson, Jeanne (1964) 'The Sociability Project: a chronicle of frustration and achievement', in Phillip E. Hammond (ed.), *Sociologists at Work: Essays on the Craft of Social Research*. New York: Basic Books.

Riessman, Catherine Kohler (1993) *Narrative Analysis*. Newbury Park, CA: Sage.

Roberts, Carl W. and Popping, Roel (1993) 'Computer-supported content analysis: some recent developments', *Social Science Computer Review*, 11: 283–91.

Robinson, W.S. (1951) 'The logical structure of analytical induction', *American Sociological Review*, 16: 812–18.

Rosen, E. (1978) *Cognition and Categorization*. Hillsdale, NJ: Lawrence Erlbaum Associates.

Roth, Julius (1963) *Timetables*. New York: Bobbs-Merrill.

Rothstein, Lawrence E. (1986) *Plant Closings: Power, Politics and Workers*. Dover, MA: Auburn House.

Rowe, J.H. (1953) 'Technical aids in anthropology: a historical survey', in A. Kroeber (ed.), *Anthropology Today: An Encyclopedic Inventory*. Chicago: University of Chicago Press.

Rubinstein, Robert A. (1991) 'Managing ethnographic data with *askSam*', *Cultural Anthropology Methods*, 3(2): 4–8.

Russell, Cynthia K. and Gregory, David M. (1993) 'Issues for consideration when choosing a qualitative data management system', *Journal of Advanced Nursing*, 18: 1806–16.

Ryan, G.W. (1993a) 'Using styles in WordPerfect as a template for your fieldnotes,' *Cultural Anthropology Methods*, 5(3): 8–9.

Ryan, G.W. (1993b) 'Using WordPerfect macros to handle fieldnotes', *Cultural Anthropology Methods*, 5(1): 10–11.

Sanjek, Roger (1990a) 'On ethnographic validity', in Roger Sanjek (ed.), *Fieldnotes: The Makings of Anthropology*. Ithaca, NY: Cornell University Press.

Sanjek, Roger (1990b) 'The secret life of fieldnotes', in Roger Sanjek (ed.), *Fieldnotes: The Makings of Anthropology*. Ithaca, NY: Cornell University Press.

Schwandt, Thomas A. and Halpern, Edward S. (1988) *Linking Auditing and Metaevaluation: Enhancing Quality in Applied Research*. Newbury Park, CA: Sage.

Seidel, John V. (1985) *The Ethnograph Version 2.0 User's Manual*. Littleton, CO: Qualis Research Associates.

Seidel, John V. (1988) *The Ethnograph Version 3.0 User's Manual*. Littleton, CO: Qualis Research Associates.

Seidel, John (1991) 'Methods and madness in the application of computer technology to qualitative data analysis', in Nigel G. Fielding and Raymond M. Lee (eds), *Using Computers in Qualitative Research*. London: Sage.

Seidel, John V. and Clark, Jack A. (1984) 'The ETHNOGRAPH: a computer program for the analysis of qualitative data', 7: 110–25.

Seidel, John and Kelle, Udo (1995) 'Different functions of coding in the analysis of textual data', in Udo Kelle (ed.), *Computer-aided Qualitative Data Analysis: Theory, Methods and Practice*. London: Sage.

Sieber, Joan E. (1991) 'Introduction: sharing social science data', in Joan E. Sieber (ed.), *Sharing Social Science Data: Advantages and Challenges*. Newbury Park, CA: Sage.

Silverman, David (1985) *Qualitative Methodology and Sociology*. London: Sage.

Skott, Hans E. (1943) 'Attitude measurement in the Department of Agriculture', *Public Opinion Quarterly*, 7: 280–92.

Smith, Crosbie (1994) 'Frankenstein and natural magic', in Stephen Bann (ed.), *Frankenstein, Creation and Monstrosity*. London: Reaktion Books.

Social Research Association Working Party (1993) 'Report of the Social Research Association Working Party on the future of training in social research', in Wendy Sykes, Martin Bulmer and Marleen Schwerzel (eds), *Directory of Social Research Organisations in the United Kingdom*. London: Mansell.

Spradley, James P. (1979) *The Ethnographic Interview*. New York: Holt, Rinehart and Winston.

Stanley, Liz and Temple, Bogusia (1995) 'Doing the business? Evaluating software packages to aid the analysis of qualitative data sets', in Robert G. Burgess (ed.), *Studies in Qualitative Computing, Volume 3, Computing and Qualitative Research*. Greenwich, CT: JAI Press.

Strauss, Anselm L. (1959) *Mirrors and Masks*. New York: Free Press.

Strauss, Anselm L. (1987) *Qualitative Analysis for Social Scientists*. Cambridge: Cambridge University Press.

Strauss, Anselm L. and Corbin, Juliet (1990) *Basics of Qualitative Research: Grounded Theory Procedures and Techniques*. Newbury Park, CA: Sage.

Strauss, Anselm L. and Corbin, Juliet (1994) 'Grounded theory methodology: an overview', in Norman K. Denzin and Yvonna G. Lincoln (eds), *Handbook of Qualitative Research*. Thousand Oaks, CA: Sage.

Tesch, Renata (1988) 'The impact of the computer on qualitative data analysis.' Paper given at the Annual Conference of the American Educational Research Association, New Orleans.

Tesch, Renata (1989) 'The correspondence between different types of analysis and different types of software.' Paper given at the Conference on Qualitative Knowledge and Computing, University of Surrey.

Tesch, Renata (1990) *Qualitative Research: Analysis Types and Software Tools*. New York: Falmer Press.

Turner, Ralph H. (1953) 'The search for universals in sociological research', *American Sociological Review*, 18: 604–11.

Walsh, B. and Lavalli, T. (1997) 'Beyond beancounting: qualitative research software for business', http://www.microtimes.com/162/research.html.

Wax, Murray L. and Cassell, Jane (1979) ' Fieldwork, ethics and politics: the wider context', in Murray L. Wax and Jane Cassell (eds), *Federal Regulations: Ethical Issues and Social Research*. Boulder, CO: Westview.

Weaver, Anna and Atkinson, Paul (1995a) 'From coding to hypertext: strategies for micro-computing and qualitative data analysis', in Robert G. Burgess (ed.), *Studies in Qualitative Methodology, Volume 5, Computing and Qualitative Research*. Greenwich, CT: JAI Press.

Weaver, Anna and Atkinson, Paul (1995b) *Microcomputing and Qualitative Data Analysis*. Aldershot: Avebury.

Weber, Robert Phillip (1985) *Basic Content Analysis*. Beverly Hills, CA: Sage.

Weitzman, Eben A. and Miles, Matthew B. (1995) *Computer Programs for Qualitative Data Analysis*. Thousand Oaks, CA: Sage.

Wellman, Barry (1990) 'Integrating textual and statistical methods in the social sciences', *Cultural Anthropology Methods*, 2(2): 1–5.

Werner, Oswald (1992) 'Short Take 8: *Hapax Legomenon*: first steps in analyzing your inter-
views', *Cultural Anthropology Methods*, 4(3): 6–8.
White, Douglas R. (1991) 'Sharing anthropological data with peers and Third World hosts',
in Joan E. Sieber (ed.), *Sharing Social Science Data: Advantages and Challenges*. Newbury Park,
CA: Sage.
Whyte, William Foote (1955) *Street Corner Society: The Social Structure of an Italian Slum*.
Chicago: University of Chicago Press.
Yuen, H.K. and Richards, Thomas J. (1994) 'Knowledge representation for grounded theory
construction in qualitative data-analysis', *Journal of Mathematical Sociology*, 19: 279–98.
Znaniecki, Florian (1934) *The Method of Sociology*. New York: Farrar and Rinehart.

Index